A deeply researched, stylishly written piece of na telling vignettes. The organisation – around the fi Book Society – works wonderfully, giving an emc enormous pleasure to read, while also deepening immeasurably my understanding of the literary business of the interwar period out beyond the well-walked squares of Bloomsbury.

Dennis Duncan, UCL, author of Index, *A History of the*

In this dynamically narrated and archivally-rich study, Nicola Wilson brings book history to life as she takes us behind the scenes to show how Britain's first book club made its choices. Wilson argues for the importance of the Book Society as an under-acknowledged powerhouse in the shaping of 20th-century literary tastes. Those tastes belonged of course to specific individuals, each with their own personal story, and Wilson shows us the intimate friendships; networks and connections; and at times bitter disagreements behind the book choices. The story of the Book Society is one that also addresses some of the most pressing issues of our own literary moment - in this era of influencers and algorithmic recommendations, whose stories are told? Whose are chosen for splashy promotions and wide distributions? What does it mean to be an 'outsider' in a cliquey literary marketplace? A must-read for today's 'busy reader,' this book is a triumph of imagination, historical research, and storytelling.

Claire Battershill, University of Toronto, author of *Circus*

This is essential reading for all those who love books and literature. The story of the Book Society, the club that in the 1930s opened up reading and book buying to the man in the street, is of course the main focus, and how good to see Hugh Walpole's pivotal role in it fully recognised. But as Nicola Wilson takes us through the Book Society's 40 year history, setting the story against a backdrop of unfolding national and world events, she displays in the process her truly astonishing depth of knowledge of 20th century literature. This is no dry academic tome but a tremendously readable and insightful account of a fascinating story. It is filled with engaging anecdotes and numerous quotations, many of which have not been published before, all gleaned from her wide-ranging research. This book is a very impressive achievement indeed.

Nicholas Redman, Chairman, *Hugh Walpole Society*

‘This original and revealing work describes not only how books were promoted to reach a wider public long before the computer age, but also explores the relationships of those people involved in the enterprise. A highly engaging read.’
Margi Blunden, daughter of *Edmund Blunden*

‘It’s been a huge pleasure to read this, and fascinating to learn more about the workings of the Book Society and my great-grandmother Sylvia Lynd’s role in that. Nicola Wilson weaves the biographical elements in and out of the Book Society story so well’
Lydia Syson, author of *Mr Peacock’s Possessions*

Recommended!

Recommended!

The influencers who changed how we read

Nicola Wilson

Holland House

www.hhousebooks.com

Hardback ISBN: 978-1-739104-75-7

Cover design by Ken Dawson

Typeset by Polgarus Studio

Published in the UK

Holland House Books
Holland House
47 Greenham Road
Newbury, Berkshire RG14 7HY
United Kingdom

www.hhousebooks.com
Cover image credits: from Centre for Ephemera Studies; Lettering, Printing and Graphic Design Collections; Department of Typography & Graphic Communication, University of Reading. With thanks to Emma Minns

For Peter, Emily, and Michael

You must love books and reading, but above all you must be interested in the people behind those books, and appreciate how they loved what they were doing and what struggles and spiritual adventures they had

Hugh Walpole, *Book Society News*, December 1938

Literary history and the present are dark with silences

Tillie Olsen, *Silences*, 1962

Contents

Author's note

The Book Society was a limited company, with tens of thousands of members, trading in Britain and the Commonwealth between 1929 and 1968. Company papers have been lost, so I have drawn on other records preserved in publishers' archives and surviving copies of the monthly *Book Society News*, plus diaries, letters, autobiographies, and biographies of the main celebrity judges involved.

Sources for quotations from diaries, letters, or other written records (published or unpublished), are given at the back of the book. Quotes taken from the judge's reviews of choices and recommendations are from the *Book Society News* unless otherwise indicated.

List of characters

Book Society Selection Committee:

Hugh Walpole (1884-1941) Bestselling novelist, screenwriter, and head of the selection committee, 1928-41. Knighted for services to literature 1937. Homes in Piccadilly and the Lakes. In long-term relationship with his chauffeur and personal assistant, Harold Cheevers.

Sylvia Lynd (1888-1952) Poet, novelist, book critic and reviewer, on selection committee 1928-51. Hampstead socialite, famous for her parties. Married to journalist Robert Lynd, with two daughters, Sigle (Sheila) and Máire (B. J.).

Jack (J. B.) Priestley (1894-1984) Novelist, dramatist, book critic. On selection committee 1928-32 and 1941-48. Married twice.

George Stuart Gordon (1881-1942) Oxford academic and broadcaster, on selection committee 1929-42.

Clemence Dane (1888-1965) Dramatist and screenwriter, pen name of Winifred Ashton. One of the original Book Society judges. Left 1937 for Hollywood.

Edmund Blunden (1896-1974) WWI poet, author, and pacifist. On selection committee 1932-52. Married three times.

Cecil Day-Lewis (1904-72) '30s communist poet and detective novelist (pseudonym Nicholas Blake). On selection committee 1937-45. Worked for the Ministry of Information during WWII. Married twice.

Others:

Arthur Barker First manager of the Book Society. Left 1932 to set up his own publishers.

Alan Bott (1893-1952) Editor and publisher. Founder and director of the Book Society. Later started the Reprint Society, Pan paperback books, and co-founder of the Folio Society.

Harold Cheevers (1893-1971) Ex-police constable, worked for his lover Hugh Walpole from 1926 until Hugh's death. Married to Ethel Cheevers, with two boys.

Aki Hayashi (1889-1962) Researcher, literary secretary to Edmund Blunden. Followed Edmund to England from Japan in 1927, after a 2-year relationship. Lived and worked in Hampstead, London. Naturalised as a British Citizen post-WWII.

Julian Huxley (1887-1975) Biologist and zoologist, on selection committee mid-1935 to early 1937. Younger brother of writer Aldous.

Sylva Blunden (née Norman, 1906-71) Journalist and writer. Married Edmund Blunden in 1933, divorced 1945. His second wife. Worked with the WAF during WWII.

Claire Blunden (née Poynting, 1918-2000) Undergraduate at Oxford, in a relationship with Edmund Blunden from 1940. Married Edmund in 1945, his third wife.

Mary Day-Lewis (née King, 1902-unknown) First wife of Cecil Day-Lewis. Married 1928, divorced 1950.

Rosamond Lehmann (1901-90) Novelist. In a notorious relationship with Cecil Day-Lewis 1941-50.

With appearances from:

Vita Sackville-West (1892-1962) Novelist, poet and journalist.

Rose Macaulay (1881-1958) Writer, best friend of Sylvia Lynd.

Victor Gollancz (1893-1967) Left-wing publisher. Friends with Sylvia Lynd.

Nannie F. Dryhurst (1856-1930) Irish nationalist, teacher, anti-imperialist. Sylvia Lynd's mother.

Robert Lynd (1879-1949) Irish journalist and essayist. Married Sylvia Lynd in 1909.

Rupert Hart-Davis (1907-1999) Publisher. Secretary of the Book Society 1932-3, following Arthur S. Frere. Friend of Edmund Blunden

Virginia Woolf (1882-1941) Writer and publisher at the Hogarth Press.

Laurie Lee (1914-97) Writer. Worked at the Ministry of Information with Cecil Day-Lewis, 1944-46.

Siegfried Sassoon (1886-1967) WWI veteran, poet and writer. Close friend of Edmund Blunden.

Illustrations

0.1 Book Society flyer, postwar. From the Centre for Ephemera Studies; Lettering, Printing and Graphic Design Collections; Department of Typography & Graphic Communication, University of Reading.
0.2 Book Society flyer, mid 1930s. From the Centre for Ephemera Studies, University of Reading.
1.1 Sir Hugh Walpole by Bassano Ltd, whole-plate glass negative, 30 September 1929. NPG x124766 © National Portrait Gallery, London.
1.2 Book Society membership booklet, early 1930s. From the Centre for Ephemera Studies, University of Reading.
1.3 Hugh Walpole by mantelpiece, 90 Piccadilly. Published in *Titles to Fame*, ed. Denys Kilham Roberts (Nelson, 1937).
1.4 Hugh Walpole and Harold Cheevers playing chess at Brackenburn, dated 27 June 1933. Sketch by Stephen Bone, first published in *The Cumberland and Westmoreland Herald*. In the collection of Keswick Museum © Estate of Stephen Bone. All Rights Reserved, DACS 2025..
1.5 *Book Society News*, May 1930. University of Reading Special Collections, Hogarth Press Archive, MS 2750/416.
2.1 Sylvia Lynd by Howard Coster, chlorobromide print, 1937. NPG x1996 © National Portrait Gallery, London.
2.2 Sylvia and Robert Lynd, with children by Unknown photographer. Vintage bromide print on brown card mount, 1913-1914. NPG x1600 © National Portrait Gallery, London.
3.1 Edmund Blunden by Rex Whistler, drawn at Siegfried's, pencil, 1929. NPG 6254 © National Portrait Gallery, London.
3.2 Edmund Blunden and Aki Hayashi in Kobe, c. 1925. Published in Sumie Okada, *Edmund Blunden and Japan: The History of a Relationship* (Palgrave Macmillan, 1988), figure 14.
4.1 5 Keats Grove, Hampstead. Photo taken by author.
5.1 Cecil Day-Lewis by Howard Coster, half-plate film negative, 1937. NPG

x10287 © National Portrait Gallery, London.
6.1 Tillies Cottage, Forest Green. Photo taken by author.
6.2 The new club rooms in Book Society House, Grosvenor Place. From the *Book Society News*, September 1937.
6.3 Henry Rushbury R.A., 'View From a balcony: Hyde Park Corner', Print Society, 1939.
7.1 *Book Society News*, February 1940. British Library.
8.1 *Book Society News*, June 1941. British Library. From Edmund Blunden's review of *Winged Words. Our Airmen Speak for Themselves*, Book Society Choice for June.
8.2 Brackenburn, looking down from Cat Bells, with Derwentwater. Photo taken by author.
8.3 Memorial seat below Cat Bells, above Brackenburn. 'To the memory of Sir Hugh Walpole OBE…erected by his friend Harold Cheevers, September 1941'. Photo taken by author.
9.1 The symbol of 'Book Production War Economy Standard', designed by R. A. Maynard of George Harrap & Co.
10.1 Book Society special edition of *Persuasion*. Choice 183, December 1944, with an introduction by Edmund Blunden. From the Francis and Margaret Crichton collection.
11.1 The club magazine after WWII. *The Bookman*, incorporating the *Book Society News*.
11.2 Book Society bookplates, from the Francis and Margaret Crichton collection.

Colour plates

Helen Beauclerk, *The Love of the Foolish Angel* (William Collins). Book Society Choice no. 1, April 1929.
H. M. Tomlinson, *All Our Yesterdays* (Heinemann). Book Society Choice no. 10, January 1930. With yellow belly band, a rare survival.
Sigrid Undset, *Kristin Lavransdatter* (Knopf's American edition). Book Society Choice no. 11, February 1930. The American Book-of-the-Month club draw attention to the rare double whammy.
Eric Linklater, *Juan in America* (Jonathan Cape). Book Society Choice no. 24, March 1930. With one of the first Book Society Choice ads integrated into the dust jacket design.

Tom Clarke, *My Northcliffe Diary* (Victor Gollancz). Book Society Choice no. 25, April 1930.

T. S. Stribling, *The Forge* (William Heinemann). Book Society Choice no. 29, August 1931.

D. Wynne Willson, *Early Closing* (Constable). Book Society Choice no. 30, September 1931.

Virginia Woolf, *Flush: A Biography* (Hogarth Press). Book Society Choice no. 55, October 1933.

George Blake, *The Shipbuilders* (Faber & Faber). Book Society Choice no. 72, March 1935.

Ann Bridge, *Illyrian Spring* (Chatto & Windus). Book Society Choice no. 77, August 1935.

Winifred Holtby, *South Riding* (William Collins). Book Society Choice no. 84, March 1936.

Rosamond Lehmann, *The Weather in the Streets* (William Collins). Book Society Choice no. 88, July 1936.

Knud Holmboe, *Desert Encounter: An Adventurous Journey through Italian Africa* (George G. Harrap). Book Society Choice no. 92, November 1936.

Helen Simpson, *Under Capricorn* (William Heinemann). Book Society Choice no. 102, September 1937.

Francis Brett Young, *Portrait of a Village* (William Heinemann). Book Society Choice no. 105, December 1937.

F. D. Ommanney, *South Latitude* (Longmans). Book Society Choice no. 108, March 1938.

Eric Linklater, *The Impregnable Women* (Jonathan Cape). Book Society Choice no. 112, July 1938.

Daphne du Maurier, *Rebecca* (Victor Gollancz). Book Society Choice no. 113, August 1938.

Nora Waln, *Reaching for the Stars* (Cresset Press). Book Society Choice no. 123, June 1939.

Ethel Vance, *Escape, a novel of Inside Germany* (William Collins). Book Society Choice no. 128, November 1939.

E. M. Delafield, *The Provincial Lady in War-Time* (Macmillan). Book Society Choice no. 131, February 1940.

Jules Romains, *Verdun* (Peter Davies). Book Society Choice no. 133, April 1940.

Louis Bromfield, *Night in Bombay* (Cassell & Co.). Book Society Choice no. 137, August 1940.
Winged Words. Our Airmen Speak for Themselves (William Heinemann). Book Society Choice no. 147, June 1941.
Hugh Walpole, *The Blind Man's House* (Macmillan). Book Society Choice no. 150, September 1941.
Ernest Hemingway, *For Whom the Bell Tolls* (Jonathan Cape). Book Society Choice no. 144, March 1941.
Evelyn Waugh, *Put Out More Flags* (Chapman & Hall). Book Society Choice no. 156, March 1942.
Lin Yutang, *A Leaf in the Storm: A Novel of War-Swept China* (William Heinemann). Book Society Choice no. 158, May 1942.
C. S. Forester, *The Ship* (Michael Joseph). Book Society Choice no. 169, May-June 1943.
Leo Tolstoy, *Anna Karenina* (Book Society). Book Society Choice no. 170, July 1943.
Storm Jameson, *Cloudless May* (Macmillan). Book Society Choice no. 172, September and October 1943.
Evelyn Waugh, *Brideshead Revisited* (Chapman & Hall). Book Society Choice no. 187, May 1945.

Introduction: Five is Better than One

I

On the evening of Friday 7 December 1928, five writers met and dined together for the first time in a private members' club off Piccadilly. The evening was wet, winter showing its hand, but inside the dimly lit club room it was warm and cosy, a soft layer of chatter draped like tinsel around the assembled guests. Our party was well-dressed, the men sporting tailcoats and white bowties, the women in smart cocktail gowns. The women and two of the men were in their forties; the third man, gruffer and more on edge, was clearly younger. Now and then a hearty laugh from the tallest man in the group, well-built and wearing glasses, with clove carnation in buttonhole, drew vague attention from the other guests dining nearby. He was the most recognisable of the five, though his companions were all popular literary celebrities. But in the hushed affluence of the club room they were not particularly remarkable. You wouldn't have guessed, to look at them, that this was the beginnings of a quiet revolution.

For as the red wine was served out, followed by whisky and cigars for the men, cigarettes for the ladies, the writers' plans began to take shape: month by month, book by book, they'd change how people thought about reading. As judges their tastes would be broad and eclectic, embracing popular genres and literary fiction, as well as history, travel writing, and memoir. They would not take themselves too seriously; books should be enjoyable and for everyone. By supporting new authors and encouraging a habit of book-buying, they'd break the back of the private subscription library market, enabling ordinary, busy people to build their own collections of first editions. They would help those without nearby bookshops to keep up with new writing and ideas, creating a wide Anglophone reading community. Their selections and recommendations would be bestsellers, making publishers, agents, and booksellers take note. They'd shake up the staid book world with their expert advice, allowing wider audiences, with a growing appetite for books, better access to a world from which many felt actively excluded

Along the way, they would gain enemies. Personal attacks and jibes about their integrity would haunt them, threatening to topple their careers. They'd be accused of dumbing down, mocked as 'middlemen' for 'conferring authority on a taste for the second-rate'.[1] Not all five would stick it out. But the Book Society they began that night would serve tens of thousands of readers worldwide for the next forty years, steering a course through The Great Depression, the rise of fascism, and the devastation of World War II. Hundreds of what we now think of as twentieth-century classics would first reach readers wrapped in 'Book Society Choice' yellow bands.

Before Reese Witherspoon and Zoella's Book Clubs, there was Oprah Winfrey and Richard and Judy. And before them, there was Hugh Walpole and the Book Society. This is the story of five writers who shaped what we read.

II

Book Society flyer, postwar

Today we are accustomed to taking advice on what to read. Tailored book subscription packages soared through the Covid lockdowns of 2020-22, providing a welcome treat through the mail each month. Millions of us continue to follow influencers – booktokkers and bookstagrammers, radio and TV celebrities – for recommendations helping us decide what we read.

But in 1928 book subscription services were unheard of in the UK, though they did exist in Germany, France, and the USA. The Book Society, in fact, was modelled on the American Book-of-the-Month Club set up two years earlier, the brainchild of advertiser Harry Scherman (it is still around today). With sixty thousand members within a year, and over ninety thousand by 1928, the American BOMC had shown that books make ideal mail-order goods which readers could be persuaded to buy (rather than borrow) if they trusted the decisions being made for them and valued what they received. There were important differences: while the American BOMC practised deep discounting, making books cheaper to buy, this was not the aim of the Book Society, which upheld the UK's net book agreement, selling publisher's first editions at retail price (the club's massive pre-orders did allow publishers to scale up and bring down production costs, but cut-price, reprint book clubs would not come until a decade later in Britain). Instead, the Book Society aimed to democratise knowledge and culture, and make life a bit easier for readers navigating the tens of thousands of new books published each year.

What was most radical about the new club was its attitude to books as consumer items to be sold to customers direct through the powers of curation, advertising, and expert opinion. To some – like socialist Margaret Cole – this meant books had joined a consumer revolution that 'in the course of a generation, has brought gramophone records, silk stockings, foreign travel, and smoked salmon...within the reach of small purses'.[2] But to others, the Book Society was standardising literature and selling out. To many with a stake in the snobbish book world of the time, readers shouldn't need to be told what to buy. The anxiety and prejudice facing the Book Society's new model of taste-forming hasn't gone away entirely. In 2001 when author Jonathan Franzen refused to appear on Oprah Winfrey's book club after *The Corrections* (2001) received a selection, he surfaced a lingering mockery, and snobbish disdain, for having your books chosen by someone else.

So, imagine you're a booklover wanting to read newly published books in the late 1920s. If money was no object, you'd probably belong to a high-end circulating library like Harrods (1914-89) or Mudie's (1842-1937), where you could browse and be seen with the upper crust. For a deposit and annual fee in the late 1920s of two pounds and two shillings (the equivalent of six days wages for a skilled tradesman), you'd be guaranteed access to all works in circulation at Mudie's Select Library on the corner of New Oxford Street (if you lived in the country or overseas, Mudie's could make weekly dispatches). If cash was a little tighter, you might belong to W. H. Smith (1860-1961) or Boots Book-lovers' Library (1898/9-66), high-street establishments with relaxing library spaces catering to a wider class of paying readers. If you couldn't afford a private library subscription, you might visit the public library in town after work, though these could be intimidating spaces, had strict rules on appearance and cleanliness, and often delayed getting the newest books in (especially fiction). More hard up, you might borrow books from a local newsagents or stationers, from the Co-operative library or working-men's institute, or perhaps pay tuppence a time to borrow a title from a local 'Twopenny' library'.[3]

But even the relatively well-off rarely bought books when the Book Society was founded. In 1935, Freddie Richardson, head librarian at Boots, wrote in an essay collection on the contemporary book world 'It is increasingly apparent that, for better or for worse, we have become a nation of book-*borrowers.*'[4] The Big Four library distributors (Mudie's, W. H. Smith, Boots, and *The Times*), accounted for between a quarter to two thirds of publishers' new sales. There were bookshops of course, though not so many outside big towns, or in the countryside, but the culture of book-buying itself was not widespread. 'There is a deep rooted idea in the ordinary English mind,' H. G. Wells wrote in W. H. Smith's new *Guide to Book Buying and Book Reading* in 1927, 'that it is extravagant and wrong to own books.'[5] In the spring of 1929 when the Book Society began, judge Clemence Dane asked:

> Why is it that well-to-do people think nothing of spending a guinea apiece on a dinner, and half a guinea or more for a stall at a revue, five shillings each way for a taxi, and a string of half-crowns for all sorts of etc and oddments, chocolates and cigars included, whereas they stare at the bare idea of spending seven or eight shillings on books?[6]

A few years later, Penguin paperbacks would change the book world forever by showing that people would buy books *en masse* if they were sold at the right price point. But the Book Society led the way in what Margaret Cole described as 'the opening stage of a real revolution' by shifting the habits of a more affluent reading public and encouraging those who could afford to buy a new, full price, book each month, to think of themselves as book-owners, and sign up.[7]

III

In the final instalment of Hugh Walpole's famous *Herries Chronicle*, one of the characters mocks a younger relative for belonging to the Book Society. They are sitting together awkwardly at a family dinner party when Phyllis Veasey tells Cousin Benjie that, thanks to the Book Society, she is reading a very long novel – *Kristen Lavransdatter* by Norwegian writer Sigrid Undset. Why would she want anyone else to dictate her reading for her, he asks, puzzled? 'Oh, I don't know. Five's better than one,' she replies, tongue-in-cheek. 'Not so prejudiced.'[8]

When he was asked to form a selection committee in 1928, Hugh Walpole answered the call with this in mind. 'I think the Book of the Month Club suggestion is most interesting and I would of course love to have a finger in it if it comes to anything,' he replied with enthusiasm to Arthur S. Frere, a director at publisher's William Heinemann. 'I hope though that you will get names on the committee that will reassure the public, people who are not cranks nor like to drive always in the direction of a special clique.'[9] This was an obvious dig at the so-called 'Bloomsberries', that group of modernist writers who, as Labour MP Ellen Wilkinson put it in her first novel *Clash*, 'bestowed fame on themselves by writing reviews of each other's books'.[10] Left to his own devices, Hugh looked to an alternative network for his panel of judges. Enter the Hampstead Broadbrows.

In E. M. Forster's *A Passage to India* (1924), Hampstead is described as 'an artistic and thoughtful little suburb of London'. One hundred years earlier, it had been home to greats of the Romantic movement: Keats and Coleridge, Constable and Linnell. In the 1920s and '30s, Hampstead was still known as a village and full of artists and writers, not yet too expensive to live in on a professional writer or journalist's salary. Hugh spent most of his London free time in Hampstead, making his literary allies there his first port of call. 'Rose joining the Committee, Jack is coming on,' he wrote in his diary after inviting them to lunch at the end of October 1928. Rose Macaulay, Jack Priestley and Sylvia Lynd (who Hugh approached by more formal letter the next day) were popular writers tarred with the brush of the 'professional scribbler', according to novelist Virginia Woolf – public intellectuals, like Walpole, being seen as distinctly at odds with the elitism and aesthetics of the modernist set.[11] That same year, Jack and Hugh had co-authored a novel, *Farthing Hall*, with the advance from Hugh's publishers, Macmillan, bankrolling Priestley's breakthrough novel, *The Good Companions* (this was dedicated to Walpole 'for a friendship that has even triumphantly survived a collaboration'). Like Hugh, Jack believed that 'criticism should address itself to intelligent men and women of the world, asking for many different kinds of pleasure from many different kinds of books and authors'.[12] 'To this end I hasten to announce that my friends and I are Broadbrows,' Jack wrote in a satirical essay 'High, Low, Broad' of 1926:

> the people who are for ever quarrelling with both High and Low, who snap their fingers at fashions, who only ask that a thing should have character and art, should be enthralling, and do not give a fig whether it is popular or unpopular, born in Blackburn or Baku, who do not denounce a piece of art because it belongs to a certain category but only ask that it shall be well done, shall have in it colour, grace, wit, pathos, humour or sublimity.[13]

Academic gravitas to bolster the committee came in the form of Scottish academic, Professor George Stuart Gordon. Gordon was a distinguished war veteran with a democratic attitude to reading who believed, like Hugh, in the power of books to do good. 'He now has Raleigh's place at Oxford', Hugh noted in his diary after meeting George in January 1928, 'A man with an odd head that goes up to a very thin peak but very pleasant and amusing.' In 1926 George, then Merton Professor of English Literature at Oxford, gave a series of talks for radio on 'Companionable Books', arguing that too many readers were fearful of old books for the wrong reasons. Some of the classics were 'much more alive and a great deal more companionable than any best seller one might care to name' he suggested. 'What most men and women are looking for all their lives is companionship,' he summed up, 'and so far as books provide it, here it was.'[14]

To Hugh, learning lightly worn was appealing, and he was delighted when George agreed to join the club. 'You know that in this charming place one wonders sometimes if one is alive or dead,' George replied in a letter from Merton at the end of October 1928. 'That you should think me alive (a state I aim at) is a satisfaction in itself. If it all comes off I shall try to do my share.'[15] The following month, George was nominated to become President of Magdalen College and he would be swamped by university administration for the rest of his career (he shared his wife Mary's opinions on the club books he'd been sent). At least until Edmund Blunden joined the judges in 1932, George was their designated serious reader, tasked with appraising the biographies, histories, and more erudite books that came in. But he was also resident expert on murder-stories and books of adventure. He was not one to get his lectures written up, shrinking (as Mary put it candidly) 'from the finality of print'.[16] But short articles and reviews for the Book Society kept him honest. They were right up his street.

When Rose Macaulay dropped out of the fledging committee before their first choice was even announced, Hugh turned to another popular woman writer, his friend Clemence Dane. Clemence (the pen name of Winifred Ashton) had made her name as a dramatist, novelist, and journalist, and was widely known as a book critic for *Good Housekeeping*. Her first novel, *Regiment of Women* (1917), was for its time a shocking bestseller about a charismatic lesbian school mistress ('Why the book was not censored I cannot understand', said one contemporary reviewer).[17] Clemence had followed this with West End successes *A Bill of Divorcement* (1921) and *Will Shakespeare* (1921). Like Hugh, she had the knack of combining an astonishing amount of reading – going to bed at night and seemingly inhaling piles of proofs before she woke up – with an impressive amount of her own work. The club billed her to members as 'one of the most brilliant of a generation of remarkable women writers'.[18]

Clemence Dane got the job because of her fame and democratic views on literature, but it helped that she was a massive Walpole fan. For most of 1928, she'd been writing a study called *Tradition and Hugh Walpole*, published in America in 1929 and in Britain the following year, which argued that Walpole's popularity with readers was part of a reawakened interest in tradition and romance at the end of WWI.[19] In private, Hugh was wary. 'She has interesting ideas' he wrote in his diary, 'but my position is too immature yet to have a book written on it.'[20] Nevertheless he offered encouragement, as he did to all writers who approached him with what they were working on, and supported her thesis in public.

Clemence Dane was not part of the Hampstead set. Coming from the stage, her social circle was made up of theatrical types – Noel Coward was a close friend – and she lived for many years by herself in a flat in Covent Garden, close to the Royal Opera House, on the fringe of the West End. Clemence knew Sylvia Lynd from the Slade School of Fine Art where they had both trained, as well as meetings for the *Prix Femina*, but the two women were not close initially. Rose Macaulay's comments on her replacement were mean (though of course, made in private). 'I should have to kick by accident under the table – hard', Rose wrote to Sylvia when she heard the news, '& apologise for thinking her leg the table's. I hope she likes all the wrong books – but the trouble is she probably likes all the right ones.'[21] Clemence was an exuberant, overwhelming personality whose enthusiasms could rub people up the wrong way. 'She takes a pre-Caxton view of books, and the sight of print on the page excites her to madness,' Jack would mock later.[22] Of them all, Hugh knew Clemence found it hardest to fit in.

IV

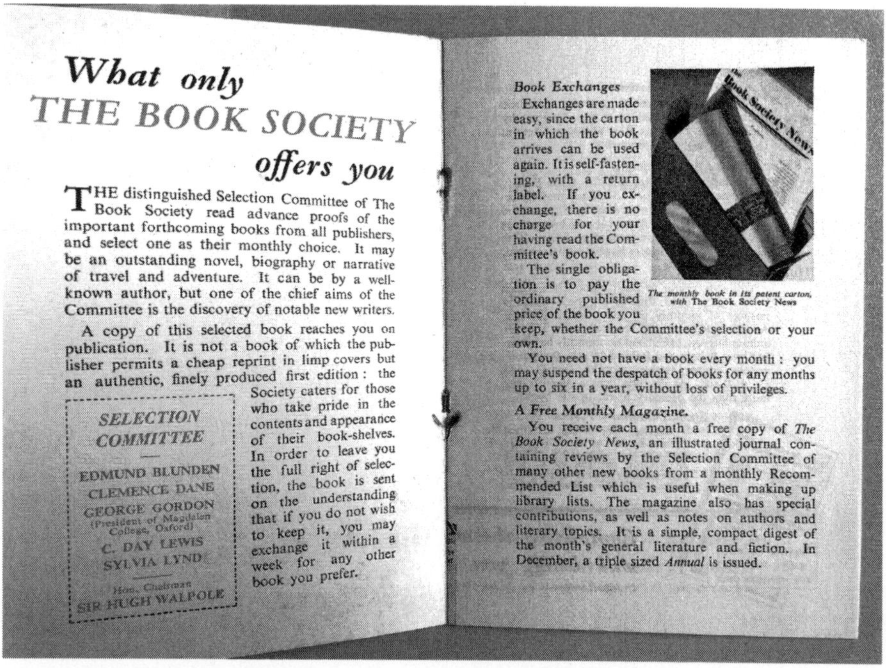

What only
THE BOOK SOCIETY
offers you

THE distinguished Selection Committee of The Book Society read advance proofs of the important forthcoming books from all publishers, and select one as their monthly choice. It may be an outstanding novel, biography or narrative of travel and adventure. It can be by a well-known author, but one of the chief aims of the Committee is the discovery of notable new writers.

A copy of this selected book reaches you on publication. It is not a book of which the publisher permits a cheap reprint in limp covers but an authentic, finely produced first edition: the Society caters for those who take pride in the contents and appearance of their book-shelves. In order to leave you the full right of selection, the book is sent on the understanding that if you do not wish to keep it, you may exchange it within a week for any other book you prefer.

SELECTION COMMITTEE
EDMUND BLUNDEN
CLEMENCE DANE
GEORGE GORDON
(President of Magdalen College, Oxford)
C. DAY LEWIS
SYLVIA LYND
Hon. Chairman
SIR HUGH WALPOLE

Book Exchanges

Exchanges are made easy, since the carton in which the book arrives can be used again. It is self-fastening, with a return label. If you exchange, there is no charge for your having read the Committee's book.

The single obligation is to pay the ordinary published price of the book you keep, whether the Committee's selection or your own.

You need not have a book every month: you may suspend the despatch of books for any months up to six in a year, without loss of privileges.

The monthly book in its patent carton, with The Book Society News

A Free Monthly Magazine.

You receive each month a free copy of *The Book Society News*, an illustrated journal containing reviews by the Selection Committee of many other new books from a monthly Recommended List which is useful when making up library lists. The magazine also has special contributions, as well as notes on authors and literary topics. It is a simple, compact digest of the month's general literature and fiction. In December, a triple sized *Annual* is issued.

Book Society flyer, mid 1930s

The Book Society changed how we read and how people thought about books. I came across it in the archives of the Hogarth Press, the club manager (followed by Hugh), writing determinedly to Leonard and Virginia Woolf asking for changes in publication schedules and format so that Hogarth Press titles could be considered and selected by the club (Virginia Woolf changed the size and format of her 1933 book, *Flush*, for the Book Society).[23] It was the most unlikely correspondence I'd found in the publisher's archives and opened up a whole new way of thinking about the Woolfs and the Hogarth Press, so often seen as somehow outside of the concerns of the marketplace, nor commercially minded. Beyond that, it questioned what I thought I knew about reading, book sales, and publishing between the wars. And the traces of the Book Society in the archives showed just how much today's celebrity book sales clubs owe to this forgotten precursor.

This book sets the record straight. Now I work as an academic in an English Literature department, I'm part of the establishment that Hugh

Walpole and the Book Society set out to change. But I am a 'first generation' prof from a former mining village and an ordinary state school, so I can regard myself as a bit of an interloper. Academia is not the stuffy place it once was, but a whiff of privilege still circles the subject I teach, not least in conservative ideas about who has a right to study and enjoy the Arts and Humanities. Shame and unbelonging can catch me out unexpectedly, over coffee with a new colleague, or in the cut and thrust of unspoken assumptions about what's important in the seminar room. But as Hugh Walpole learnt the hard way, there's something liberating about seeing things as an outsider. And that's part of the wider story about value and whose stories we privilege that this book seeks to reclaim.

As a commercially savvy bestseller, Hugh Walpole made a career out of championing books and reading for everyone. In the 1920s and '30s, he filled lecture halls from Doncaster to Dallas with his gospel that books were for the 'Man in the Street plus a little culture'.[24] Nowadays, when public libraries are being cut, writers from working-class and minority backgrounds continue to struggle to get published, and entire regions and segments of society are overlooked as potential reading audiences, we know equal access to books is still not guaranteed. Early influencers like the celebrity writers on the Book Society, willing to take privilege to task, still matter. As do the books they chose and the readers they sustained.

For 'it takes all sorts to make a world', Hugh Walpole once said. 'At least it does in my library.'[25]

Chapter 1: Hugh, 1928-30

Life comes back to the novel

I

Sir Hugh Walpole by Bassano Ltd, whole-plate glass negative, 30 September 1929 © National Portrait Gallery, London

If you were looking for a literary celebrity to host a new book club in the late 1920s, you couldn't do much better than Hugh Walpole. Charming and charismatic, tall and 'very big, upright' – a 'rosy-faced man', as Sylvia Lynd put it, 'glossy with health, as it seemed' – Hugh had been at the heart of the book world since the early 1920s, smoothing relations between authors, publishers, and booksellers through monthly gatherings of the Society of Bookmen, a 'little dining club' he'd set up that met in his bachelor flat at 90

Piccadilly 'to talk "shop"'.[26] The Society of Bookmen (still in existence and now, confusingly, known as the Book Society) was a frank-talking sounding board between the various trade bodies, aiming to present a united front to promote and sell books. Along with cricket and the Lakes, books were Hugh's sustenance. Putting himself at the centre of selling them cemented his influence.

While he was in London, Hugh lived at breakneck speed: dashing off articles and reviews in the morning; entertaining up-and-coming authors over lunch; popping out for drinks at the club with the Great and the Good, his pocket engagement diary always on hand. He was renowned as an 'excellent guest' and 'excellent host', deeply invested in the publishing world and all its doings.[27] 'He kept an eye on a sort of stock market of literary reputations,' Jack Priestley recalled, 'where that novelist's shares were going up, this critic's going down.' 'He may have been desperately anxious to succeed,' Priestley admitted, 'but even so he was far less self-centred than most writers are. He ran to welcome new talent in all the arts.'[28]

One reason Hugh worked so hard to maintain his position in literary London was because he had not grown up in it. Born in Auckland, New Zealand in 1884 where his father, the Reverend Somerset Walpole, had a position in the Anglican Church – 'a New Zealand very different then from the civilized country of to-day', Hugh wrote in his late forties – Hugh had endured 'an odd childhood and upbringing'.[29] When Hugh was five, the family followed his father to New York where he had accepted a new position, and four years later, aged nine, Hugh was separated from his parents and younger siblings when he was shipped to England as a public school boarder. 'I went to three schools', he would say later of his lonely school days (these were Marlow; King's School, Canterbury; and Durham): 'at the first of them I was tortured, at the second I was happy, at the third I was miserable, being a day-boy. At none of them was I educated.'[30]

Hugh's relationship with his parents was not unusually distant for his time and class, but his sexuality was a cause of tension and confusion between them, especially for his father. 'He did not then or ever understand morbidities or eccentric twists,' Hugh wrote of his father; his own language clearly influenced by the guilt-laden attitudes of the time. 'Life was as clear to him as a bowl of shining glass and what one must do was to serve God and do one's Duty.' Hugh's mother Mildred – who had barely left Cornwall before she embarked on a peripatetic life as the wife of a colonial missionary, with a young family in tow – was often anxious, according to Hugh. 'My own small person', it seemed to him, 'distressed and bewildered her.'[31]

From a young age, Hugh relied on books to provide comfort and escape. Looking back, he described reading compulsively as a schoolboy, 'like a little criminal for whom the whole world was hunting', slipping away to the town library and climbing the ladder to dig for treasure. Mary Shelley, Ann Radcliffe, Walter Scott, Charles Dickens 'became to me friends and companions so real that they moved with me everywhere', he wrote later in his autobiography.[32] Loving books first as 'friends and companions' meant, as an adult, despising 'literary snobs' and the 'clever critic'. 'The fact remains', he wrote in an essay on *Reading* for a series on 'Diversions' edited by Jack Priestley, 'that on looking around you it is the books that you have loved that count, not the books that you have criticised.'[33] Importantly for the success of the new club, Hugh was passionate about the personal and social good of reading.

At twenty-four, Hugh moved to London after rejecting his father's clerical vocation and an unsuccessful bout of school teaching, a Third-Class History degree from Cambridge under his belt (despite, he thought, having 'a second-class amount of knowledge'[34]). He launched himself on the literati, as he would later put it, 'with thirty pounds in my pocket and the manuscript of a novel'. Landing a part-time job at the Curtis Brown literary agency, starting at £2 a week, Hugh saw first-hand the power of networks and personal recommendations that would encourage him to support the Book Society. 'Many a good book has been lost because there were not enough voices raised on its behalf to direct it towards those who would care for it', he wrote in his reminiscences.[35]

His first novel, *The Wooden Horse*, was published in 1909, and for the next thirty odd years Hugh produced almost one book a year (sometimes more). Grateful to his own mentors – and to Henry James especially, whom he'd approached with reverence as an unknown writer at the start of his career – Hugh loved easing others' path to success. His papers are full of thanks and gratitude from authors to whom he gave a leg up; many in return gave him manuscripts or dedicated their own books to him. 'I don't think,' Osbert Sitwell said, 'there was any younger writer of any worth who has not at one time or another received kindness of an active kind, and at a crucial moment, from Hugh.'[36] 'Hugh Walpole must have helped more people to their place in the sun than any writer of his generation,' agreed Clemence Dane. 'He would always be on the side of the under-dog, always the energetic friend of the people or the ideas in need of help.'[37]

As far as the wider public was concerned, Hugh Walpole was a popular writer whose name guaranteed a good read. Across the counters of high street libraries Boots' and W. H. Smith, his books flew off the shelves. 'The works of such a writer as Hugh Walpole go on for ever,' confirmed Freddie Richardson, head of Boots Book-lovers' library between the wars.[38] It wasn't common to buy books interwar, but tens of thousands of readers did buy Hugh Walpole. In the UK, his books had respectable sales, averaging 15,000 or so with each new hardback title, but in the larger American market he was massive, regularly nearing the 100,000-figure mark.

With close to thirty books out by the late 1920s, Hugh made good money from writing, which he spent lavishly, supplementing his author's income with after-dinner speeches and working the international lecture circuit tour, plus giving talks for the new BBC radio and later, in the 1930s, writing scripts for Hollywood. 'I am not quite sure what the word "success" means,' Hugh would demur in 1937, the same year he was awarded a knighthood for services to literature.[39] But by then he had been stung by W. Somerset Maugham's painful depiction of him as a grasping, popular novelist in *Cakes and Ale* (1930). His reputation, along with his self-confidence, never really recovered from the smear. However, when he was asked to lead the Book Society in May 1928, aged forty-four, Hugh Walpole was at the top of his game.

II

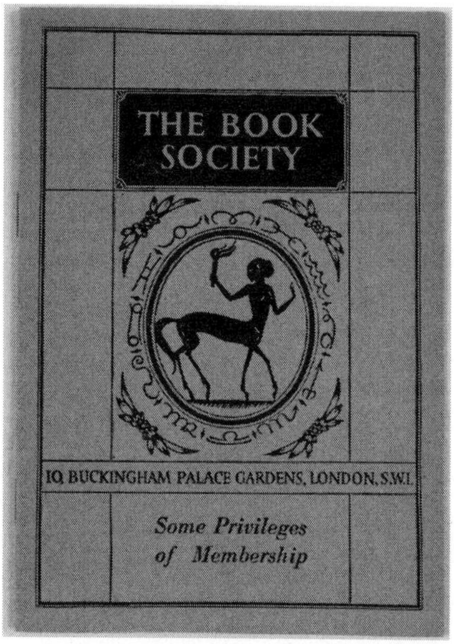

Book Society membership booklet, early 1930s

Early adverts announced the club as 'An Aid to the Busy Reader.'[40] At a press conference held in their offices on Grosvenor Place, Arthur Barker, the club's first manager, described how the Book Society would help readers find the best out of the ten thousand plus books published annually. Anticipating criticism of inertia selling, marketing would emphasise readers' choice to take the selected book 'on approval' or return it in favour of another recommended title. 'The great advantage of this scheme from the member's point of view', Barker outlined, 'is that they will not only get the benefit of the brains of the Selection Committee, but will also have the book on the morning of publication instead of having to wait for it. Further, readers may be perfectly certain they will have a book about which there will be considerable discussion, and will be in the lucky position of being able to read it before anyone else.'[41] Promoting new books to read-and-keep as a way of investing in yourself became a staple of the club's literature. Here was a 'modern, highly-efficient service' that would help you build 'a modern library for yourself and your children', one advert sold the Book Society.[42] 'You never miss a book of outstanding importance' ran an ad in *The Times*.

'You never have to "wait your turn" at the library.'

The club was set up as a private limited company with directors and a secretary, fronted by Walpole's literary selection committee (each judge was paid £250 a year, the equivalent back then of nearly two years' work for a skilled tradesman). The directors were, as Hugh described them in a letter to Sylvia Lynd, 'certain City men, big financiers and advertisers'.[43] Initially this included writer and publisher Alan Bott (author of bestselling WWI memoir *An Airman's Outings* and escape story *Eastern Flights*), and American journalist R. D. Blumenfeld (editor of the *Daily Express*).[44] Subscribers were enticed with various perks: a free monthly illustrated magazine; bookplates designed by famous artists and engravers (Edmund Dulac, Rex Whistler, Robert Gibbings) to personalise your new book collection; an invitation to visit the West End clubrooms near Piccadilly if you were ever 'up' in town. Despite some noise from the bookshops, fearful they'd be pushed out, subscriptions came in steadily. Two thousand readers had signed up to receive the first Book Society choice in April 1929.

***

For Hugh, the club's first choice was a mess. On the first Monday of March 1929, he received a telegram from his sister Dorothy in Edinburgh with news of their father's sudden death. Dashing up on the night train, Hugh was bewildered by an 'odd sort of loneliness', he told fellow judge Sylvia Lynd, in losing his last surviving parent, his mother having died four years earlier after suffering a long illness.[45] Hugh's father had been Bishop of St Mary's Episcopal Cathedral in Edinburgh for the last nineteen years of his life, and was a well-respected public figure (an obituary in the *Daily Mail* dubbed him 'The Kindest Person in Scotland'). Hugh was incensed by what he saw as his father's lack of foresight over Dorothy, knowing 'he would leave her practically penniless' (there is some brotherly over-protectiveness here: Dorothy had qualified recently as a Doctor, thanks partly to Hugh's financial support through medical training).[46] The children buried their father next to their mother in the churchyard of St Mary's, Dalmahoy, on the 'most lovely day' Hugh could remember in Edinburgh: 'the rooks flew cawing over our heads, the ground was covered with snowdrops'.[47] But the days either side of the funeral were a blur of visiting properties, trying to find Dorothy a new home now they'd lose the church residence on Eglinton Crescent. 'My one desire now is to find a good home for my sister who is magnificent and adorable,' Hugh wrote Sylvia in answer to her letter of condolence. 'Now as to the Book Society,' he continued...

So the launch of the club came at the worst possible time for Hugh. Barker wrote to him in Edinburgh pressing for an immediate decision, leaving Hugh 'reading frantically, everything...' They did not have as many manuscripts to choose from as would later become common, and they'd started the reading back in January once enough publishers were on board. But despite this, at the start of March 1929, several books were still in play. 'I'm afraid that unless something turns up I'm rather in favour of *The Cradle of The Deep*,' Hugh told Sylvia. 'I agree with your argument that it will shock our subscribers but only to a point,' he admitted. 'I think it more genuine than you do and I really don't feel it very nasty.'[48]

The Cradle of the Deep by American film actress Joan Lowell was already a bestseller in the States, thanks to the American Book-of-the-Month Club. It was sold as the autobiography of a young girl growing up on her father's schooner, sailing the Pacific, and learning to steer and spit like a sailor. Sylvia advised Hugh that the book was overly sensational: 'the author of *The Cradle* is a victim of the Ethel M. Dell complex' she wrote, saying she thought Helen Beauclerk's second novel, *The Love of the Foolish Angel*, a much safer bet.[49]

Distracted by the family crisis in Edinburgh, Hugh was forced to rely on Sylvia's judgement, consequently sparing the Book Society an embarrassing first choice. For American readers were scandalised when *The Cradle of the Deep* was exposed as a literary hoax soon after its release. The Book-of-the-Month Club issued an apology, conceding 'there is considerably more fiction in this book, and less fact, than our judges and the publishers had been led to believe'. Trying to dodge the heat, three judges on the American committee signed a statement saying it was 'commonplace as writing' and 'there was no agreement', making visible the rift.[50] Subscribers were encouraged to return the book in exchange for another at the same price, an administrative nightmare that would have been disastrous for the new Book Society. Hugh was aware that Sylvia's tastes were quite different to his own, and the near miss brought home her perceptiveness. His deferral to her on this first choice set the tone for their relationship.

So it was with Sylvia's favourite, *The Love of the Foolish Angel*, that the club launched in April 1929. The book was beautifully put together, with decorations by illustrator Edmund Dulac, Beauclerk's partner since he had separated from his wife. However, the story was odd, a historical fantasy based loosely on Anatole France's *La Revolte des Anges*, not likely to be everyone's cup of tea. Hugh revealed to Sylvia that he'd been persuaded despite himself. 'It is charming and in spite of being in a genre that I generally detest it's thrilling and touching', he acknowledged.[51] But it was soon clear the book had not gone down well. 'Very happy lunch' Hugh wrote in his diary after the May 1929 selection committee, 'but our Beauclerk choice has obviously been a bad one. Very doubtful this will go on over ten years.'[52]

The judges' second choice, Valentine Katacv's *The Embezzlers*, was another flop. Hugh had pushed this one onto the others, declaring it 'the first *funny* novel about Russia to reach England since Gogol'.[53] Hugh had been passionate about Russia since spending time there during WWI. Going out initially as a journalist, having been refused service by the British army because of his eyesight, Hugh worked with the Russian Red Cross and was awarded the medal of the Order of St. George for rescuing wounded soldiers under fire, seeing out the latter part of the war in Russia working for the Foreign Office (he was in Petrograd to witness the first revolution in March 1917 but left as the Bolsheviks took power in November). To the Book Society, Hugh billed Katacv's book about two embezzling officials as 'the best ambassador from Soviet Russia to the outside world that we have yet had'. But readers were not impressed and exchanged it in droves. According to Sylvia at least, who was away in Dublin and missed the selection, *The Embezzlers* 'though a clever and amusing little book...made as many people resign from membership of the society as the first book had made decide to join'.[54]

The book to put a flag in the sand and set a direction for the club was choice number four, Francis Hackett's non-fiction 'narrative-biography', *Henry the Eighth*. In his preface, Hackett described himself as a 'psycho-historian' who aims to be '*then*-minded': 'To use imagination and intuition, to suggest life', as he put it, while remaining faithful to the facts.[55] Hackett was part of what was known at the time as the school of 'new biography', writing 'thrilling and authentic history' as Hugh put it, on a par with anything 'any contemporary novelist could succeed in creating'.[56] They had listened to what their members and booksellers had been telling them about the popularity of History and Biography, Hugh confirmed, taking a chance on a solid, 550-page history book. In her review for the club, Clemence Dane described the book's style as cinematic. Hackett and the new biographers had found a way of writing, she argued, that centred storytelling, holding 'the man or woman who is fond of reading but is also busy, tired'.[57] It was the most popular choice of the first six months.

The club's sizable pre-order reduced the price, enabling publisher Jonathan Cape to charge 12 shillings and sixpence, rather than the projected guinea (12s and 6d is approximately £28 in today's money; a guinea was 21 shillings). 'This is exactly one of the Society's aims,' Hugh told readers, 'that it should bring certain books to a wider audience than they would have had without the Society's help.'[58] It was an important signal to the trade, showing publishers of works chosen by the Book Society they could stretch costs – printing more and charging less – thanks to the thousands of advance sales and extra publicity. Today, many publishers would say the influence of book clubs has gone too far, restricting the market, limiting innovation and risk. But in the late 1920s when publishers were facing 'a nation of book-*borrowers*', the scale of potential sales through curated book clubs was a revelation.[59]

III

Hugh Walpole by mantelpiece, 90 Piccadilly

Six months in, the judges were finding their feet. Membership numbers were still rising, with more publishers coming onboard, ensuring greater variety and better books to choose from. When the selection committee met in August 1929, they had Ernest Hemingway's *A Farewell to Arms* to consider as well as important new books by Aldous Huxley, Frank Swinnerton, and Virginia Woolf (all of which would be recommended), but for Book Society choice, there were two obvious forerunners. Richard Hughes's thriller *A High Wind in Jamaica*, about a group of children getting taken captive by pirates might just be the next *Treasure Island*. This was 'a work of genius but of a decidedly, not to say dangerously, mad genius', Sylvia had written Hugh before they met. 'We must recommend it as a thoroughly disconcerting book – it seems to me the most interesting we've had so far.'[60]

For Hugh meanwhile, the standout title that first summer was *Whiteoaks*, the second novel in Mazo de la Roche's Canadian family saga. Mazo was a new and glamorous friend, already famous in the States, currently on a European tour with her partner, Caroline Clement. The series followed an Anglo-Canadian family living in Jalna, a stately manor in rural Ontario (the house is named after the Indian military station where Grandfather Whiteoak was based with the British Army). In *Whiteoaks*, the Victorian sympathies of the older generation are challenged by the modernity of the younger characters: Byronic hero Renny, a symbol of modern Canada defining itself against the British; his younger brother Finch, a musician who queers Renny's model of heterosexual patriarchy; Alayne Whiteoak, a New York working girl who marries (unsuccessfully) into the family group. Recognising the story's dramatic potential, Hugh championed *Whiteoaks* on the selection committee and, with *A High Wind in Jamaica* lined up as choice for September 1929, it was duly chosen for October. Suitably grateful to her influential new ally, Mazo dedicated *The Master of Jalna*, the next but one book in the series, to Hugh. 'My books do not seem to be properly launched till they have made their bow to you', she confessed several years later.[61]

Wearing his heart on his sleeve in a glowing review of *Whiteoaks* that autumn, Walpole told readers that 'No selection that the Book Society has made has given me so much pleasure as this one.'[62] Mazo de la Roche had used creativity and imagination to produce a book that was compulsively readable, he argued. 'I am not speaking with exaggeration', Hugh went on, 'when I say that I know of no English novel since *Jalna* two years ago that has so extraordinary a power of taking you into the very heart of a family's life as this one.' Thanks partly to such fanfare from the Book Society, *Whiteoaks* became a publishing sensation, by Christmas 1929 selling over eleven thousand copies (the series would go on to be a literary phenomenon, sprawling into sixteen volumes published between 1927 and 1960, turning Mazo de la Roche into a global superstar). 'After ten years of autobiographical bitterness and sterility', Hugh asserted in his review, here 'Life Comes Back to the Novel.'

'Life' and the question of what that was, and the novel's relationship to it, or otherwise, was a topic of fierce debate for critics in the culture wars interwar (known as 'the battle of the brows'), fuelling column inches, public stand-offs, and heated radio spats. Hugh, like Mazo de la Roche, was pitched on one side of the equation, celebrated for capturing authenticity through life-like character, plot, and dialogue. 'Shapely and full of life' said *The Spectator* of Hugh's new novel, *Hans Frost*, published that September. 'Good plot, good talk, interesting people, humour, and a wealth of observation' reported the *Daily Mail.* This language mirrored the aesthetic values for which de la Roche was widely celebrated. *Whiteoaks*, said Clemence Dane, was 'more like real life than any book has the right to be'; 'here is life at first hand', wrote the *TLS*, 'not merely a novel about life'.

For others, and most famously Hugh's new friend Virginia Woolf, 'life' in the novel was something to be got at differently. 'Life is not a series of gig lamps symmetrically arranged' Woolf said in her essay 'Modern Fiction'. 'Life is a luminous halo, a semi-transparent envelope surrounding us from the beginning of consciousness to the end.'[63] This radically disrupted traditional ideas of character, plot, and verisimilitude. As Walpole would satirise such views in his *Letter to a Modern Novelist* (commissioned by the Woolfs as a polemical statement for their Hogarth Press):

> Now to all this you will say at once: 'but of course – the Theme of my book is that there *is* no Theme. Life has no Theme. Do you not know that we have got beyond that *arrangement* of the older novelists, the placing of things in order, the punctual rising of the sun, the crisis at its proper time, the ending neatly rounded off? Life was never like that. What we have to do is to render life as it is. To be Real.'

Privately, Hugh worried about his romantic style and being labelled old-fashioned. But publicly, he was the popular voice for the 'simple genius for story-telling', apparently under threat.[64]

Hugh and Virginia Woolf had crossed paths in the early 1920s but they didn't become friends until Hugh presented Virginia with the *Prix Femina* for her novel *To the Lighthouse* in May 1928. 'A frightful occasion,' Hugh reflected afterwards in his diary. 'Rows of old female novelists glaring at me. I made a rotten speech. Everyone desperately nervous.'[65] Invitations to tea at the Woolfs to 'discuss Reality' followed, and while Hugh was aware of being tested out by Virginia and her circle and remained in awe of her intellect, he grew fond of her company. That November 1929, Hugh reported in his diary: 'Tea with Virginia, Vita, Daddy Rylands. Heavenly! Virginia discussed whether she was real or no. Decided no.'[66] Virginia meanwhile was animated by Hugh's 'bustling vigour' and 'talk of Russia, & war & great doings & famous people', his 'talk about reviews and sales and dingy dirty literary shop'.[67] It was a friendship of opposites that lasted until their deaths, tragically just a couple of months apart.

Hugh's 1929 novel *Hans Frost* included a thinly veiled portrait of Virginia.

'She looked like the wife of a Pre-Raphaelite painter, her dark hair brushed back in waves from her forehead, her grey dress cut in simple fashion, her thin pale face quiet and remote.' 'She wrote the most beautiful prose in the most beautiful way', we are told.[68] Virginia described in a letter to Hugh how she had read the story compulsively. 'We had visitors and I had an article to write and books to read', she wrote him that September 1929, 'and there I sat reading on and on and on, pretending that I would only read one more chapter and then stop; and then arguing that as there were only five more chapters I might as well finish.' 'How do you do it?' she asked him, 'What is your lure?'[69] Later, after hearing of Harold Nicolson's talk on BBC radio in which Hugh (along with John Galsworthy and Priestley) was described as 'definitely old-fashioned', Virginia wrote to him, 'Lord – how tired I am of being caged with Aldous, Joyce and Lawrence!'[70] 'Can't we exchange cages for a lark?'Yet despite the artificialities of such rifts, there was enough truth in them to ground perceptions of literature and animate public debate for much of the Book Society's existence. In his own talks and lectures, Hugh made the most out of them. '*Ulysses*, by James Joyce, is an enormous volume of closely-written pages of great length,' he told audiences in Minnesota and Michigan on his second US lecture tour during 1922-3. 'We are getting so that we can expect the adventures of a snail crawling a few feet to appear in 500 volumes.'[71]

In his society novel *Wintersmoon* (published on his forty-fourth birthday, in March 1928) Hugh depicts a character called Wildherne. Though a war veteran, and well-regarded in London club rooms, Wildherne is made to feel stupid by modernity:

> Some of his Oxford acquaintances moved among writers and painters, but these seemed to care for things that he did not understand. He was not modern at all. [...] The modern arts, when he touched them [...], seemed to him all negation. He felt himself slow, behind the times.[72]

It was readers left behind to whom Hugh and the Book Society spoke. For while some contemporary writers were seen to have turned their backs on the 'New Reading Public' (as the early twentieth century working and lower-middle class readers, with more education and higher literacy rates, became known), Hugh and his 'broadbrows' addressed them specifically. Club reviews and recommendations were life-affirming, celebrating the pleasures of good, honest reading that united Tolstoy and Austen and Dickens. Deliberate, self-conscious complexity was no good for a reading democracy, they believed, and writers like Mazo de la Roche should be 'compelled by law' to write a new Whiteoak every year, Jack Priestley joked. For while Proust, Joyce, and Eliot had 'their own genius and depth' as Jack argued, 'it would be absurd to pretend that they have the old broad appeal on many different levels, beginning with anyone who wants a book to read. They only begin where the average reader wants to stop.'[73]

* * *

The Book Society was set up during a boom in World War I literature. The ten-year anniversary of the war's end had brought runaway bestsellers like Erich Maria Remarque's *All Quiet on the Western Front* (a German anti-war novel) and R. C. Sherriff's West End hit, *Journey's End*. Alongside the more modest success of Siegfried Sassoon's *Memoirs of a Fox-Hunting Man* and Edmund Blunden's *Undertones of War*, these fuelled what became known in publishing circles as the 'war books boom'.

For the club, mindful of catering for a wide mainstream audience, the question of whether to amplify such writing presented a dilemma. Rejecting the more controversial interventions, like Richard Aldington's *Death of a Hero* (this was printed in the UK with obscenities blanked out by asterisks), was relatively straightforward. In Hugh's eyes, Aldington typified a trend in some younger novelists towards 'autobiographical bitterness and sterility', depending too much in his anti-war novel on 'personal and generally peevish reactions to personal disappointments and exasperations'.[74] Oftentimes, language and subject were an issue. In Hemingway's *A Farewell to Arms*, for instance, Sylvia saw 'filthiness'; a shame in her eyes when his *Men Without Women* 'tackled everything so inoffensively…and this could have been so admirable'.[75] But despite the apparent deluge in war books (Hugh admitted to a general reluctance to open another one), readers' taste for critical reflections on the First World War ten years on proved insatiable and the club was compelled to offer a steer. They did so by directing readers towards what they perceived as more humane, less disillusioned, interventions. So Compton Mackenzie's *Gallipoli Memories* was selected as November 1929 choice and H. M. Tomlinson's *All Our Yesterdays* brought in the New Year.

Compton Mackenzie was the best-known of all the writers the Book

Society had selected so far. A popular novelist pre-war, he was famous for the semi-autobiographical *Sinister Street*, made into a film in the early 1920s. The selection committee justified the choice (apparently contrary to the club's aim to promote new writers) on grounds of Mackenzie's humility in a flood of bitter war writing. *Gallipoli Memories* was the first of a planned trilogy on the Entente defeat in the Turkish straits between 1915 and 1917, billed by Hugh as 'a war novel with wit and humanity,' in which Mackenzie 'combined his personal narrative with the larger sweep of the war'.[76] George Gordon had visited the Gallipoli Peninsula in 1919 for the War Office during research for their official military history and like Hugh, he admired Mackenzie's sensitive mingling of drama, facts, and humour.

H. M. Tomlinson's complex novel, *All Our Yesterdays*, was promoted to readers as a work of art and an important literary intervention. Hugh argued that Tomlinson's prose matched the finest poetic realism of Blunden's *Undertones of War*, while Jack Priestley went further, announcing that *All Our Yesterdays* 'contains some of the best writing of the century'. The yellow Book Society band, wrapped around all the club's choices, carried their shared endorsement: 'This goes to the head of war books with a bang,' pronounced Jack. It was Tomlinson's 'finest book' according to Hugh.

IV

Hugh Walpole and Harold Cheevers playing chess at Brackenburn, dated 27 June 1933. © Estate of Stephen Bone. All Rights Reserved, DACS 2025

Hugh saw out the last days of 1929 onboard the *Berengaria*, the Cunard's flagship ocean liner. Setting sail for America on Christmas Eve, he arrived seven days later, greeted at the dock by a press pack and former heavyweight world champion boxer Gene Tunney, a fan who reported 'he owed his taste for good literature to the novelist'.[77] It had been 'a marvellous year', Hugh reflected in his end-of-year summary, 'the best of my life so far'. Tackling family, work, and friendships in that order, Hugh was thankful his father's death had been relatively 'happy and peaceful', while Dorothy was now settled in a new house in Edinburgh. Workwise, he'd started the Book Society and finished writing *Rogue Herries* – due to be published next spring – which had taken the best part of two years. Jack Priestley was one of the friends he'd 'loved especially' that year, Hugh noted; he'd just got him elected to the Society of Authors. But at the top of his list of First Fifteen friends, for the second year running, came Harold Cheevers. 'Both Cumberland and HC are better than ever,' Hugh confirmed in his diary, adding with a flourish: 'HC is miraculous.'

Hugh had met Harold Cheevers (HC) in 1924, the year Hugh turned forty. Two years later, Harold had left his job as a policeman to join Hugh full-time as his 'secretary-chauffeur-friend and ROCK!'[78] Harold was tall and well-built like Hugh, but fitter – a champion swimmer – and Hugh was drawn to his 'quiet imperturbability', a grounding influence and contrast to the drama of literary life.[79] In an age when gay men could be imprisoned (in Rupert Hart-Davis's authorised biography, first published in 1952, Hugh's sexuality is only hinted at, but Harold is there in the dedication) theirs was a delicate, vulnerable relationship, which for both men and their families meant edging their way into unknown territory and unfamiliar ways of being. As Hugh wrote to Harold on Whit Monday 1926, working out how they could be together and formulating the basis of their new relationship:

> I've been thinking these two days a great deal about you and your family as I'm sure you have of me. Such a friendship as you and I now have is very rare in the world; in fact I see no other sign of it anywhere. I think it's a sign of this new world where we are all going to be so much more equal as man to man. I welcome that as the happiest thing that can happen to the world. But I'm sure you will agree with me that our affection for and trust in one another is now so precious to us that we won't let <u>anything</u> hurt it.[80]

Hugh continued to have relationships with other men – renowned Danish opera singer Lauritz Melchoir (Hugh called him David) was a glamorous acquaintance whenever he was in town – but Harold would become Hugh's life-long partner. 'Hate leaving HC even for two days. Feel in danger when he's not with me' Hugh wrote in his diary in March 1928. The two men enjoyed a loving relationship that respected and included Harold's wife Ethel and the Cheevers' two sons, who were encouraged to think of Hugh as a surrogate uncle and spent holidays at Hugh's second home in the Lakes. 'You and he have changed my whole life' Hugh wrote Ethel five years into the relationship. 'I was a very lonely man before and now I am perfectly happy. I can never be grateful enough.'[81] In 1928, Hugh took a house on long lease for the Cheevers in Hampstead Garden Suburb, kitting out a writing room for himself there. 'I have never been in the heart of a family as I am in this one,' he confessed in his diary.[82] Harold would become central to Hugh's household management and financial affairs. Before he left for America that Christmas Eve 1929, Hugh took out a power of attorney in Harold's name.

The American tour began in New York and progressed through Pennsylvania down to Washington, going back up the east coast to Toronto and Montreal, then spreading to Illinois, Iowa, and Missouri before concluding in Massachusetts. It was Hugh's fourth American lecture tour and, though it still sounds a lot, he took it more steadily than previously (his first tour in 1919-20 lasted six months; his second in 1922-23 lasted eight). $5000 equalled twenty lectures over two months, with at least four out of every seven days free of speeches. His Book Society commitments and the diabetes with which he had been diagnosed five years earlier meant Hugh could set the pace a bit more, insisting this time on less than three months away.

In New York, Hugh touched base with the *Saturday Review* and Book-of-the-Month Club people – the Canbys, Christopher Morley – finding out only towards the end of the trip that they had refused *Rogue Herries* 'at which I am not surprised' he confessed. 'Its sombre mood is against it.'[83] But he got a new commission to write monthly pieces for the *Golden Book Magazine* and lunched with publisher Blanche Knopf and his American publisher George Doran (recently bought out by Doubleday). He caught up with old writer friends Robert Frost and Carl Van Vechten, and made new ones in novelists Thomas Wolfe and Thornton Wilder, agreeing to a series of talks with Wilder asking 'Is fiction or history more real?' By Saturday 8 March, Hugh was back at the docks with Doran, delayed from leaving by a 'tiresome fog' but thankful that 'The American tour this time has been a complete success.'

On the way out he'd treated himself to reading Shakespeare's history plays straight through, but on the way back he got stuck into work for the Book Society, catching up with the choices the judges had made in his absence. 'I like this ship greatly' he wrote three days in: 'Trying to plough my way through the books.' 'Reading Bloch's very brilliant '*& Co.*' he noted with pleasure the next day, 'But I don't think it a good choice for the Book Society.'[84] Telling the story of a Jewish family from the annexed territory of Alsace who refuse to become German subjects and move to France before

WWI, Jean-Richard Bloch's *& Co* was an epic canvas of industry and society. Written by one of France's leading novelists and celebrated by critics, the translation was announced on publisher Victor Gollancz's bright yellow covers as 'The greatest French novel since Balzac.' But Hugh's instincts were correct. It wouldn't do so well with the Book Society.

The following weekend Hugh was back in London. Hampstead with the Cheevers on Sunday (tea at Jack's), then all Monday morning at Macmillan's, signing copies of his new book. Published the next day, 18 March 1930, *Rogue Herries* was 'the most important book of my life so far' Hugh wrote in his diary: his tribute to the tradition of Fielding, Walter Scott and Thackeray. Reviews were good – bar one exception in the *Daily Express* – and sales proved excellent, with *Rogue Herries* becoming Macmillan's bestseller for March, still selling 'hundreds a week' a year later.[85] The booksellers got behind it: Selfridges had a full window display, Bumpus chose it as one of their Easter books to advertise everywhere. Visiting his sister that April, Hugh reported happily to Harold Macmillan that 'every bookseller in Edinburgh [...] had a grand display'. John Buchan wrote to Walpole that it was 'the best novel published in English since *Jude the Obscure*', leaving Hugh deeply satisfied. 'Of course it was a risk to bring out so romantic a novel in these realistic days', he wrote to his publishers, who were initially sceptical.[86] But there was clearly a huge audience for what they'd feared was an 'enormous historical novel'.[87] Hugh was already part-way through the next one, *Judith Paris*, about Rogue Herries's headstrong daughter. Working constantly, and producing several short books in-between, Hugh would deliver the following two volumes over the next three years, creating an epic love letter to the Lakes that would come to define him.

In a patriotic foreword to *The Herries Chronicle* written two weeks into WWII (Macmillan brought the four books out in one volume at the end of 1939), Walpole positioned the work's genesis in the First World War. 'In the middle of the last War' he wrote, 'sitting in the mud in trenches near the Carparthians, I comforted my soul with visions of an English Chronicle that would stretch, without break, from the days of Elizabeth to our modern time.' Conceived as an escape from the present, the dramatic saga, covering a period of two centuries, from 1730 to 1932, transported readers from the day-to-day of The Great Depression. Francis Herries, the brash head of the family who brings them to Keswick, is dubbed by his neighbours 'a rogue, Herries – a fantastic rogue' after he sells off his mistress at a fair ('Even to that country tradition in that uncouth time the event was memorable', we are told).[88] Smuggling, cockfighting, more mistresses, and the Jacobite Rebellion follow. 'This is not merely a land of placid lakes and green hills and pastoral calm,' one admiring critic wrote, 'but it is also one of bareness and scars and restless energy.'[89] Even now, *The Herries Chronicle* is regarded as Walpole's masterpiece, and still celebrated in the Lakes. 'That I love Cumberland with all my heart and soul is another reason for my pleasure in writing these Herries books' Hugh wrote in his 1939 foreword. 'That I wasn't born a Cumbrian isn't my fault,' adding, 'that Cumbrians, in spite of my "foreignness", have been so kind to me, is my good fortune.'

Hugh had first visited the Lake district in his teens during summers away from Durham school, staying with a farming family near Gosforth, close to the sea, in south-west Cumberland. In his late thirties, he rediscovered his love for the place while on holiday and decided to buy a home near Keswick. Brackenburn, Manesty Park, Derwentwater, was 'Above Grange in Borrowdale. A little paradise on Cat Bells' he wrote excitedly in his diary. 'Running stream, garden, lawn, daffodils, squirrels, music-room, garage, four bedrooms, bath – All!'[90] Balancing out his life in Piccadilly, Brackenburn was a safety net, where he got most of his writing done; he had a new room built on top of the library to give himself a writing room so he could look over the trees and see Derwentwater. He could read and take the train up to Brackenburn, or motor there with Harold in the new thirty horsepower Daimler. 'All my own ambitions have come to this,' Hugh wrote in his autobiography, 'that I have been able to connect myself with a small square of country, the most lovely to me in the world, & to put on record for everyone who loves it as I do, my gratitude and the peace that I have found there.'[91] *Rogue Herries* was stamped with his two loves: Harold and the Lakes, dedicated 'For a trusted friend and in love of Cumberland.'

V

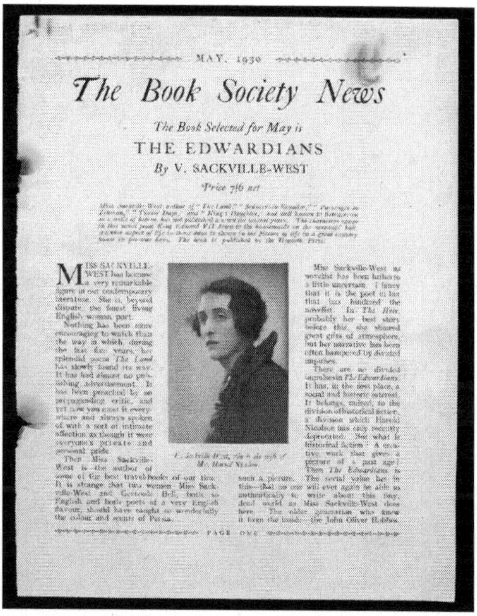

MAY, 1930

The Book Society News

The Book Selected for May is

THE EDWARDIANS

By V. SACKVILLE-WEST

Price 7/6 net

Book Society News, May 1930

The Book Society's first birthday party fell just over a month after the launch of *Rogue Herries*. 'This a great success' Hugh confirmed in his diary.[92] All of their authors were invited to a swanky dinner, plus publishers who'd tasted what one described as 'the Book Society bun'.[93] 'It was a lavish banquet, with wine flowing in rivers', publisher Harold Raymond wrote the next day to his author Margaret Irwin, whose novel, *None So Pretty*, they'd hoped might make a choice. 'How the booksellers would have gnashed their teeth if any of them had been present', he added.[94] Alan Bott arranged some additional publicity, asking famous German photographer Eric Salomon to attend with his 'candid camera' (Salomon was heralded as an innovator in celebrity photography, notoriously hiding his camera in unlikely places – bowler hat, hollow book – to catch his subjects off guard). Salomon got a series of photographs of his 'victims' in double (reflected upside down, taken with camera hidden at table level) which were later published by Bott in *The Graphic*.[95] There was Vita Sackville-West, author of the May 1930 choice, *The Edwardians*, smoking, looking on knowingly. Clemence Dane is in discussion with Fryniwyd Tennyson Jesse, great-niece of Alfred, Lord

Tennyson and author of *The Lacquer Lady*, the December 1929 choice, set in Burma. And Sylvia Lynd was captured by Salomon with eyes smiling wide, with friend *Punch* satirist A. P. Herbert, author of June 1930's *The Water Gipsies*.

Hugh is not in Salomon's birthday pictures. He arrived late, tired after seeing potential secretaries in the morning, meeting with the Society of Authors in the afternoon, then a film. But he was keen to see Vita Sackville-West, a literary celebrity known for her travel writing, radio broadcasts, and prize-winning poetry, as well as her open marriage to Harold Nicolson (diplomat, politician, and writer) and still, like her recent lover, Virginia Woolf, a relatively new friend. *The Edwardians* was her first book for six years and widely anticipated; an upstairs-downstairs novel set in a big country house, caught between critique and nostalgia for what seemed like the lost world of England before the war. Even without the Book Society, the book was likely to do well, but the Society's recommendation guaranteed success. Vita – like her publishers, Leonard and Virginia Woolf at the Hogarth Press – was delighted. They agreed to rush the production and trust the printer to make corrections without asking for a second set of proofs, so that they could publish for the Book Society in May, rather than June as had been planned. Hugh gave it a powerful send-off in the club magazine. 'No one will ever again be able so authentically to write about this tiny, dead world as Miss Sackville-West does here', he told readers. The social portrait of a house and its history was on a par with what Woolf had achieved in *Orlando*, it seemed to him. 'I wish', he wrote, 'what I very rarely wish, that her book had been twice as long as it is.'

However, the path to Book Society choice hadn't been easy. Though all the selection committee were in favour of *The Edwardians*, Sylvia had nursed doubts and put it to Hugh (as closest personally to the author) to persuade Vita to make changes to the text before it came out. These ranged from minor points of historical fact to worries about defamation. 'The references to King Edward will cause needless offence and are hardly fair since the ladies' names are altered', Sylvia pointed out. But then she went further, giving editorial advice and arguing that the conversation on the roof between the characters Sebastian and Leonard was 'silly'; 'much better let them talk in arm chairs afterwards', she thought.[96] Vita agreed to some modifications, changing the parts about Edward that Sylvia objected to. But the iconic conversation on the roof remained.

The episode flagged the judges' editorial power behind-the-scenes. In one sense this wasn't surprising. The selection committee were reading proofs direct from the publishers, before books came out, and as professional critics paid to read for a living, they were used to expressing their opinions. But ringing through suggested changes to authors and publishers after meetings – as, the archives show us, they started to do more and more – meant crossing a line. 'Don't know what upset Sylvia', Eric Linklater asked in a telegram to his publisher after the Book Society's deliberations on *Juan in America* left him with suggested edits to make.[97] Scottish writer George Blake changed language and dialect in his Clydeside novel *The Shipbuilders* to guarantee a Book Society choice. As Chair, Hugh was uncomfortable about asking authors for changes and persuaded Sylvia that they must choose *The Edwardians* once Sackville-West had made their revisions. 'I wrote to Mrs Nicolson and she replied that all the bits about Edward were now modified. I don't think we can well ask her to do more' he made clear in a letter from his sister's home that spring.[98] Novelist Richard Aldington had complained to his publishers about the cautious literary climate between the wars, saying there was a 'pre-publication censorship that is imposed upon you and me'.[99] Hugh and the Book Society contributed to this with varying degrees of unease.

Hugh's honeymoon with the club lasted a little over a year. On Tuesday 20 May 1930, three weeks after the first birthday party, he had tea with the Woolfs. They were just back from a tour, hawking their books around the Southwest, and full of news of opposition. 'The booksellers are often very rude', Virginia explained in a letter to Vita, 'all violently against the Book Society and say it is ruining them.'[100] Sales of *Rogue Herries* were slowing, and Hugh shared the Woolfs' report with Macmillan in panic, asking if they thought the opposition to the club only temporary, or if he should quit? 'So tell me honestly', Hugh pleaded, overtaken by anxiety, 'Is my chairmanship of the Book Society a nuisance to you as publishers?' Wondering if the stress was worth it, he told himself that now the club was established it could get on just as well without him. 'I can easily retire on the charge of my diabetes which is genuine enough,' he added.[101]

On the Friday that same week, Hugh told the other judges he might leave and was gratified by the 'Great bewailings' that followed. 'I won't this year anyway,' he noted after the meeting in his diary. He confirmed this conclusion in a letter to Macmillan the next day. 'In any case I must stay on till the end of the year,' he wrote him. 'Then I hate the idea of making the booksellers think they've won.' 'But I'm tired', he confessed, on the back of another rollercoaster year. 'I've been doing too much.'[102] Summer in Brackenburn beckoned however, punctured by a fortnight's lecture tour in Germany, and briefly Switzerland, where he had lunch with author Thomas Mann at his house ('very friendly but speaks almost no English', Hugh noted afterwards) and met psychologist C. G. Jung after he attended Hugh's lecture in Zurich.[103] The building work at Brackenburn was done when he arrived and Hugh found himself invigorated by the new writing-room and in re-arranging his books on the 'new glistening bookshelves'.[104] He bought a Bokhara rug in Manchester for the new room and enjoyed the wash of renewal and creative energy. He had a holiday with Harold in France and Spain to look forward to at the end of August. Panic over, he wrote to Macmillan from Brackenburn that June: 'Now I'm fit and ready to carry on the Book Society for ever.'[105]

VI

Hugh was back in London mid-September 1930 and hosted a Book Society meeting on Thursday 25th at his flat. With the Society touching nearly 11,000 members, the judges that day were 'very jolly, Jack especially', Hugh felt, and they agreed on some promising works for the autumn.[106] G. B. Stern's *Mosaic* was part of a Jewish series inspired by Galsworthy's *Forsythe Saga*, and for November they'd selected *The Fortunes of Richard Mahoney*, a great Australian trilogy whose three parts were now published in one volume, representing excellent value for money. That month, members would receive *Grand Hotel* by Vicki Baum, translated from the German by Basil Creighton. *Grand Hotel* was 'coarse in places', Hugh had conceded to Sylvia, but its cinematic style ensured a good read.[107] A stage adaptation was underway – due to open on Broadway that November – and the film rights had already been sold (this would come out in 1932, starring Greta Garbo).

After the meeting, Hugh dined out then went to the Palace Theatre to watch Franz Lehar's biographical operetta, Friederika, about the young poet Goethe's doomed love. He returned home to the flat, alone. Writing in a shaky hand in his diary the next day, still 'dreadfully upset', Hugh described what followed afterwards: 'Then home and half-undressed sitting on my bed, picked up idly Maugham's *Cakes and Ale*. Read on with increasing horror. Unmistakable portrait of myself. Never slept.'[108]

The portrait of Hugh as popular novelist Alroy Kear in W. Somerset Maugham's *Cakes and Ale*, was, as Virginia Woolf put it, 'a clever piece of torture' that Hugh never recovered from.[109] Like Walpole, Maugham's character was the author of 'some thirty books' and as a young man had 'laid his book at the feet of a great artist'. Alroy Kear lunched at the Savoy and had 'many friends in literary circles', with 'a pretty gift for after-dinner speaking'. He toured the United States and 'lectured up and down Great Britain. Now and then he revised his lectures and issued them in neat little books...' The similarities were obvious, the satire damning. 'His career might well have served as a model for any young man entering upon the pursuit of literature', the narrator states. 'I could think of no one among my contemporaries who had achieved so considerable a position on so little talent.'[110]

The next day, Hugh went into overdrive, calling Jack first, then Clemence Dane. Both shared a publisher with Maugham and they agreed to get onto Charlie Evans, Heinemann's managing director, about the potential libel right away. 'It had never occurred to him that there was any resemblance between the Alroy Kear of my novel and you', Maugham explained to Walpole during the fall out, flatly denying any link. Maugham had ten years on Walpole, and both had attended The King's School Canterbury, though at different times. 'Really I should not have been such a fool', Maugham protested in a long letter, swearing Alroy Kear was a composite figure of the writer, 'made up of a dozen people and the greater part of him is myself'. But as Hugh would say later, going over and over with friends 'his piteous, writhing & wincing & ridiculous & flaying alive story of Willie Maugham's portrait,' what he minded most were the little things: the engagement diary Alroy kept in his upper left-hand waistcoat pocket; the snide comment about his being in love with 'a duchess' (a dig at Hugh's relationship with opera singer Lauritz Melchoir).[111]

Later, after Hugh's death in 1941, Maugham's portrait was dredged up in various obituaries, and eventually came to define him. In 1950, Maugham admitted in a new introduction for the Modern Library that the character was based on Hugh.[112] But at the time, Hugh could be sure of only paranoia and uncertainty; plus a general sense that everyone was laughing at him. For how could Maugham deny it, he asked himself in his diary, 'when there are in one conversation the very accent of my voice?'[113]

The *Cakes and Ale* debacle knocked Hugh off his perch. For twenty years he had grafted his way into the literary establishment, brazening it out with good humour and charm. He knew some critics sneered at him. But Maugham's portrait, coming from a fellow writer who had attended the same school, was a body blow. 'My self-consciousness this year has leapt up like the damned trees that hide the lake from my window,' he wrote in his journal at the end of the following month, the new first floor rooms at Brackenburn not quite fulfilling their purpose.[114] 'The hardest business of the year was *Cakes and Ale*' he confirmed in his end-of-year summary.[115] Chairing the Book Society catapulted Hugh to a level of fame that made him an obvious target, but now he'd seen how power and influence could work against him, and he blamed the club for increasing the number of his detractors. Give or take a little time out in Hollywood, he'd stay on with the Book Society until his death in 1941. But it wouldn't be an easy ride.

1929

1	April	*The Love of the Foolish Angel*, Helen Beauclerk
2	May	*The Embezzlers*, Valentine Katacv, trans. by Leonide Zarine
3	June	*The Adventures of Ralph Rashleigh. A Penal Exile in Australia, 1825-1844*, ed. by Lord Birkenhead
4	July	*Henry the Eighth*, Francis Hackett
5	August	*Nicky, Son of Egg*, Gerald Bullett
6	September	*A High Wind in Jamaica*, Richard Hughes
7	October	*Whiteoaks*, Mazo de la Roche
8	November	*Gallipoli Memories*, Compton Mackenzie
9	December	*The Lacquer Lady*, F. Tennyson Jesse

1930

10	January	*All Our Yesterdays*, H. M. Tomlinson
11	February	*Kristin Lavransdatter*, Sigrid Undset, trans. by Charles Archer and J. S. Scott
12	March	*Three Daughters*, Jane Dashwood
13	April	*And Co.*, Jean-Richard Bloch, trans. by C. K. Scott Moncrieff
14	May	*The Edwardians*, Vita Sackville-West
15	June	*The Water Gipsies*, A. P. Herbert
16	July	*Bengal Lancer*, Francis Yeats-Brown
17	August	*A Note in Music*, Rosamond Lehmann
18	September	*Grand Hotel*, Vicki Baum, trans by Basil Creighton
19	October	*Mosaic*, G. B. Stern
20	November	*The Fortunes of Richard Mahoney*, H. H. Richardson

Chapter 2. Sylvia, 1930-1932

Everybody talks about books

I

Sylvia Lynd by Howard Coster, chlorobromide print, 1937

At the end of October 1930, Sylvia Lynd's mother, Nannie Florence Dryhurst, died at her home in Hampstead, three doors up from the Lynds. Sylvia had been nursing her mother for the last few months, sitting together each evening before the night nurse arrived, talking of the trip they'd made to Ireland the previous year, reminiscing about family and friends. On the night of her mother's death, Sylvia went home to write a review for *Time and Tide*, before coming back to find her asleep. 'I held her head on my hand and heard her breathe her last,' she recalled later of her profoundest experience of grief. Sylvia took ill and was too overcome to attend the funeral held a few days later in Golders Green. 'For two years I wept every day for her' she wrote later in her diary. 'She had always been my closest friend and to live near her was my greatest joy.'[116]

Nannie Dryhurst (born Hannah Anne Robinson) was a woman ahead of her time. 'Passionate, volatile and responsive to every new idea', as her granddaughter Sheila (Sylvia's eldest) remembered, Nannie was a formidable influence on those around her and a powerful role model for the women in her family. Born in Dublin in 1856, Nannie had worked initially as a governess and went to London in her twenties (where she met her future husband, Alfred Robert (Roy) Dryhurst, whom she married in 1884, aged twenty-eight), making a name for herself in the anarchist circles around Russian exile Peter Kropotkin, and, as a prominent Irish nationalist, involved with the Inghinidhe na h'Eireann [Women of Ireland] movement and the Gaelic League. She was renowned as a teacher, artist, translator, and anti-imperialist (in 1907 she gave an eye-witness account of Tsarist Russia's oppression of Georgia at an international conference at the Hague), raising awareness of the subjection of India, Egypt, and Ireland under the British. In 1910, she co-organised a conference for the 'Defence of Nationalities and Subject Races' in Caxton Hall in Westminster – there were sessions on modern-day slavery, Empire, and racism – and edited the volume of papers that came out the following year. Had she been born a generation or two later, her family believed, Nannie would have been 'conspicuously active in Parliament or some better source of human improvement'.[117] As it was, Nannie F. Dryhurst turned her home in Hampstead into campaign headquarters. The family drawing-room, as Sheila later recalled, was 'always full of Indians, Persians, and other plotters of the downfall of the British Empire', rubbing shoulders with actors from the Purcell Operatic Society and other writer friends (George Bernard Shaw, Ellen Terry, Gordon Craig). 'Sinn Féiners, Egyptian nationalists, Armenians, Georgians and Finns', writer David Garnett remembered gathering at Nannie's lively meetings on Downshire Hill.[118] According to family lore, Roy would return home from work at the British Museum, 'open the drawing-room door an inch or two, enough to look in on the Irishry, and disappear again at once'.[119]

Nannie's 'rebel spirit' deeply influenced her daughter Sylvia, demonstrating what was possible for an educated, middle-class, married woman of her time to achieve.[120] Sylvia Lynd had turned thirty and had two daughters by the time the Sex Disqualification (Removal) Act of 1919 was passed, which gave women the right to join the professions, to sit on juries, and be awarded degrees. But thanks to her mother, Sylvia knew how to combine meaningful work with home and family (building what we might now call a portfolio career), using her power and privilege in the domestic sphere to undergird her professional influence and reputation.

Sylvia hadn't planned to become famous as a book judge and critic, but she was primed from a young age to make a name for herself in the Arts. With both parents invested in literature, she'd read widely and began writing poetry in her teens (her first poem was published in the *Westminster Gazette* when she was fourteen or fifteen). Sylvia's parents were (as her youngest child later commented) an 'ill-suited pair, in agreement about having no religion and about the need for socialism (though not how this was to be achieved) and both enjoying music, but with very little else in common' and Sylvia's childhood was rocked by her mother's affair with journalist Henry Nevinson (this was discovered when Roy followed Nevinson along Downshire Hill one day and watched on, aghast, as Nevinson's dog turned automatically in at the gate).[121] During the rift that followed, her parents opted to divide and rule, taking responsibility for one child each, so Sylvia – under her mother's charge – had an unconventional schooling at the new, co-educational King Alfred School in Hampstead where she learnt how to paint but not to spell (so she told her own daughters). Afterwards, Sylvia trained at the Slade School of Fine Art and then – inheriting her mother's love of drama – as an actress at the equally prestigious Royal Academy of Dramatic Art. The stage furnished material for Sylvia's second novel, *The Swallow Dive*, published in 1921, but marriage and maternity put an early end to her acting career. 'I was deeply in love with a beautiful young actress and could not bear the thought of her being embraced, even in make-believe', her husband Robert said in his sixties.[122] Like her mother, Sylvia challenged many patriarchal codes facing women of the time, but they were still part of a society inevitably shaped by them.

Sylvia had first met Robert Lynd, then 'a perfectly penniless Irishman' from Belfast, at a meeting of London's Gaelic League which she attended, aged fifteen, with her mother.[123] Robert was the Irish-language tutor, nine years older than Sylvia, tall, wiry, and good-looking, dark curly forelock falling tantalisingly over his eyes. By the time she was seventeen, they were engaged to be married but her parents forced her to wait while Robert was still living 'hungrily on freelance journalism'.[124] Sylvia finally wed Robert in Hampstead Registry Office in April 1909, she not quite twenty-one, he just turned thirty and now with a regular post at the *Daily News*; he would stay there for the rest of his career, becoming literary editor after five years, as well as contributing a weekly essay as 'Y.Y.' (two wise) to the *New Statesman* from its founding in 1913 until 1945. They honeymooned in Ireland, Robert finalising material for his book on *Home Life in Ireland*, due out later that year (this was his first book dedicated to Sylvia Lynd, not Sylvia Dryhurst). Sígle (Gaelic for Sheila) was born the following year in 1910, Máire (known throughout her life as B. J., Baby Junior) in 1912, and the girls were raised bilingual, with the Irish cultural revival central to their childhood. As Sheila remembered, 'I myself was brought up to speak Gaelic first – in Hampstead; we were dressed in homespun and linen smocks from Achill, and among our earliest fairy tales were Lady Gregory's wonderful translations of Cuchulain and the stories of the Fianna.'[125]

Sylvia and Robert Lynd, with children by Unknown photographer, vintage bromide print on brown card mount, 1913-1914
© National Portrait Gallery, London

Sylvia and her family were 'passionately Irish', according to author Arthur Ransome (who once proposed to her), and the fate of Ireland, what was known at the time as the 'Irish Question', was a defining presence in their lives.[126] Nannie had edited the first volume of *Bean na h'Eireann* [*The Woman of Ireland*] and was a frequent visitor to Dublin's Scoil Éanna [St Enda's], the Irish language school Pádraig Pearse, one of the leaders of the Easter Rising, had founded in 1908, and his girls' school, Scoil Íde (Sylvia and Robert squeezed in a visit during their honeymoon). Robert Lynd was a socialist and nationalist – a London delegate for Sinn Féin (Sylia was also a member at the time of her marriage) – who believed, like Sylvia and her mother, that the Irish nation was best run by the Irish, not by an oppressive foreign power.[127] In his books and journalism, Robert campaigned for Ireland's right to Home Rule and independence, believing it his purpose in life, as Sheila later put it, 'to persuade the English how wrong they were about Ireland, and the Irish how wrong they were about each other'. 'England is in Ireland not as a matter of right but as a matter of power', he argued in his *Ireland. A Nation* of 1919. The only way to end war was to end Empires and imperialism. And that meant the English freeing Ireland from eight hundred years of colonial oppression, as much as fighting for Serbia, Belgium, and other small nations in World War I.

Like many others, Sylvia and Robert had been shocked by the Easter Rising of 1916, as Robert said, 'so obviously incapable of success'.[128] His *New Statesman* essay, 'If the Germans Conquered England' – a satire of colonialism, widely interpreted as a coded appeal for Irish freedom – was reprinted on the cover of the *Irish War News* by Pádraig Pearse to spread news of the Dublin rebellion. But the Lynds thought the uprising misguided, if noble, when so many of their fellow Irish were fighting alongside the English in the trenches (Robert had tried to sign up but was refused on health grounds). Nevertheless, the severity of the English response to the uprising was itself shocking, and the Lynds fought hard to clear Roger Casement, one of the insurgents. Casement was a well-respected anti-imperialist diplomat, knighted for his exposé of human rights abuses in the Congo and Peru. He was also a family friend, often meeting the Lynds for walks on the Heath (he always brought chocolate for the children, Sheila remembered). When Casement was tried for high treason for sourcing arms from Germany to support the Rising, Sylvia and Robert petitioned alongside Nannie for his reprieve, Robert visiting him in Pentonville prison the day before he was hanged. They kept a photograph of Casement on the wall in their bedroom. 'Dear Roger', Sylvia mourned years later in her autobiography, 'a tall, dark-haired man with pale blue eyes. I remember seeing him and Robert come striding down Downshire Hill together, and our grief when 1916 had brought all the old fierceness and danger back into the Irish and English scene.'

Watching the 'old fierceness and danger' wreck their homeland after 1916 devastated the Lynds. Sylvia and Robert took the girls with them to visit Ireland at the height of the War of Independence in 1920, Robert reporting daily to the London papers on the latest horrors, visiting Balbriggan in September the day after it was burned by the Black and Tans. They knew Michael Collins and Arthur Griffith personally through the Irish Literary Society in London (Collins would tease Robert when they met about his non-conformist protestant roots) and the Lynds were in favour of the Treaty negotiated with the British Government to end the war in December 1921. The Civil War that followed between June 1922 and May 1923 (as Eamon de Valera led nationalists who refused the terms of the Treaty) changed Sylvia and Robert, pushing them towards moderation in middle-age. 'Though he never wavered in any aspects of his radicalism', publisher Victor Gollancz recalled of Robert, 'he became one of the gentlest of all the men I have known, and one of the most tolerant.'[129] For Sylvia too, the Irish Civil War was a dividing line. There is no doubt that her experience of Ireland and the turbulence of Irish politics in her thirties shaped her response to the rise of fascism when serving on the Book Society the following decade in her forties.

Tall and slim, wearing her short hair in a fashionable perm, Sylvia was 'handsome, immensely energetic, ambitious, and a trifle ruthless and domineering' according to her friend, publisher Victor Gollancz, a regular at her Friday night soirees.[130] Like her mother's gatherings that she had grown up with, Sylvia's at-home salons in Hampstead were places to be seen. In the early 'irresponsible days' of her marriage, Sylvia and Robert mingled with the glamourous, up-and-coming set of Katherine Mansfield, John Middleton Murray, D. H. Lawrence, Rebecca West, and artist Mark Gertler (whom Sylvia knew from the Slade), as well as Robert's hard-drinking journalists from the *New Statesman*: Jack Squire, Clifford Sharp, Desmond McCarthy.

When they settled at 5 Keats Grove in her mid-thirties with the joint finances a little more stable though they still ran up medical and household bills that were difficult to pay, the parties got bigger ('if fine' was always the caveat, reliant on spilling out into the garden for space), the guests older and more establishment, but still raucous enough to annoy the neighbours. As well as Sylvia's writer colleagues on the Book Society, the Lynds' parties attracted journalists, literary agents, and publishers: essayist and caricaturist Max Beerbohm was a regular, along with cartoonist David Low, *Punch's* A. P. Herbert, novelist Rose Macaulay, and Victor Gollancz and his wife Ruth. A series of photographs in Gollancz's reminiscences capture the so-called lifting game in the Lynds' garden: Sylvia in the thick of it with a group of men, applying pressure on Gollancz's head to then miraculously lift him up in his chair. To a writer like Virginia Woolf, Sylvia's set were 'thinblooded'. Too '"nice", "kind", respectable, cleverish & in the swim' for her own tastes, Woolf reported in her diary.[131] But for Sylvia, glittery parties where she would 'play Puck' and set the world to rights were a saving grace, for even if her own star was fading and she didn't make much money from her own books, bringing people together brought in other types of literary work, helping shore up her career.[132] After her death in February 1952, aged sixty three, friends would call attention to Sylvia's legendary hospitality and ability to make guests happy 'with such apparent ease'. 'Few women can have left so large a number of devoted and grateful friends to keep her memory green,' J. B. Morton wrote in *The Times*.[133] It is one of the ironies of fate – though not untypical for literary women – that it is for her parties that Sylvia Lynd is now best known, where she is remembered at all.

II

During the hard months of her mother's lingering illness, Sylvia had read and admired E. M. Delafield's story, 'The Diary of a Provincial Lady', in the journal *Time and Tide*. Like many other middle-aged women of a certain class stretched by conflicting responsibilities, Sylvia empathised with the provincial lady's daily lot: obnoxious neighbours, a noncommittal husband, servants, children away at boarding school. This was on top of the endless trials of domesticity: planting bulbs, shopping, catering, the pressure to look good herself and keep up to speed. Privately, Sylvia thought her own erratically kept diary might be amusing to read one day. If, that is, 'all the tale-telling' were cut out, as she put it, leaving 'the diary of a delightful woman with many faults, and with a delightful if not wholly perfect family'.[134]

Lynd had known E. M. Delafield for years. They had moved in the same literary journalist circles since 1922, when Sylvia and Robert returned to London after a spell in rural Sussex during and after the First World War, and Sylvia had picked up her journalist contacts, writing for several papers including the *Nation*, the *Bystander*, and Lady Margaret Rhondda's *Time and Tide*. Dubbed 'The Modern Weekly for the Modern Woman', *Time and Tide* was an important venue for female journalists interwar, boasting an all-female board of directors, of which Delafield was one. Sylvia became one of their lead book reviewers, her apprenticeship on the paper helping establish her reputation as a serious – but accessible – critic, with an eye for spotting important new writing by women (Sylvia celebrated Virginia Woolf's breakthrough modernist novel *Jacob's Room* in 1922 for instance as 'the book that her admirers have hoped she would write', and championed Sylvia Townsend Warner's debut novel *Lolly Willowes*).[135]

Sylvia's talent for spotting the best writing by other women didn't necessarily help her own work. There was always someone better to be aware of, writing something more worthwhile, making her doubt herself. But it cemented her reputation as an influential critic. Joining the Book Society in 1928, Sylvia had been forced to give up her regular slot at *Time and Tide* (along with several other commitments), but she'd kept in touch by contributing the occasional poem or short story. Early 1930, during her mother's illness and while Delafield's fictionalised diary was being serialised, Sylvia was invited back for a high-profile slot, representing 'The Critic' in a series of articles published in *Time and Tide* on contemporary publishing. Sylvia took a generous line, arguing that critics should look for achievement rather than failure (not something her earlier, more ambitious self, keen to make a name, might have recognised). In the 'lowly branch of book-reviewing' that she belonged to, she added, the critic's most important job was simple: to let the potential purchaser know what they were buying.[136]

Through her connections, Sylvia knew that Delafield's serial was supremely popular, helping to broaden *Time and Tide's* readership, and leading to a clamour of protest when its first run came to an end. The serial was ripe with book club potential: 'a humorous masterpiece' in Clemence Dane's words; its author was 'our nearest Jane Austen', according to Hugh.[137] Consequently, the Book Society advised Delafield's agent that they'd make it a choice if it were longer when it came out in book form. 'Since there is no particular reason why a Diary should not go on just as long as its writer has strength to hold the pen,' Delafield recalled, 'I naturally agreed to write another 20,000 words.'[138] All went to plan, with Book Society members receiving *The Diary of a Provincial Lady* for Christmas 1930, two months after the death of Nannie Dryhurst.

As their twenty-first choice, *The Diary of a Provincial Lady* marked the club's own coming of age via its seepage into popular culture. In the story, the fictional heroine is a member of the Book Society and its choices puncture her diary, with books – or rather discussion about keeping up with new books – part of her social currency. So alongside 'talk about the Riviera, the new waist-line, choir-practice, the servant question, and Ramsay MacDonald' sit Vita Sackville-West's *The Edwardians* and T. S. Stribling's *The Forge*. Satirising the social milieu she was part of, Delafield captures brilliantly the competitive edge to her characters' book talk:

> Conversation becomes general. Everybody (except Robert) talks about books. We all say (a) that we have read *The Good Companions*, (b) that it is a very *long* book, (c) that it was chosen by the Book of the Month Club in America and must be having immense sales, and (d) that American sales are What Really Count. We then turn to *High Wind in Jamaica* and say (a) that it is quite a short book, (b) that we hated it-or, alternatively, adored- it, and (c) that it Really *Is* exactly *Like* Children.[139]

Amusingly, at the start of the diary the heroine is returning that month's book selection (Compton Mackenzie's *Gallipoli Memories*, if we take the dates straight). 'Arrival of Book of the Month choice, and am disappointed' she confides. 'History of a place I am not interested in, by an author I do not like.' Opting for an alternative recommendation, she finds herself thwarted. 'Find, on reading small literary bulletin enclosed with book' she continues:

> that exactly this course of procedure has been anticipated, and that it is described as being "the mistake of a lifetime". Am much annoyed, although not so much at having made (possibly) mistake

> of a lifetime, as at depressing thought of our all being so much alike that intelligent writers can apparently predict our behaviour with perfect accuracy.[140]

It makes sense that the provincial lady is a member of the Book Society. As a busy, well-to-do woman living in rural Devon, without easy access to bookshops, she would have been prime target material. We only have traces of the club's original members from its in-house journal (official membership records haven't survived), but according to research carried out for the BBC at the end of the 1930s, sixty to seventy percent of members lived outside of any town (both in the UK and what were then colonies: thirty to forty percent lived outside England).[141] Before signing up to the club, the provincial lady has been a regular book-borrower and admires the new book 'without library label' as a symbol of affluence.[142] Like Laura Jesson of *Brief Encounter*, the provincial lady uses Boots' Book-lovers' Library to borrow new books during her shopping trips, occasionally sending off for ones she can't wait for from *The Times*. Book Society marketing and promotional materials played on the social anxiety she experiences, asking how often you had to admit to your friends that you hadn't read the new book of the season? But Delafield also captures the pervasive social snobbery and doubts haunting readers who valued this new form of guidance. 'Decide not to mention any of this to Lady B.', the protagonist concedes, after the palaver with sending that months' book back:

> Always so tiresomely superior about Book of the Month as it is, taking up attitude that she does not require to be told what to read. Should like to think of good repartee to this.[143]

III

After her mother's death, Sylvia suffered over the winter of 1930-31 with a flair up of the chronic health problems she had endured for many years; her daughter B. J. believed her mother's serious illness, which often forced her to bed, may have been Crohn's Disease – a condition she had herself – only named by doctors in 1932. In January 1931, an operation on Sylvia's sinuses led to a spell of temporary deafness that resulted in a few weeks stay in a nursing home near Harley Street. Before Christmas, she'd helped the judges identify some strong choices for the new year. Stella Benson's *Tobit Transplanted* headed up a good run that included Tom Clarke's portrait of Lord Northcliffe (owner of the *Daily Mail* and *Daily Mirror*: the 'Napoleon of Fleet Street' according to the *New York Times*), and A. J. Cronin's debut novel, *Hatter's Castle*. But, grieving and still recovering from the operation, Sylvia was absent when the selection committee chose *Red Ike: A Novel of Cumberland* co-authored by J. M. Denwood and S. Fowler Wright. It was the club's most controversial decision of the early years, and it soon came back to bite them.

Red Ike is a gothic thriller about a poacher, the story marked by passion, murder and revenge. Its main author, Denwood, was a Cumbrian dialect poet, known as a local genius and the 'Burns of the Lake District'.[144] Denwood's father (who inspired the character of Red Ike) was also a self-educated poet, a man 'as poor as Job', his son Denwood remembered, whose own poetry had fallen into oblivion.[145] Hugh Walpole had come across Denwood when he was up in the Lakes and encouraged him to try writing prose (more money in it than poetry). After reading an early version, Hugh agreed to write a preface, believing Denwood's book remarkable for a working-class poet '*not* a professional novelist' by training, who'd achieved something special with the writing 'because of its feeling of place'.[146]

Unfortunately, this preface was written before the manuscript was passed to S. Fowler Wright, tasked (as he put it) with correcting 'a radical defect of construction' and knocking it into shape by 'changing it to the third person throughout, and placing the incidents in chronological order'.[147] Hugh's endorsement advertised the book all the same. 'All his life long he has breathed the air of these hills and dales as though he were part of them,' Hugh told Book Society readers.

Red Ike was selected at a quiet judges meeting late April 1931, with only Hugh, Clemence Dane, and George Gordon present. Clemence was wary, feeling the book flawed and the change from first person to third problematic, losing the narrator's personality and vividness of the original style. But she found herself persuaded by Hugh's enthusiasm. Sylvia – always firmer with Hugh – was predictably furious when she found out ('I hope you weren't too annoyed?', Hugh tiptoed by letter, well knowing the answer). It would have been better if the 'poacher had written about poaching', Sylvia replied clearly, and if 'Fowler Wright hadn't transposed what he did write' into something else.[148] Sylvia and Clemence's reservations about the book were echoed in the wider press, rammed home by some reviewers in the first real challenge to the club beyond the bookselling trade. Helen Fletcher's damning review for *Time and Tide* was especially hurtful to Sylvia. *Red Ike* was a 'semi-successful return to Victorian melodrama', Fletcher argued, 'funny if it were not so tragic'. Ominously, *Time and Tide* used the selection to question the club's judgement overall. Before *Red Ike*, 'Mr Walpole's committee seemed a valuable safeguard', Fletcher conceded, 'a kind of sorting-house for the classics of to-morrow.' 'What jars is the lost affinity between the Book Society and modern literature,' she went on.[149] *Red Ike* was a genuine bestseller between the wars, selling over forty thousand copies in two years, landing Denwood a publishing deal and a much wider platform than he'd had previously. But its selection opened up a faultline which first undermined, and finally led to the collapse, of the Book Society's credibility with serious critics. The episode demonstrated just how much they needed Sylvia.

***

That April 1931, Sylvia brought out her fourth collection of poems. *The Yellow Placard*, published by her neighbour and ally, Victor Gollancz, was dedicated to family friend Geraldine Wildon Carr, whose husband, the philosopher Herbert Wildon Carr, was dying. It was an intimate volume of reflective, formally traditional lyrics – largely about nature – shot through with a bitter sense of loneliness and grief:

> Oh it is dark and cold
> In this green wood alone
> The grave is not a colder place
> To shut me from the sun. ('The Seeds of Love')

Sylvia Lynd's poetry of the late 1920s and '30s is full of dark nights, lonely interiors, and solitude. Trees become objects of terror; the domestic fireside becomes a 'prison'. In 'October Evening', 'Lime and Ash and Chestnut tree / In darkness drown' as the viewer sits while dusk falls. In the poem's second stanza, night takes over as love, death, and human separation merge in an image of desire and despair:

Intangible all-whelming sea!
Night after night I watch and mark
The shadow of oblivion
That makes all shapes and meanings one,
And you and me. ('October Evening')

Sylvia shared advance copies among her friends cautiously, writing to Hugh with modesty: 'Here is a book for you – a drop in the ceaseless deluge but not a large one.'[150] He replied two days later, full of reassurance and praise, affirming he'd read it through 'in a gulp'. 'But it's a shame that you don't write more', Hugh pointed out, unnecessarily, 'and how well you know it's a shame!'[151] Publicly, there was no major fanfare – poetry was always a difficult sell – but Gollancz found enough good copy for further publicity. 'What beauty she makes out of her dreams!' glossed a review in the *New Statesman*; 'Jewels that are flawless' said the *News Chronicle*. Lynd had corrected some of the minor flaws of rhythm that (according to the *TLS*) had tripped readers of her debut volume in 1916, *The Thrush and the Jay*. Since then, she'd had two further collections out: *The Goldfinches* with Richard Cobden-Sanderson in 1920, and a volume in Ernest Benn's prestigious series of Modern Augustan Poetry in 1928. But there was just enough criticism to needle Sylvia's fragile sense of her worth as a poet. *The Yellow Placard* was in the main tradition of 'English minor poetry' wrote 'Baskerville' in a mean review in the *Birmingham Gazette*: 'The cumulative effect is that of a charming mind finding careful and adequate expression in limpid and exact poetic phrase.'[152]

IV

That summer of 1931, Sylvia Lynd hosted one of the biggest parties of her life. On Saturday 4 July, after nearly twenty-seven years of living together, James Joyce and Nora Barnacle were married quietly in Kensington Register Office to ensure their children's inheritance. Robert Lynd helped Joyce to try and keep it out of the papers, hosting a modest, rather sombre, lunch for the Joyces at 5 Keats Grove after the service. But once the press had got wind and whipped up a scandal – questioning both Nora's listing in the register as 'spinster' and Joyce's solicitor's statement about his supposed marriage to her in Austria in 1904 – the Lynds' did them proud with a proper do the following Thursday. Sheila and B. J. helped decorate the garden, hanging Chinese lanterns from the weeping ash and dotting night-lights in coloured glass jars around the flowerbeds. Hordes of guests were squeezed in (no Hugh, already holidaying in Cornwall with Harold). 'It was the high point of my mother's literary parties', B. J. remembered. 'Sometime after midnight…we all went into the drawing-room…and then Joyce went to the piano.'[153] 'He sat down,' Victor Gollancz recalled in his memoirs, 'and I shall always remember what followed as among the rare experiences of my life.'[154] As Joyce sang traditional Irish songs and folk tunes - Phil the Fluther's Ball, the sad and beautiful Shule Aroon – and recited parts of *Anna Livia Plurabel* from his 'Work in Progress' (later published as *Finnegan's Wake*), the room hushed. 'The sound of it was lovely beyond description,' Gollancz recalled. Sylvia was in her element.

Despite the mockery in the press over *Red Ike*, the club itself was still pleasing readers. Like the rest of the industry, the Book Society had assumed The Great Depression would negatively impact book sales yet membership held out, mirroring what the press dubbed 'an amazing increase in the amount of reading done by the general public', with less cash to spend on other consumer items during the crisis, or on going out.[155] Before the summer holidays, the judges selected their first American book with T. S. Stribling's much-anticipated *The Forge*. This had come out in the States in the spring in midst of The Great Depression but was already a bestseller thanks to the American Book-of-the-Month Club, celebrated as an important book that challenged the nostalgic codes of writing about the South typical of Antebellum literature. Stribling was known to American readers as the writer of *Teeftallow* (1926) – a 'tale of religious fanaticism and village herd-poison' as Christopher Morley, one of the Book-of-the-Month Club judges, flagged in a letter to Hugh – as well as *Birthright* (1922), critically acclaimed as one of the first Southern novels to treat the experience of Black Americans seriously.[156] Trained as a teacher and lawyer, Stribling had travelled in Venezuela and other parts of South America and was not afraid of taking an unpopular line. As he explained to one reader, 'when I write of people nobody likes very much, I know I have done a human thing'.[157]

The Forge was the first volume in what became known as Stribling's Alabama trilogy, set during the American Civil War and Reconstruction era. The story centres on a household of pioneer farmers called the Vaidens and the people they have enslaved, exposing societal hypocrisy and corruption and satirising the confused moral codes of the South. As Augustus Vaiden is challenged by a Union hill farmer when he runs away to join the Confederate army:

> "You deserve to be tuk out!" stated the old man harshly, "joinin' up to fight to keep human beings in servitude...chain up men an' womern an' children in slavery generation after generation!"[158]

The book spoke to America's racist Jim Crow laws that continued to enforce racial segregation in the South, and the country's long-running problems with white supremacy, making the point of view of the Blacks – as Clemence Dane pointed out to the Book Society – 'the real basis of the story'.[159] The 1920s had seen the resurgence of lynching and the Ku Klux Klan (one of the Vaidens joins up in *The Forge*), while the notorious Scottsboro Boys case of April 1931 resulted in nine African American teenagers in Alabama accused of rape condemned to death before an all-white jury in a clear miscarriage of justice. In August, when *The Forge* was published in the UK, African American writer W. E. Du Bois declared that confederacy monuments in the South should be inscribed honestly as 'Sacred to the memory of those who fought to perpetuate Human Slavery.'[160] The following year, 1932, Stribling was awarded the Pulitzer Prize for *The Store*, the second volume in the Alabama trilogy.

The Book Society followed *The Forge* with some lighter choices by new authors, largely promoted by Sylvia. Dorothy Wynne Willson's first novel, *Early Closing*, about an English boy's school, was 'as fresh as the proverbial daisy and as clever as the unproverbial paint' Sylvia wrote Hugh: it 'couldn't be wittier or charminger'.[161] After this came conservative Arthur Bryant's first trade book, an entertaining history of *King Charles II* that began dramatically with Charles's escape after the Battle of Worcester. And in December 1931, the club selected Kate O'Brien's 'peculiarly beautiful and arresting' fiction debut (Priestley's words). *Without My Cloak* is an epic family saga exploring the strictures of Irish society and Catholicism, and how a family can 'own one another'.[162] Sylvia was an early champion and one of its most important backers, telling both the Book Society and the *Prix Femina-Vie Heureuse* committee 'to expect something that was, so to speak, the guinea and not the pound'.[163] As well as accolades from both of Sylvia's literary committees, the book went on to win the Hawthornden and James Tait Black literary prizes (it was reissued as a Virago Modern Classic in 1986). Today, Kate O'Brien is celebrated as a foremother to contemporary women's dominance in Irish fiction and a pioneer of queer writing. She 'seems to me extraordinarily good...' Sylvia wrote to Hugh in a persuasive letter, overflowing with enthusiasm.[164] Here was an Irishwoman who could really benefit from Sylvia's connections. And, more importantly, the novel spoke to her heart.

Kate O'Brien's *Without My Cloak* explores love, duty, and desire across two generations. Caroline Considine's attempt to leave an unhappy marriage (only to return days later) and her nephew Denis's struggle to break from family convention, are imaginative possibilities that the story opens out to readers: bids for personal freedom that we know are, nevertheless, doomed to fail. For Sylvia, these were dreams close to home. As a child, she had seen what happened when two people in a marriage were fundamentally unsuited. Now, as a mother herself, she worried about her own daughters' settling down. Sheila had shut her out recently after being 'jilted' by Gerry Young (a Baronet), to whom she'd been engaged from the age of nineteen. But Sylvia was also invested in *Without My Cloak's* four-hundred-and-fifty-odd pages because of her own personal loss and heartbreak. The book was a cry for happiness from a writer who knew what it felt like to be trapped. For though she might dream of beginning another life sometimes, Sylvia knew that – like Kate O'Brien's Caroline Considine – she'd never go through with it.

Ten years into her marriage, in 1919, Sylvia had fallen for the married Irish barrister, Gordon Campbell. If Robert had stayed sober, she protested in her diary, 'I shouldn't have fallen out of love with him.' 'And then I shouldn't have had an empty heart for G. to walk in to.' As a civil servant, Campbell had been a key figure in the government of the Irish Free State (in 1922, his Dublin home had been attacked by anti-Treaty forces who let his wife Beatrice save the children's Christmas presents before they burnt it down). A friend of Robert's initially, Gordon and Sylvia met through mutual friendships with John Middleton Murry and Katherine Mansfield. Gordon was a keen sailor and literary man (he had a play performed in 1928 under a pseudonym), on the board of Dublin's Gate Theatre. He was also part of the Irish aristocracy. In March 1931, just before *The Yellow Placard* was published, Sylvia had learnt that he'd become Lord Glenavy, succeeding to the title on his father's death. Not having seen him since before her own mother's death the previous year, Sylvia mourned his absence. 'Always to think of him & never to see him' she wrote in her diary. 'How unreproachful I feel, though he has, in one sense, helped to spoil my life. (So many things have done that, though). Really he has been my life. Never out of my thoughts for more than ten minutes in the last sixteen and a half years.'[165]

Gordon Campbell was married to the Irish artist Beatrice Elvery in a union arranged by their families. Beatrice was talented and well-connected, dubbed 'the beautiful Miss Elvery' by writer Lady Gregory, and close to Sylvia's own great Dublin friend, artist and patron Sarah Purser.[166] But Beatrice was unhappy in the marriage according to Mark Gertler, in whom she confided (he then passed this news on to Sylvia), 'living with Gordon like complete strangers in the same house'.[167] Despite their love affair, neither Sylvia nor Gordon were prepared to lose their homes and family or scandalise society. As Gordon would later admit to Robert in his office: 'the thing is, I want to enjoy myself and your wife wants me to behave myself'. 'Oh, God, had I forseen what it would all be I could not have lived', Sylvia wrote in anguish, a regular refrain in her diary. 'What folly. We could have been so happy just knowing one another, if he had not insisted on making me fall in love with him.'[168]

Sylvia's own marriage to Robert was known to be challenging. By her account, they lived amicably for the first eight years until 'one day, on my suggesting that three whiskies instead of four would be better after dinner, I found that we did not agree.' Robert was a notoriously hard drinker, like his father, and battled against alcoholism all his life. Fleet Street was not an easy place to stay sober, and his friendship with the editors of the *New Statesman* (Squire and Sharp especially, according to Sylvia) made his drinking problem worse. To outsiders, Robert's drinking may have appeared benign. 'At the Lynd parties he became gentler and gentler as more and more whiskey passed through him,' Gollancz remembered in his memoirs, 'until at midnight he just looked at you with faintly quivering nostrils and a smile like a Seraph's.'[169] But to Sylvia, it was difficult to bear. In her diary, she recounts how Robert would come home late at night, disturbing her sleep, waking her in a rage ('it isn't himself but the whisky fiend who howls abuse at me', she rationalised). After one particularly embarrassing party, when Alan Herbert had plied Robert with drink and he'd been sitting 'like an imbecile half asleep on the sofa by half-eleven', Sylvia wrote, he woke her 'as usual' 'about five o'clock muttering in an obscure rage'. This time she fought back. 'I said if he didn't stop at once & let me go to sleep again I'd hit him in the face with my fist, take my bed clothes into the study & this time never come back.' 'Robert is killing himself and killing me' she despaired privately. It was like 'the strain of living with a madman'.[170]

***

Book Society members received *Without My Cloak* in December 1931, as the club oversaw its first change of judges. Now three years in, it was little surprise that one of them wanted out, and Jack Priestley was the first to jump ship. Jack's own personal life had gone into meltdown that summer when an affair with the young actress Peggy Ashcroft (then wife of Rupert Hart-Davis, who would replace Arthur Barker as the club's assistant early 1932) prompted Jack to temporarily leave his second wife, Jane, and their four children (two were from Priestley's first marriage). Hugh had found himself in the middle of the break-up: 'the complications are almost more than I can follow, poor bachelor that I am', he protested.[171] By August 1931, Jack had 'chucked everything – "*Standard*", "Book Soc:" – everything!' But by the end of the year, he and Jane were reconciled and made plans to move into a four-storey house across the Heath (a former home of Coleridge) before their next baby was due in the spring. Jack set himself up in the Romantic's 'pokey' study and continued to write at a prodigious rate but remained determined to leave the Book Society.[172] He'd been invited to take over Arnold Bennett's job as lead book reviewer on the *Evening Standard*, one of the most influential, and best paid, book jobs of the day. 'I am delighted about the *Standard* of course', Hugh congratulated him on his appointment. 'More power to you!'[173] Hugh and Jack remained close, with Hugh becoming part of the extended Priestley family as godfather to his children. 'I've never had a writing man for a friend before who has been so close a companion', Hugh reflected on their friendship early on.[174] 'He is so gruff, ill-mannered', Hugh wrote of Jack towards the end of his life. 'But, through all and everything, there is a deep sweetness that pervades his whole nature, which is why I love him.'[174]

Finding the right person to replace Jack was hard, and the judges toyed with possibilities for months. But by the December 1931 meeting ('everyone at their nicest', wrote Hugh), where they chose Charles Morgan's WWI novel set in Holland, *The Fountain*, for the new year, they'd whittled it down. Sylvia was pleased. Poet Edmund Blunden (proposed by George Gordon) was a new fellow in English Literature at Merton College, Oxford. Blunden had left school in 1915 – delaying an Oxford scholarship for the Officer Training Corps, Flanders, and France – and was sent to the Front in May 1916, aged nineteen. By his twenty-first birthday he'd survived continual action in the Front lines, taking part in what he described as the war's 'vast machine of violence' including the 'holocaust of the Somme' and the Battle of Passchendaele.[176] After the war, Blunden worked on *The Athenaeum* and taught in Japan and was now established, in his mid-thirties, as a literary editor and prize-winning nature poet (like Sylvia, he was part of Benn's Augustan Books of Modern Poetry). Robert Lynd had been on the panel that awarded Blunden the Hawthornden Prize in 1922 for *The Shepherd (And Other Poems of Peace and War)*, anticipating 'promise here of a permanent contribution to English Literature'.[177]

Sylvia knew Edmund from *Time and Tide* where, like her, he was an occasional contributor. She'd hugely admired his bestselling memoir, *Undertones of War*, published in 1928, and praised the poetic sensitivity in the book, declaring 'the indictment of war seems more complete here than any we have yet encountered'. 'One thing is certain', she'd concluded in a major review for *Time and Tide*, 'after this book there can be no ignorant war-makers.'[178] Already during 1931, Blunden had brought out a limited edition of Keats's Letters – Sylvia had seen him promoting it at the reopening of Keats's House, just down the road from them, that July – and edited a new, wide-ranging collection of poems by Wilfred Owen (this would be the standard edition of Owen's poetry for the next thirty years). Edmund Blunden was a serious, quietly dignified man – 'a cross between Julius Caesar and a bird', as Robert Graves captured him – who, Sylvia agreed with Hugh, would be useful in helping them find more good criticism and biography.[179] They'd miss Jack Priestley in meetings: mocking all their enthusiasms, slighting everything on the lists, railing at Barker and Bott to get better books in from the publishers. But having a poet and scholar like Edmund Blunden in his place signalled the club's critical ambitions. They were still here providing a service to readers. And they intended to be taken seriously.

V

Four months into her membership, E. M. Delafield's provincial lady resigns from the Book Society, blaming the 'wide and ever-increasing divergence of opinion between us as to merits or demerits of recently published fiction'. In the next volume, *The Provincial Lady Goes Further* (published in book form in 1932, after being serialised in *Time and Tide* again), we get a candid appraisal of the club's record to date:

> We talk about Italy, the Book Society - *Red Ike* a fearful mistake, but *The Forge* good - and how can Mr. Hugh Walpole find time for all that reading, and write his own books as well?[180]

'I hear you don't like the Delafield', Hugh wrote Sylvia, discussing who would write the review (*The Provincial Lady Goes Further* was recommended as an alternative, rather than a main selection). 'Wonders will never cease! I should have thought it just what you would like, but do, do something else if you'd rather.'[181] For Sylvia, the sniping was getting too close to home. And Delafield had benefited enough from club reach and publicity.

The criticism on *Time and Tide* that had begun with Delafield's playful satire and hardened as it mingled with Helen Fletcher's attack on *Red Ike* the previous year, came to a messy head for Sylvia early 1932. On Saturday 13 February, sat up in bed with the papers, Sylvia was pouring out the tea carefully (her housekeeper had left a note warning her to be careful with the broken teapot handle) when she came across the front page of *Time and Tide*. 'The Book Society' announced the lead article. There was a double page spread further in, analysing the club's impact, with a table of figures breaking down club choices and recommendations by publisher between January 1930 and that month's *The Fountain*. Victor Gollancz came out top (with five selections and twenty-four recommendations equalling twenty-nine books in total), then William Heinemann (twenty) followed by Jonathan Cape (totalling thirteen). 'We will only say that the gifts of fortune seem to have fallen with an unevenness that does not always bear relation to merit' the anonymous author reflected.[182] 'The really important point in the criticism which has been...directed against the Book Society' the article went on, 'is that literary merit – we use the word "literary" in its widest sense – has not always been given its due weight.'

For the next three weeks, a flurry of letters from readers and the trade fed a public debate on the club. Were judges paid? Did publishers influence the selections? How much was it harming the bookshops? For the club, it was all publicity, ultimately, offering a chance to settle the score. 'The Book Society is a private limited liability company not, and has never set up to be, an Academy of Letters' the judges wrote in a joint statement published the following month. Yes, judges were paid a stipend to read and write reviews but held no shares and had nothing to do with the business direction of the company. Nor had they ever used the word 'best' to describe their selections: they were the judges' personal recommendations to members – readers who were free to resign at any time or exchange that month's choice for another selection. In fact, the spat gave the selection committee and their allies an opportunity for grandstanding. 'But live and let live', Rose Macaulay wrote in defence of her friends, comparing club membership to taking your fishmonger's advice on the day's catch, 'Let anyone chose anything for anyone who wants to be chosen for, and let no one else give a damn about it.'[183]

But for Sylvia, the attack on her integrity was personal. Everyone on *Time and Tide* staff knew how close she was to Gollancz and his wife Ruth. There were the weekly parties at her house that they came to, and now Victor was her own publisher (Sylvia was at work on two anthologies for Gollancz coming out later that year: an omnibus of stories for children and a selection of stories for Christmas). 'Did you not take our leader for more of an attack than it actually was?', Lady Margaret Rhondda, founding editor of *Time and Tide*, asked after Sylvia's impassioned right-to-reply was published the following week. 'Our object was to extend the pleasure of reading and possessing books, and in this we have succeeded beyond our wildest expectations,' Sylvia declared in an overly long rant (published in full, the editor pointed out, despite exceeding the space usually allotted to any one correspondent), accusing *Time and Tide* of inaccuracies in its reporting and suggesting it had its own bias towards certain publishers in its choice of book reviews. 'Might it not be more sensible to question the disinterestedness of the anonymous critics of the Book Society Committee rather than to question the integrity of Mr Hugh Walpole, Professor Gordon, Miss Clemence Dane, Mr J. B. Priestley, and, in all humility, your old contributor?' Sylvia signed off in a flurry.[184]

The apology was clearly written in haste and did Sylvia no favours, only fanning the flames while the spat ran its course. But it was all helpful fodder to a recently qualified PhD in Cambridge, writing up her thesis on *Fiction and the Reading Public* for her publishers, Chatto and Windus. Queenie D. Leavis's caricature of the Book Society as part of the 'middlemen' responsible for dumbing down and standardising taste would damn the club far longer than the *Time and Tide* furore. 'By conferring authority on a taste for the second-rate, a middlebrow standard of values has been set up (to the Book Society the publication of *A Modern Comedy* is "a real event in the story of modern English literature")' Leavis wrote with disdain in her influential survey of cultural change and interwar reading patterns (still in print).[185] The club was a minefield in the contemporary culture wars. And Edmund Blunden was wading straight into it.

1930

21	December	*The Diary of a Provincial Lady*, E. M. Delafield

1931

22	January	*Morning Tide*, Neil M. Gunn
23	February	*Tobit Transplanted*, Stella Benson
24	March	*Juan in America*, Eric Linklater
25	April	*My Northcliffe Diary*, Tom Clarke
26	May	*Hatter's Castle*, A. J. Cronin
27	June	*Red Ike*, J. M. Denwood & S. Fowler Wright
28	July	*Humour and Fantasy*, F. Anstey
29	August	*The Forge*, T. S. Stribling
30	September	*Early Closing*, D. Wynne Wilson
31	October	*King Charles II*, Arthur Bryant
32	November	*Festival*, Struthers Burt
33	December	*Without My Cloak*, Kate O'Brien

1932

34	January	*The Brothers*, L. A. G. Strong
35	February	*The Fountain*, Charles Morgan

Chapter 3. Edmund, 1932-5

Chapters of Literary History. Very Little Known

I

Edmund Blunden by Rex Whistler, drawn at Siegfried's, pencil, 1929

As he stepped off the Oxford train into the crowds of Paddington station, he stole another glance at his watch. Slim and relatively small in stature at five foot six, his precise movements revealed the habits of a keen sportsman as he darted through the throng, an unremarkable figure in a shabby suit. The battered suitcase he was carrying was empty, waiting for treasures like the signed Charles Dickens he'd found the previous summer. If he hurried, he might have enough time for some book-hunting in the Farringdon Road book-barrows before that afternoon's meeting at Hugh Walpole's flat.

For Edmund Blunden, the previous six months had been overwhelming.

March 1932, he was approaching the end of his first two terms as a Fellow of English at Merton, gradually becoming accustomed to the grind and routines of college life, plus the incongruity of high table. Oxford was 'a mixture of luxury and privation,' as he put it to his mother, 'not a job for anyone whose hopes and previous labour were poetry and good literature'.[186] He enjoyed the companionship and stimulation of living with other scholars in Fellows' Quad and liked talking about the eighteenth century, or cricket, with the undergraduates he befriended during informal tutorials along the River Cherwell (or more often with a pint in the pub). He was endlessly patient and a good listener, with a dry wit. But academia was pulling him every which way. Since February that year, Edmund had delivered the Clark Lectures in Cambridge (his topic was the essayist Charles Lamb, whom he was attempting to recover from critical neglect and condescension), in addition to talks in London and the new lectures he was obliged to give in Oxford. These were prepared largely, as he admitted privately, 'on my nerves and alcohol'.[187]

On top of all this new work was the journalism. He was still writing weekly for the *Nation* and *TLS*, as well as trying to find time for his own research and poetry. 'My head burns, my body shakes – and yet I am not getting things done' he confessed to Aki Hayashi, his literary assistant, early February 1932.[188] And now there was the Book Society. But he needed the money. Edmund's university salary was swallowed up by his personal commitments, with payments to his ex-wife, Mary, and the children, to Annie, his German sister-in-law; as well as Aki. 'Do not damn me' he wrote his old friend Siegfried Sassoon on joining the club's selection committee. 'I am always considering the possible necessity of my stealing off into solitude; this Univ. is a little crushing to me.'[189]

Edmund's first Book Society meeting on Friday 4 March was inevitably dominated by the *Time and Tide* fallout. Hugh was in a flap, complaining about being made 'general Whipping Boy!' yet again and worrying about the impact on his own book sales, while Sylvia was, it seemed to Edmund, 'malicious and gentle by turns,' clearly feeling herself stabbed in the back.[190] Edmund knew George Gordon already from sherry after tennis at Oxford, and admired how his good humour helped steady the ship. Alongside the others, Edmund put his name to the joint 'Manifesto' (Hugh's words) agreed on that day.[191] 'We are entirely uninterested in the names of the publishers; their books are our sole concern' the judges declared to *Time and Tide* in a carefully worded right-to-reply. All published criticism was intended both to guide opinion and make someone a profit, they reminded the paper's readers. Perhaps partly out of bravado, they chose another Victor Gollancz title that day, adding to readers' already prominent collections of bright yellow dust jackets. Hilda Vaughan's *The Soldier and the Gentlewoman*, a tale of post-WWI marital conflict, was 'much more than a story of a woman of breeding who murders her husband', read the cover. Edmund agreed to write the review, and Gollancz used the new judge's endorsement to lead his advertisements.

But more important to Edmund personally on that first day in March 1932 was meeting another new recruit to the club. Rupert Hart-Davis – former actor turned office-boy at publisher William Heinemann – had been appointed to relieve Arthur Barker of the club's management (Barker was leaving to set up his own publishers). Rupert was twenty-five, ten years younger than Edmund, but Edmund was immediately drawn to him, impressed by Rupert's charisma and ideas, and friendship developed fast. By April, Rupert had visited Edmund's parents' home in the village of Yalding near Maidstone in Kent, appreciating the rural community that continued to nurture his new literary friend. 'I enjoyed very much my visit to Yalding, for which a thousand thanks,' Rupert wrote Edmund after Easter on Book Society letterhead. 'Fine books, beer, food and company. What a treat!'[192] Rupert was sympathetic to Edmund's term time workload and grateful to be accepted 'as a contemporary and a literary and intellectual equal' by such an esteemed mentor.[193] 'I hate to think that you begin each day tired,' Rupert wrote him the following month. 'We must get you right somehow. Oxford is clearly bad.'[194]

For his part, Edmund found Rupert's youthful enthusiasm a tonic. Blunden was only thirty-five when he joined the Book Society that spring, but his traumatic experiences on the Western Front – surviving the disasters of the Somme, Ypres, and Passchendaele during 1916 to 1918 – had made him feel 'ancient', so much so that he could describe Rupert in a letter to fellow veteran Siegfried Sassoon as 'a great discovery to my mind' who had 'brightened' his 'old age'.[195] As new boys at the Book Society, the pair quickly became allies. Edmund commiserated with Rupert on having to find copy for the monthly club magazine, sending him one of his own poems to print whenever he could. 'Here we are all busy casting clouts and catching colds,'

Rupert wrote Edmund in May 1932, 'while over all hangs the black threat of the Book Society News. I wonder whether any single one member ever opens the bloody thing?'[196] The following April, 1933, Rupert would leave the Book Society to join publisher Jonathan Cape. But their friendship became one of Edmund's most important relationships, lasting for over forty years and leaving a huge correspondence. In 1934, Rupert became Edmund's own publisher, supporting his then wife Sylva's writing career too. Edmund would dedicate his biography of John Taylor – *Keats's Publisher* – to Rupert when it came out with Cape in 1936. Of his scores of books, it was the academic achievement of which he was most proud.

***

Joining the Book Society at the beginning of 1932, Edmund Blunden was in the throes of a new love affair, 'passing through (perhaps 'through')' as he put it in a letter to Sassoon, 'a period of deep inward disturbance'. In February 1931, Edmund's divorce from his first wife, Mary, had finally been granted. He and Mary – whom he'd married aged twenty-one, after two years of war, in 1918 – had two children, Clare (born 1920) and John (born 1922), named after rural poet John Clare (their first daughter, Joy, born in 1919, had died at five weeks). Since 1929 they'd been separated, driven apart by affairs on both sides, Edmund's bookish lifestyle, and his three-year stint in Japan between 1924 and 1927. During the protracted legal wrangles since he'd filed for divorce, Edmund had been courted by writer Sylva Norman, a journalist and novelist he'd met via the staff of the *Nation*. Confiding to Sassoon about the affair, Edmund protested that Sylva's love had 'defeated my two years' attempts to prevent it from development'.[197]

Sylva Norman was from an Armenian background (she changed her name from the family Nahabedian) and was brought up in Manchester. Her first novel, *Nature Has No Tune*, was published in 1929 by the Woolfs' Hogarth Press. Reviewing her second, *Cat without Substance*, in September 1931, Edmund had critiqued what he saw as cleverness and a modern 'wrist-watch sense in it', leading to a passionate exchange of ideas.[198]

Sylva was adamant about the role of the modern writer and what she was trying to achieve in her work. 'It's as though, for example, one had a vision of a South Sea Island, or Japan, or Florida, & longed to be there,' she explained to him wistfully. 'But one can't avoid starting in a train through the London suburbs, reckoning with tickets, luggage, passports, getting on a probably overcrowded boat...'. 'I didn't, in this book, reach what I was aiming for,' she admitted. Sylva challenged Edmund's own ideas about art and the writer's duty to society. 'Quite useless, I feel,' she expanded, 'to turn away from the dim & bustle, to write (even if one could) a simple earnest story of quiet country life that might be recognised at once as "good".' Despite Edmund's reticence and some unanswered letters the previous autumn, Sylva had not been put off. 'I am myself much of her mind,' Edmund had admitted his feelings awkwardly in confidence to Sassoon. 'But my general situation and especially my peaceful love for Annie and all her works complicate.'[199]

Edmund's 'general situation' when he joined the Book Society, as he put it, was indeed complex. In addition to his long-term responsibility towards Mary and the children, Edmund was also financially supporting his brother's German wife Annie, who had looked after him during the divorce and kept him a room (along with many of his books) in her farmhouse, Hawstead, outside Bury St Edmunds in Suffolk. Annie had a difficult, on-and-off relationship with her husband, Edmund's younger brother Gilbert. 'She looks on me as her salvation and promise to that end,' Edmund explained in an expansive letter to Sylva early February 1932, outlining his 'long-sustained loyalties'.[200] 'To her I own most of the calm and sweetness which I have had for the last four years...She is in love with me, I think; and she is not the only one.'

The other woman in love - and financially reliant upon him - was Aki Hayashi, his dearest 'Autumn' (the meaning of Aki in Japanese), now working as his literary assistant. Aki had been a teacher of English when she met Edmund at a summer camp in Karuizawa where he was lecturing in 1925. She was thirty-six, he twenty-eight, both were lonely and dissatisfied with work, an affair began. Keen to keep her close, but not provoke gossip, Edmund suggested that Aki join him to work as his secretary: a plan that involved Aki moving from Nagoya to Tokyo initially, taking separate rooms in the Kikufuji Hotel, then applying for a visa to travel and work as Edmund's permanent secretary when he returned to England in August 1927. 'You must be my refuge if ever my friends forsake me,' Edmund had written Aki in August 1925, worried that Sassoon might not support him financially when he returned to England if he knew of the affair. 'But it will help us, if we can keep a secret,' he'd reassured her.[201]

Edmund Blunden and Aki Hayashi in Kobe, c. 1925

In Japan, Aki had sorted Edmund's letters and his WWI poems, which would later form the last part of his *Undertones of War*. In England, she did extensive research, transcription, indexing, and copyediting for his many books and lectures: hunting out rare books, letters, and obscure articles in the British Museum reading room, transcribing Wilfred Owen and Keats's poetry, working on Coleridge's manuscripts. This was detailed, highly skilled bibliographical research and editorial labour, highly unusual for a Japanese woman to undertake for an English writer in this period. Pleased with the arrangement, Edmund set Aki up in a flat in Hampstead, paying her regular 'okane' for her assistance, as well as sending work her way from other writers (including Sassoon, Graham Greene, and George Orwell). But he betrayed his promise to marry her if he ever divorced from Mary. 'I have wished that she would find somebody to charm her, but she cannot' Edmund protested to Sylva. 'She is a child,' he added, 'though not a young woman and having no special allurements but character.' Nonetheless, Aki was his responsibility. '[T]o injure her by throwing her aside is unthinkable,' he told Sylva. 'I do not know what you will make of this situation.'[202]

For Aki, Edmund's new relationship with Sylva Norman that spring was galling. Before they had left Japan together in 1927, Aki had made Edmund promise his good intentions. 'In case I should ever marry a second time I should all in probability/likelihood marry Aki,' she had coaxed out of him, onto paper at least.[203] Aki preferred the skilled, literary research she did for Edmund to teaching English to non-committal high school students in Japan. But living alone in London interwar on a precarious salary – a Japanese woman with an only-occasional gentleman-caller – was not easy, and Aki found herself increasingly isolated, the monotony of daily life broken only by interactions with staff at the British Museum, or the odd research trip out of town.

Aki looked forward to Edmund's London visits and hoped the monthly meetings for the Book Society might help regularise them. But she soon realised her diminished status in her lover's priorities as Edmund's relationship with Sylva Norman blossomed. Three days after his first meeting with the Book Society, Edmund apologised to Aki for leaving her standing at Paddington station. 'Indeed I arrived by the 5.50, and was met by my Miss Norman, who took me up to Hampstead to dine with her father and mother; I had appointed that evening for her as you know, & so did not look out for you.'[204] Aki received another letter from Edmund two days later, again trying to defend his behaviour. 'It is not fair to me [...] that I am to be the only object and support of your total personality,' he declared, more severe this time, attempting to draw a line under the affair:

> I may ask you to be absolutely content with working for me, and with having my friendship and my continued care and trust: to avoid all attempt at a love affair with me; to behave quietly and respectfully towards me, as a secretary should; to expect that I shall not visit you alone as much as I have done.[205]

We do not have Aki's replies to Edmund from this period. In fact, only a handful of her letters have survived (plus a few pages of her diary, scrappily torn out), preserved in Edmund's voluminous archive. Later in August 1932, Edmund took Sylva on what became for him an annual pilgrimage to the battlefields of Northern France. There, the new lovers decided to collaborate on 'almost a novel' (this became *We'll Shift Our Ground, or Two on a Tour,* published 1933), roping Aki in to help. 'There is something dear A which you can usefully do at once for me at the Museum,' Edmund wrote to her early September 1932, requesting she copy out passages from Jean Froissart's *Chronicles* to inspire him and Sylva during the writing process.[206] By the end of that month, while thousands of protesters on the National Hunger March advanced on London, Aki and Sylva had met. 'I am very glad that you liked Sylva, & she likes you,' Edmund wrote Aki, grateful for the temporary reprieve.[207] In July 1933, the following summer, Edmund and Sylva married at Willesden registry office, with a small reception held afterwards at Rupert Hart-Davis's flat. Aki was busy in the British Museum, sourcing materials on Charles Lamb.

II

Edmund Blunden's next collection of poetry, published in 1934 as *Choice or Chance*, begins with a poem 'To Sylva'. Towards the end of the book, there is a satirical sonnet on the Book Society. 'Chapters of Literary History. Very Little Known' begins:

> LED by great WALPOLE, at th' accustomed Task
> The Book Society's Committee sat,
> And neared the session's close. 'Again I ask,'
> The Chairman called (and I put down my hat),
> 'Whether we all agree upon this Choice–
> It is a work of genius, there's no question;
> No one can doubt that this authentic voice
> Will thrill–has anyone a fresh suggestion?
> Of course, some readers will not like the topic,
> But still...The author's a deserving man,
> But we are critical, not philanthropic.
> He's an old hand? True, let's have, when we can,
> New writers. But this month there's such a frost
> Where they're concerned. Agreed? Good: PARADISE
> LOST.

Edmund's position on the Book Society was challenging. Brought in for his scholarship and respected reputation as a literary critic, he often found himself going against the grain with the other judges, pleading to recommend more poetry, for instance, rather than what he saw as the 'commercially prepared Fiction' that Hugh (like many of the club's readers) preferred.[208] Hugh was a strong personality, and though Edmund would warm to him, admiring his 'inexhaustible energy and ardour,' he found some of his enthusiasms and repeated calls for '"the most important Book of the Year"' baffling, as he reported to Sassoon.[209] Sylvia Lynd meanwhile, Edmund found testy. She had a habit of goading him in meetings – being rude about John Clare for instance – just to wind him up. Clemence Dane, suffering from overwork and ill health through late 1931 and much of 1932 (which put her in a nursing home in August that year), was rarely there. After *Wild Decembers*, her new play about the Brontës, began to do well in the West End, from 1933 she spent more and more time in Hollywood, courted by the studios, recognised for her talent in scriptwriting. Edmund would travel down to Book Society meetings on the train from Oxford with George Gordon whenever he could, both happy to escape the classroom (in his contribution to George's wife's biography of her husband, Edmund remembers fondly the time they were so animated in conversation about a lecture George was preparing that neither realised they had been stopped 'a good while' at Reading station and needed to change trains).[210] But unless they worked around his schedule, George struggled to attend the monthly gatherings at Hugh's flat. So, it was mainly Hugh and Sylvia whom Edmund had to deal with.

From looking at the selections after Blunden joined the club, it's clear he sought to get more serious non-fiction onto the lists. Members received hefty biographies of *Sir Walter Scott* in 1932 (the centenary year of his death), followed by studies of Cecil Rhodes and Lady Blessington d'Orsay in 1933. Virginia Woolf's *Flush*, Book Society Choice in October 1933 and her first club selection, was also a kind of biography: this written playfully from the perspective of Elizabeth Barrett Browning's cocker spaniel. Edmund's detailed notes on early club reading are preserved in the archive as part of his burgeoning friendship with Rupert Hart-Davis ('my dear R. H. D.'), and show that he approved the selection of another Hogarth Press title with the choice of William Plomer's boarding-house murder mystery, *The Case is*

Altered for July 1932, but that he was against Margaret Irwin's historical novel *Royal Flush* (despite him, Irwin would become a club favourite, with five Book Society Choices over the next thirty years).[211] Like Sylvia Lynd, Edmund was cautious about offending subscribers. American poet James Oppenheim's *Wild Oats* was 'not a practical proposition for the Society,' Edmund wrote Rupert. 'Passages about homosexuals, harlots &c. may be sincere but most readers are alarmed by them. I don't like them,' he went on, 'unless there's much more involved than a mere account of incidents; but I'm not arguing on that, simply on the type of readers I know.'[212] Though he may have had a turbulent love life himself, like many others, he didn't necessarily relish seeing modern ideas about sex and sexuality on the page.

Edmund and Sylvia were proved right to be wary about the more traditional tastes of some Book Society members when in December 1932 large numbers of Graham Greene's breakthrough thriller, *Stamboul Train*, were returned. 'Are none of your members pure in heart?' one subscriber asked. 'This may be like life, but if it is I don't want to read it,' said another.[213] Clemence Dane and George Gordon had been against this one. 'It is a failure in my opinion' George wrote Rupert during discussions that September, 'and its feeble unpleasantness doesn't make the failure any better.'[214] Edmund meanwhile had absented himself from the decision, declaring a conflict of interest now he and Sylva were living in an adjoining flat to Greene in Woodstock Close in North Oxford (Sassoon paid for their first year's rent as a wedding present).

Greene had conceived of *Stamboul Train* explicitly as 'entertainment', under financial pressure as a writer and with bankruptcy looming, hoping it would be 'a book to please which, with luck might be made into a film' (interest from the American studios was in fact quick, with a film out by 1934).[215] Interestingly, the novel is now seen as a successful example of literary fiction written for a large audience, as Greene combines elements from the popular forms he enjoyed (including melodrama and the thriller) with his particular aesthetic, political and social critique. *Stamboul Train* touched many raw nerves of the time: with two lesbian characters (one said to be modelled on Clemence Dane), a communist revolutionary, murder, social snobbery, and antisemitism, all mixed up with the gloom of The Great Depression. But Hugh and Sylvia were firmly in favour of its selection, recognising Greene as an important new writer who would appeal to a younger audience, and Rupert Hart-Davis worked on Greene's behalf behind the scenes. When Jack Priestley – no longer a judge – read a review copy of *Stamboul Train*, he recognised himself in the character of popular author Mr Quin Savory and threatened to sue Greene for libel. '13,000 copies were all printed and bound and they all have to be unstitched and some pages printed over again,' Greene confessed after 'a frantic day on the phone arranging for alterations,' dictating revisions.[216] Had Jack still been a judge on the Book Society, it would have been three to two against the choice. Greene's subsequent fame and writing career might have panned out very differently.

III

Ten days after Hitler became Chancellor of Germany on 30 January 1933, students at the Oxford Union passed what became known as the 'Oxford pledge'. The resolution 'That this House will in no circumstances fight for its King and Country' was an 'ever shameful' vote according to Winston Churchill in his memoirs, and immediately taken up by the press. 'You will have followed something of the wars that inkmongers have started about the pacifist vote at the Union,' Blunden signed off a letter wearily to Sassoon at the end of February 1933. 'I am sure it won't be much use being trained for eighteen months at Ripon or Newmarket next War!' 'How the old men are raising their heads now, Sieg,' he went on, more angrily, reflecting on the media frenzy, 'it is quite forgotten that some of us know what war is by long and mournful intimacy'.[217] Like many other veterans and non-combatants who had lost loved ones during the war, both men were shocked that such recent experience seemed in danger of being forgotten. 'One can't do more than lift one's voice and warn,' Siegfried consoled him, 'but oh, the futility of it,' like 'shouting at a Cup Tie Crowd,' he joked, "Have *none* of you ever read Shelley"'?[218] 'Neither will they understand' Blunden had begun his bestselling memoir, *Undertones of War*. 'That will not be all my fault.'[219]

As a survivor of WWI, Blunden's *raison d'etre* throughout the 1930s was to stop the world from falling into a second global disaster. During his youth, he'd witnessed some of the worst fighting on the Western Front, trauma that would define him for the rest of his life. Even twenty years later, Edmund's diary shows that he began each day with memories of the Front: the weather the soldiers were facing, or the ridges and fields they were expected to take. Death and destruction stayed with him, bringing nightmares most nights. To Sassoon, Edmund relived guilt-ridden dreams of cowardice and survival: 'The shell dropped behind somewhere, and the War went on seemingly for years, and the gun went on, and presently hit the house, and left me safe, with a beam propping up the ruins.'[220] He would be 'going over the ground again' until his death-bed, he knew, as he'd written from Tokyo in the preface to *Undertones of War* in 1924.

So when the world began contemplating 'the next war' in the early 1930s in light of Japanese, German, and Italian aggression, Edmund pledged to fight for peace and to honour the dead. Watching the failure of the League of Nations to curb Japanese aggression towards China (Japan withdrew from the League in March 1933 after refusing to hand back territories they had invaded in September 1931), followed by Hitler's consolidation of power over the Reichstag and Germany's withdrawal from the international Disarmament Conference, Edmund put his hopes in the growing anti-war movement. The Oxford Union resolution was 'tactlessly worded' (as Sassoon pointed out to him) but many people were driven by the desire to avoid war through the 1930s, with both pacifism (the absolute renunciation of military force) and pacificism (reforming global politics to remove the causes of war while retaining defensive force) part of the influential, mainstream movement for peace. When Reverend Dick Sheppard – a respected establishment figure as Canon of St Paul's Cathedral – invited people to join him in renouncing war and pledging never to support or sanction another one, Blunden and Sassoon both voiced their support (by late 1936, the Peace Pledge Union had received 118,000 postcard pledges). Edmund shared a platform with Sheppard at the first gathering of the Peace Pledge Union at the Albert Hall in June 1935, when an estimated seven thousand men 'of all ages (many of them ex-service men), most professions, and very different circumstances gathered from all parts of the country to register their determination to have nothing more to do with war'.[221] Personally, Edmund found it impossible to square the evidence of Japanese aggression in China or the Nazi party's increasingly obvious antisemitism with his knowledge of his Japanese and German friends and acquaintances.

***

Through the early 1930s, with unemployment rocketing to reach record levels, the Book Society largely steered away from contemporary politics with their choices, bar an occasional dab of social realism thrown into the mix. Sylvia we know in particular was less enamoured of the so-called proletarian writing which emerged from the mass unemployment and Hunger Marches of the early '30s – seeing off support for Walter Greenwood's bestselling *Love on the Dole* (1933) and Ralph Bates's *Lean Men* (1934), for example.[222] A handful of club choices did engage directly with the contemporary moment. Elizabeth Cambridge's *Hostages to Fortune* addressed postwar hardship and economic difficulties from a woman's perspective (Sylvia thought it dull and 'not really a literary book').[223] And some chosen titles looked outwards to the wider world. R. C. Hutchinson's novel *The Unforgotten Prisoner* exposed a defeated, depressed Germany at the end of WWI and 'a people starved to the point of rebellion' that some reviewers (Edmund included) thought shed a light on what was happening in contemporary Europe.[224] Peter Fleming's *One's Company: A Journey to China* was a travelogue from the apparently hapless Far East Special Correspondent of the *Times* that explored what was happening (from an outsider's perspective) in Japanese-occupied Manchukuo and the battle between Nationalists and Communists in 'Red China'.

But these were exceptions during the Slump and the years in which Hitler became Führer, when for the most part it was long historical novels that dominated the club's lists. David Garnett's *Pocahontas* (one of a long line of stories about the famous indigenous Princess); Philip Lindsay's *Here Comes the King* (about Henry VIII and Catherine Howard); Nis Peterson's *The Street of the Sandal Makers: A Tale of Rome in the Time of Marcus Aurelius* (translated from the Danish by Elizabeth Sprigge and Claude Napier); and Margaret Irwin's *The Proud Servant: The Story of Montrose* (on Charles I) were popular Book Society Choices through 1933 and 1934. Blunden had been estranged from Robert Graves, a friend from undergraduate days at Oxford, since 1929 when his 'gross and silly war book', *Goodbye to All That*, had come out (Blunden and Sassoon had judged the book a desecration to ordinary soldiers and renamed it *The Welsh-Irish Bull in a China Shop*. Edmund's copy, with marked-up corrections and comments, including additions from Sassoon, was deposited in the New York Public Library to set the record straight).[225] So Edmund watched on, quietly seething, as Hugh and Sylvia plumped for *I, Claudius*, the first of what Edmund mocked as Graves's ponderous 'Claudiuscations'. 'I have given up the sad task of combating such selections' he admitted to Sassoon in March 1934. 'Any long book with some sort of narrative seems to do.'[226]

IV

On 15 May 1934, Hugh Walpole lunched at the Savoy with a group of film magnates. American producer David O. Selznick, director George Cukor, and others from Metro-Goldwyn-Mayer were visiting England on a research trip for their adaptation of *David Copperfield*. Hugh was invited as an expert on Dickens (he'd been made Vice-President of the Dickens Fellowship the previous year) and was delighted to receive a call four days later with an offer to go to Hollywood to work on the script. He'd been asked to write film scenarios when he was younger and had visited Hollywood during previous lecture tours, but now, just turned fifty, and encouraged by Clemence Dane's reports of life on the West Coast, he saw this as his 'grand opening in films'.[227] Three weeks later he was sailing to New York with the MGM party when they left Plymouth on 6 June, grateful for the opportunity and the £200 a week salary plus travel. After a few days in California, he signed a contract to stay until November that year, arranging for Harold to come and join him at the end of the summer. 'I'd have him earlier if it weren't for his August holiday with the boys,' he explained to his sister Dorothy. 'Everyone asks me out – Charles Laughton, Katherine Hepburn, Charlie Chaplin.'[228]

Hugh relished the charms of Hollywood, visiting the homes of the stars, thankful for the warm climate which suited his diabetes, and enjoying being free of the petty jealousies of other writers in London. Enthusiastic and keen to learn, he sat in on dictation sessions with screenwriter Lenore Coffee who was adapting his novel *Vanessa* (they began to collaborate on the script in September and the film would be released in 1935, the following year) before dashing over to work on the set of *David Copperfield*. He was amazed by the long hours and hard graft the actors and crew were obliged to put in. But Hugh was fascinated by the whole process. 'His enjoyment was infectious,' Lenore Coffee, one of the leading women film writers of the day, remembered in her memoirs, 'it was all a new world opening up for him'.[229]

The new world of the sound 'talkies' needed celebrity writers like Hugh and Clemence Dane who understood the power of storytelling and were adept at writing for different mediums, producing scenarios and dialogue. Walpole was a big name in the States, and Cukor decided to give him a cameo as a vicar in the film of *David Copperfield*, as well as have him introduce it. But the genuinely collaborative nature of film making – Hugh called it 'an omnibus art' – wasn't for all writers, and Hugh reflected that the film author needed 'a hard skin'.[230] The work itself was chaotic ('I love the craziness, the theatricality', Clemence Dane wrote Hugh), with scenes written over and over, last-minute changes, and script conferences liable to turn everything on its head.[231] In mid-August 1934, for instance, Hugh thought that he'd done working on Copperfield, but two months later was still writing new dialogue. In November 1934, shortly after finishing the script of *Vanessa* and signing a new contract with Louis B. Mayer on a 'fabulously high salary' for the following year, Hugh was hospitalised in Palm Springs, suffering from an infection and acute arthritis in the wrist that put a stop to any writing (his diary, written most days, has a two-month gap).[232] Harold had him transferred by plane to New York, and brought him home early December.

The following year, from August 1935 to June 1936, Hugh enjoyed a second stint in Hollywood. This time Harold accompanied him from the off. Again, Hugh worked on several projects concurrently, including the film adaptations of *Little Lord Fauntleroy* and *Kim* (Kipling died while Hugh was out there, in January 1936. The film was announced in 1938 but didn't come out). Now, Hugh decided to resign from the Book Society, and at the end of July 1935 they saw him off with an official farewell dinner (he sat next to H. G. Wells, and Jack Priestley made an excellent speech, Hugh reported in his diary). 'So that's that, after 6 ½ years!' Hugh signed off after writing what he thought was his last review for the club, on the posthumous edition of T. E. Lawrence's *Seven Pillars of Wisdom*, published July 1935. 'How we shall get along without you I really don't know', George wrote to him on hearing of his retirement. 'I can't tell you how I have enjoyed it all, and especially the companionship with yourself. Certainly I shall never get used to the change.' 'No substitute is conceivable.'[233]

1932

36	March	*Sir Walter Scott*, John Buchan
37	April	*The Life and Adventures of Aloysius O'Callaghan*, Thomas Washington-Metcalfe
38	May	*The Soldier and the Gentlewoman*, Hilda Vaughan
39	June	*Royal Flush. The Story of Minette*, Margaret Irwin
40	July	*The Case is Altered*, William Plomer
41	August	*Golden Horn. Plot and Counterplot in Turkey, 1908-1918 as seen 'from the inside' by a prisoner of war*, Francis Yeats-Brown
42	September	*Greenbanks*, Dorothy Whipple
43	October	*Black Mischief*, Evelyn Waugh
44	November	*Memoirs of a British Agent*, R. H. Bruce Lockhart
45	December	*Stamboul Train*, Graham Greene

1933

46	January	*Pocahontas, or the nonparell of Virginia*, David Garnett
47	February	*The Seventh Age or Saint Saturnin*, Jean Schlumberger, trans. by Dorothy Bussy
48	March	*Rhodes*, Sarah Gertrude Millin
49	April	*The Street of the Sandalmakers*, Nis Peterson, trans. by Elizabeth Sprigge and Claude Napier
50	May	*Twenty-Years A-Growing*, Maurice O'Sullivan, rendered from the original Irish by Moya Llewlyn Davies and George Thomson
51	June	*Hostages to Fortune*, Elizabeth Cambridge
52	July	*Here Comes the King*, Philip Lindsay
53	August	*Ordinary Families*, E. Arnot Robertson
54	September	*The Woman on the Beast*, Helen Simpson
55	October	*Flush. A Biography*, Virginia Woolf
56	November	*Blessington D'Orsay. A Masquerade*, Michael Sadlier
57	December	*The Unforgotten Prisoner*, R. C. Hutchinson

1934

58 January *A Warning to Wantons. Setting forth the not undeserved but awful fate which befell A Minx*, Mary Mitchell
59 February *Queen Elizabeth*, J. E. Neale
60 March *Matador*, Marguerite Steen
61 April *Five Silver Daughters*, Louis Golding
62 May *I, Claudius*, Robert Graves
63 June *The Ginger Griffin*, Ann Bridge
64 July *Harvest in the North*, James Lansdale Hodson
65 August *One's Company. A Journey to China*, Peter Fleming
66 September *Barnham Rectory*, Doreen Wallace
67 October *Experiment in Autobiography. Being the Autobiography of H. G. Wells, vol. I*
68 November *The Proud Servant: The Story of Montrose*, Margaret Irwin
69 December *Heaven's My Destination*, Thornton Wilder

1935

70 January *This Was Ivor Trent*, Claude Houghton
71 February *A London Story*, George Buchanan
72 March *The Shipbuilders*, George Blake
73 April *National Velvet*, Enid Bagnold
74 May *The Angel of the Assassination. Charlotte de Corday*, Joseph Shearing
75 June *The Jury*, Gerald Bullett
76 July *George the Fourth*, Roger Fulford
77 August *Illyrian Spring*, Ann Bridge
78 September *Borzoi*, Igor Schwezoff

Chapter 4. Sylvia, 1935-6

What upset Sylvia

I

5 Keats Grove, Hampstead

In late October 1935, Sylvia Lynd began keeping a regular diary.

It was a cold Monday, post-party, and she was feeling anxious, suffering from a mild dizzy headache having been up later than two thirty the previous evening, seeing off guests and organising lifts. She had the bedroom fire lit to get dressed by, putting on a vest she'd left out to air overnight. The party had ended on a sour note with a drunken debate about communism between Alan Herbert and Victor Gollancz, Sylvia putting her oar in, as she said, 'in the cause of peace and occasional hope of bed'.[234] Rose Macaulay's new Morris Ten had refused to start so they'd all helped to push it downhill in the direction of town. Afterwards Sylvia had pottered around tidying, 'removing glasses – rings of moisture – tobacco ash'. Then she'd lain awake most of the night, replaying conversations, dreaming up better arguments.

They'd discussed habits of diary-keeping at the party, alongside just about everything else. William Morris's 'unruly' wallpapers had been up for debate, as well as Thomas Hardy, modern poetry, fashions in slang ('Words for drunkenness', Sylvia remembered. 'Tight a permanent word. Blotto now out of date. Squiffy quite out.'). It was said that Harold Nicolson wrote his diary up every morning after breakfast and had done so for many years: an appealing prospect to Sylvia, who never seemed to have a moment to herself. Just contemplating the previous day for instance – a typically full Sunday – included two visits to check on her mother's elder sister, Aunt Emilie, now in her early eighties, who had recently been ill (they'd called her Aunt Tatushka since childhood, muddling the Russian for aunt). In between times, Sylvia had promised to sit for a young woman artist, a protégé of Thomas Sturge Moore, who wanted to draw her and Robert 'as Hampstead celebrities' (Robert had sat for three hours already that day).[235] And then there'd been preparations for the evening party, 'the usual ringing up by men to know whether they should change or not'. They'd catered for Max and Florence Beerbohm, Alan and Gwendolyn Herbert, Lionel Hale, Rose Macaulay, plus themselves, then after supper had the children in – 'Sheila looking her old self again,' Sylvia noted – plus 'the David Davieses, Alan Thomas, Ruth Gollancz, Bryan Guinness & after midnight, Victor'. Despite mounting debts, she'd ordered two extra leaves for the dining room table so they could seat ten at parties, rather than eight, and was looking forward to replacing their 'old rattle-trap' with a second-hand Austin Twelve later that week.

At twenty-odd pages, Sylvia's first diary entry was exhausting. She couldn't keep it up.

The Austin was a luxurious black saloon 'with a bright green lining and every conceivable gadget' she noted with pleasure, 'marvellously silent after our old roarer'. Sylvia had learnt to drive at forty (she was privately scornful of women like her sister who still hadn't), so while she was admittedly nervous about trying out the new car, she took heart from her daughters' example: B. J. had set off to dine at Virginia Woolf's house 'after only being shown the knobs'. On the last day of October 1935, Sylvia drove into town for the Book Society meeting. She had rushed through the last of her reading in the morning; backing out the driveway, running late, she clipped a glass fin off the car. 'A horrible drive in the dark afternoon and rain to Buckingham Palace Gardens,' she confessed in her diary that evening. 'Couldn't tell which gear, forgot how to work the wiper and so forth. Of course everything achieved in time, but after the fin – so hot, such a hammering heart.' She prayed Robert wouldn't notice before she got it replaced.

The selection committee was going through another period of change that autumn. Hugh, still away in Hollywood, had been renamed as honorary chairman and had proofs sent out to him, while Julian Huxley (Aldous Huxley's elder brother), was drafted in to fill his shoes. Julian was Sylvia's contemporary and lived across the Heath in Highgate, not far from the Priestleys. He'd enjoyed an academic career up to his forties (working in Oxford, Texas, and at King's College, London), before the success of *The Science of Life* in 1929 – co-authored with H. G. Wells and regarded as the first popular guide to biology – gave him a public platform as scientist and broadcaster. Shortly after joining the club, Julian was appointed Secretary of the Zoological Society, a well-paid appointment that came with a study and flat in London's Regents Park Zoo, giving him the chance to influence policy while continuing writing and research. Sylvia appreciated Julian's 'brisk decisive ways' in meetings but there was no love lost between them, and they rarely saw eye to eye. After only a couple of months on the committee, Julian was complaining about the amount of reading the judges were expected to do. Like George Gordon, he often relied upon his wife to fill him in on the scores of proofs that came through the post.

Sylvia found that day's judges meeting frustrating, though pleasant enough in itself. Julian had regaled them with an account of the obscenity trial of sexologist Edward Charles's book, *The Sexual Impulse*, laughing at how a bed had been wheeled in to try and dispute the judge's suggestion that beds 'were intrinsically obscene'. Clemence shared a story from Hollywood, revealing how her scenario of *Anna Karenina* had come back from the censor with the report that though he would permit adultery in the film as it was part of the plot, the adultery must take place in the boudoir or living room – not in the bedroom. There followed debate about the current use of asterisks in books, a strategy some publishers were using to avoid costly obscenity trials (this did not always succeed; James Hanley's *Boy*, for instance, in print since 1931, had been tried for obscenity earlier that year after the cheap edition with asterisks blanking out the obscenities became widely available). But Sylvia, as she freely admitted in the privacy of her diary, generally preferred asterisks. At the start of that year, she'd asked Scottish author George Blake to modify the speech of his Glaswegian working-class characters in *The Shipbuilders*, a novel about the struggling Clydeside industry during The Great Depression. He'd done it willingly ('these people do speak a foul idiom', Blake wrote in apology), though he retained some edge to the football and pub scenes. There was 'no desire on my part', he'd assured Sylvia, 'to be the shocking young man'.[236] Sylvia had little time for anything too realistic or what she saw as salacious. And she would not recommend books like that to members of the society.

Already irritable after damaging the car on the way in that day, Sylvia was annoyed that the judges couldn't agree on a choice for the new year. George Gordon, normally able to take the meetings in hand, had collapsed during a recent lecture and was recuperating in Spain. Clemence was full of enthusiasm for Rose Macaulay's essays, *Personal Pleasures*, even though they couldn't be a choice, having been out for more than a fortnight already. Sylvia meanwhile admired American journalist Negley Farson's autobiography, *The Way of a Transgressor*, a colourful account of his intrepid adventures as a foreign correspondent and his varied encounters with world leaders, from Gandhi to Hitler. 'One of the best books we've had this year,' she wrote with frustration in her diary that evening 'so, of course, rejected as a choice.'

Like Edmund, Sylvia was often disappointed by individual club decisions, but she had more experience to draw on than he did in managing committees. For the last ten years, from the mid-1920s, before the Book Society began, Sylvia had benefited professionally from having been a part of the *Prix Femina-Vie Heureuse Anglais*. This was a French initiative established in the spirit of rapprochement in June 1919, where an English committee of twenty-five literary women selected three books to be translated for a French audience; a French committee of literary women then chose one of these and did the same for the English committee in reverse. This prize for the best work of French letters was awarded as the Northcliffe Prize. Sylvia had been President of the *Prix Femina* in 1929 and was currently the Vice President. Here she was valued for her insights into new and contemporary writing and renowned as an independent judge who didn't suffer fools – or last-minute changes to the list of recommendations – gladly. The *Prix Femina* was in theory gender blind (E. M. Forster, David Garnett, Charles Morgan, and Richard Hughes were some of the male writers whose work they backed) but women authors were firmly in the majority. For Sylvia, the two committee roles were complementary, sometimes meaning she could back an author before one set of judges if she felt they had been overlooked by the other. Her involvement in both also ensured that many Book Society choices were supported in the lists put forward by the *Prix Femina*. Always, for Sylvia, her decisions came back to the power of storytelling. It was not the 'critic's cherished masterpieces' that keep us 'standing at the dressing-table' late at night, as she declared in the *Book Society News* regarding Daphne du Maurier's gothic masterpiece *Rebecca* (1938), but a book's power to transport the reader, making us desperate to know what happens next.[237]

II

The following month, November 1935, Sylvia travelled alone on a ten-day holiday to Dublin. She had finally accepted an invitation from her old friend, artist Sarah Purser, to stay in her Georgian mansion, Mespil House, and join one of her renowned Tuesday 'at homes'. Sarah was now eighty-eight and Sylvia knew she couldn't postpone the visit much longer. The trip meant a crushing workload beforehand, making the thought of going away hideous, but Sylvia rushed through her club articles and a piece for the American magazine *Harper's*, splashed out on a new Shetland wrapper from Harrods to sleep in, and duly found herself blessed with a calm Irish sea. The prospect of meeting Gordon Campbell in Dublin was agonising; she had heard that he had visited London recently and not reached out to her, unless he had been 'the gentleman who rang up and left no name but said he would ring up later – but I need not flatter myself', Sylvia wrote in her diary. Nevertheless, she consoled herself, it would be 'nice to walk the same pavements for a few days'. She hadn't seen Gordon now for the last six years but was constantly thinking of him.

Sylvia found the trip to Ireland refreshing and enjoyed staying up late with Sarah, gossiping like a 'wild pair of conversational gluttons'. She took some roses to her mother's grave and caught up with Dublin society, enjoying the whirlwind of gatherings and luncheons that Sarah had lined up. She was quizzed by Lady Fingal among others about B. J.'s relationship with Bryan Guinness (the 2nd Baron Moyne, heir to the Guinness fortune, and recently divorced from Diana Mitford). 'All Dublin talks to me about them,' Sylvia despaired: 'Ireland is a lovely clearing house for gossip.' She had done her motherly duty, begging B. J. not to go to Biddesden, the Guinness family home, so often and asking her not to stay with Bryan in Ireland. 'Alas, I can only say that they are not going to get married, not that they are,' she confessed. Sylvia worried constantly (they would have said excessively) about both of her daughters' reputations. Sheila was currently living with David Granville, separated from his wife, but still married; a 'worthless little match' Sylvia noted bitterly, when 'she might have been Lady Acland or Lady Young'. 'There is something unlucky about our falling in love in this family,' Sylvia mourned in her diary. 'We haven't much more than half a reputation to go round – 2/3 to be exact - & can't risk losing another. I must bear this in mind too, on my own account.'

So, there was no Gordon Campbell for Sylvia in Dublin, and just a brief chat with Beatrice, his wife, as they were surrounded by a crowd. Whether by accident or design, Sylvia received an invitation to tea at the Campbells' house only after she had departed Ireland. But, with living under such stress, she did confess to Sarah about the affair, opening up on what she called her 'long widowhood'. After she returned home, the strain took hold of her nerves, and Sylvia spent her first days back in Hampstead confined to bed. When she got up, still suffering from a high temperature and high blood pressure, the room was swaying and she had 'jabs in my arm to help my heart, so that I could get my reviews done for the Book Society.' She finally posted a letter she had drafted many times, asking Gordon to return all her letters.

* * *

Earlier that summer, Sylvia had written a glowing club review of Ann Bridge's third novel, *Illyrian Spring*. Bridge (pseudonym of Lady Mary Ann O'Malley) was already successful in Britain and America after receiving the Atlantic Monthly Prize for her first novel, *Peking Picnic* (1932), drawn from her experience living as an attaché's wife in Beijing in the mid-1920s (before Chaing Kai-shek's Nationalists launched their Northern Expedition to reunify China). The Book Socicty had boosted Bridge's fame by selecting her second novel, *The Ginger Griffin*, two years later. Again, this centred on the insular, privileged world of the diplomatic corps and expatriate society.

Illyrian Spring was perfect summer reading, and the ideal kind of romance in Sylvia's view. The story centres on Grace Kilmichael, a woman in her early forties who feels trapped by 'her main job' as wife and mother and takes off to Dalmatia on her own, deserting her family - a husband who is possibly having an affair, a difficult older daughter, sons at Cambridge.[238] Grace is a successful artist in her own right and plans to finance her time abroad through drawing sketches for the American magazines. On the Adriatic steamer leaving Venice, she meets and almost falls for a much younger man called Nicholas, who is also on the run from family duty. Nicholas shares Grace's passion for painting, archaeology, and the Dalmatian coastline and they become travelling companions, enjoying long days painting, picnicking, and driving out to little-known beauty spots, revelling in the thrill of 'space and travel' and in each other's conversation.[239]

Grace is too sensible to give everything up for an affair, but she is stimulated by Nicholas and admires him. Being in his company allows Grace to reassess her strained family relationships and helps her better understand the generation gap she perceives between her children – the Bright Young Things of the 1920s and '30s – and her own middle age. The novel is especially poignant on Grace's relationship with her grown-up daughter Linnet, who Grace admits to finding infuriating. In her review for the club's readers, Sylvia appreciated the charm of the setting and sense of adventure, predicting that *Illyrian Spring* would 'fill its readers' hearts with longings for Dalmatia' (this turned out to be true. The book was said to have inspired Edward VIII's notorious yachting trip down the Adriatic with Wallis Simpson the following summer, provoking a rush of American and British tourists). In the novel's closing pages, Grace and her husband are reconciled;

he gives her more credit for her work, recognising her autonomy in the marriage and need for independence. Nicholas meanwhile is happily paired off with Grace's daughter. *Illyrian Spring* was a satisfying holiday romance, offering all the pleasure, without the inevitable mess, of following through.

III

Through the first eight months of 1936, Sylvia handled lead reviews for half of the club's selections. Hugh was still 'picture-making' in Hollywood so she took the lion's share until the summer, when she and Robert took a long-awaited holiday with a seven-week trip through Canada and the States.[240] In March 1936, Sylvia penned an obligatory celebration for Winifred Holtby's *South Riding*, an enormous novel on local politics set in Yorkshire, animated by its feisty heroine (said to be modelled on Labour MP Ellen Wilkinson), widely compared to *Middlemarch* in ambition and scale. Holtby had died tragically from a kidney problem, aged only thirty-seven, in September the previous year, and the novel was edited and published posthumously by her friend, Vera Brittain. There was one vote against it on the committee (either Edmund or Clemence, Sylvia didn't know who). In private, Sylvia confessed to being puzzled by the importance that people had attached to Holtby since her death, worrying that it reflected her own inability to judge a younger person, another sign of middle-age. But she compensated in her review for club readers, declaring *South Riding* 'one of the best novels that have ever reached this committee, indeed, one of the best of the present generation'. No one could accuse her of being out of step.

Her next lead article was more controversial, announcing the club's selection of Joyce Cary's sensational novel, *The African Witch*. This was only chosen, as Sylvia admitted in her diary, 'after considerable obstinacy on my part,' it being clear at the committee meeting that she was the only real fan. Joyce Cary was an Anglo-Irish writer who had published short stories and a couple of novels in the early 1930s based on his experience working as an official in colonial Nigeria. Sylvia saw Cary as a genius – as talented as E. M. Forster in giving dignity and complexity to foreign characters – and she compared *The African Witch* favourably to Forster's celebrated *A Passage to India* for Book Society readers. 'Like Mr Forster's Indians, his Nigerians are not merely a decorative background for his story, or, as in novels of a cruder sort, the villains or butts of the piece, but people with characters as varied as the characters of white men and with fears and ambitions as comprehensible as our own.'[241] Cary duly sent her a copy of the book with personal inscription.

Julian Huxley was firmly against Sylvia on this one. Cary's novel was a good story, he conceded, but a misguided choice for the club because it offered an inaccurate portrait of Nigeria. Julian had not yet been to West Africa (he would first visit Nigeria in 1944), but he was a recognised expert, having spent time in British East Africa in 1929 travelling through Kenya, Uganda, Zanzibar, and Tanganyika (then a colony, protectorates, and a mandated territory respectively), as well as the Belgian Congo, in order to report for the Colonial Office on African education, biological science, and conservation. He had shared the fruits of his four-month visit with a wider audience in *Africa View* (published 1931), underlining the 'almost unbelievable variety' he'd encountered 'in one small portion of Africa'.[242] Recommending more secular education and the establishment of national parks in the East African territories to protect wildlife, he had recently been drafted onto the committee advising Lord Hailey's *African Survey*, a huge report on economic and social conditions in sub-Saharan Africa published in 1938, said to be on the desk of every colonial administrator.[243]

Julian's strength on the Book Society lay in recognising serious, creditable travel writing and judging the sensitivity of European encounters with Empire and the wider world. Through 1936, for instance, he recommended travel writing by Ernest Hemingway (*Green Hills of Africa*, on the big game country of East Africa); Geoffrey Gorer's *Bali and Angkor*; Freya Stark's account of her travels through Yemen in *The Southern Gates of Arabia*; and Peter Freuchen's story of living in Greenland and marrying among the Inuits, *Arctic Adventure*. It was Julian who pushed for Danish writer Knud Holmboe's critique of Mussolini's invasion of Abyssinia, *Desert Encounter: An Adventurous Journey through Italian Africa* (translated by Helga Holbek), as choice for November 1936. Holmboe's 'intolerance of injustice and white exploitation turns him into a Mahomedan,' Julian explained to Book Society readers. 'Here was - and doubtless is - white imperialism at its most intolerant and its most brutal,' he went on in a noticeably polemical review for the club. 'It is good to have this picture of the "civilising mission" of European nations drawn by a European with such unique opportunities for discovering the non-European point of view.'

The Book Society had a complicated record on Empire and what Julian Huxley dubbed the 'non-European point of view'. On the one hand, the club no doubt provided a valued service to readers living and working across what was then the British Empire and dominions, with estimates that between thirty and forty per cent of members lived overseas (outside England) in the late 1930s.[244] Thanks to the 'Empire markets' (that in 1947 became the 'Traditional Market Agreement'), British publishers had priority access over American publishers to sell and distribute English-language books in former colonies: a distributive arrangement the Book Society could take advantage of.[245] Book Society collections have been discovered in readers' homes from Canada to Tanzania, while embassies, colonial libraries, and clubs throughout British-controlled areas of the Caribbean, Asia, and Africa took out subscriptions, providing access to the latest reading from London to diplomats, expatriates, colonial administrators, and perhaps, some communities of indigenous readers. Mindful of its sizeable membership across the British Empire (and later Commonwealth), the club frequently chose books set in Australia, India, South Africa, Canada, seeking to connect with readers and their families who may have been a long way from 'home'.

But while the club promoted writing from a variety of international authors, as well as much writing in translation, this was predominantly from a white, western perspective (reflecting the broader structures of Anglophone publishing before WWII). In general, the club's view on Empire – like Sylvia's – was representative of its time: patriotic and unquestioning, upholding a colonial arrogance that is unthinkable today. Francis Yeats-Brown's *Bengal Lancer* (1930), a swashbuckling autobiography of an officer's life in the British Raj, was a popular early choice typical of English readers' take on Empire, and European superiority, in this period. ('India understood!' pronounced Gollancz's eye-catching dust jacket with confidence).[246] Ann Bridge's well-received Chinese novels of the early '30s – which are really about upper-class Englishmen and women – are best understood as 'a pageant performed against a brightly decorated Chinese screen,' the introduction to a later issue of *The Ginger Griffin* advises.[247] They depict a time and way of life that is for most modern readers unthinkable, and unreal.

The judges worked around one another when they were particularly disgruntled by a choice. For Julian, giving in to Sylvia on *The African Witch* was a mistake, and he tried to make amends by recommending *Ten Africans* to Book Society readers in August 1936. This was a collection of life-stories by African men and women 'written by themselves or taken down from their own lips when they could not write,' Julian pointed out. It was edited by Margery Perham, lecturer at Oxford in colonial administration, giving, as Julian wrote in the club magazine, 'a direct insight into the minds and lives of African people, members of the British Empire'. This was still centred by a European gaze, clearly. But it was a long way from Cary's novel with its sacrifices and *ju-ju* house.

IV

On Saturday 4 October 1936, there was 'disorder in the East End' (as *The Times* put it mildly) in what became known as the 'Battle of Cable Street', when thousands of demonstrators clashed with fascists and the police to prevent Sir Oswald Mosley's Blackshirts from marching through Jewish areas of the East End. The Spanish Civil War had broken out that July, and many anti-fascists and communists in London adopted the Spanish Republican motto, 'The fascists shall not pass! No Pasaran!' Mosley – a Member of Parliament between 1918 and 1930, first as a Conservative, then Independent, then Labour – had founded the British Union of Fascists in 1932 and, despite formally adopting a policy of antisemitism since 1934, he had been operating in British society with relative impunity (police efforts, for instance, were geared towards clearing the way for Mosley's Blackshirts to pass, and using mounted and foot police to prevent the disruption of fascist meetings).

Earlier that year, Sylvia had gone with Rose Macaulay to protest against Mosley's last rally at the Royal Albert Hall (Mosley was only refused use of the Albert Hall after March 1936). She hadn't known where to park – all the usual approaches had been shut by the police – so she'd ended up outside the Lycée Français where she parked for the *Prix Femina* meetings. Walking back down Exhibition Road, she and Rose found themselves merged with a large crowd of 'Reds', as Sylvia put it. The police had made cordons across the street barring the way to the hall and they were turned back several times before they could enter. 'It looked like a medieval battlescene,' Sylvia wrote in her diary. There were the 'usual theatricalities,' she noted dryly, 'Black Shirts blowing trumpets, the crowd standing up, drums rattling and a spotlight for Mosley as he walked down the hall.' She had asked him a written question – 'Has not racial tolerance always been a British characteristic?' – which went unanswered, drowned out by 'a long speech advocating friendship with Japan and Germany and persecution of the Jews'. Protesting outside, Sheila and B. J. were charged at by mounted police, B. J. hit on the shoulder. Sheila's partner David was violently thrown out of the hall, along with many others, after trying to interrupt the meeting.

Sylvia was active in the various internationalist, feminist circles of the 1930s, supporting the Women's International League for Peace & Freedom (founded 1915), and part of charitable efforts to help Spanish workers and children suffering famine during the Spanish Civil War. In December 1936, she went to the House of Commons to listen to reports from a group of MPs who had visited Spain and were campaigning for the Government to offer financial aid: the Allied governments adopted a policy of non-intervention, despite tens of thousands from around the world volunteering to join the International Brigades. But Sylvia had experienced the devastation of Civil War and sectarian violence in Ireland and was scared by the growth of extremism on both sides in the 1930s. She was vehemently against her daughters' communist sympathies, so contrary to her own mother's anarchist views. Friends had returned from Soviet Russia with dismal accounts of bullying and oppression (Eileen Squire had gone out a Communist 'but loathed it', as Sylvia had her repeat the story in front of B. J.). 'A free & merry Russia does not seem to have been achieved,' Sylvia noted in her diary in September 1936, observing the start of Stalin's purge of Trotskyists from the party in what became known as the Moscow show trials. The following spring, she would recommend E. M. Delafield's *Straw Without Bricks* to the club for making public 'the sort of facts that have hitherto, in my experience, been told only in private'. It was hard to see 'the fine shade of difference' between Communists and Fascists according to Sylvia. 'I see nothing to choose', she confirmed in her diary. 'A plague on both your houses.'

So in addition to being concerned about her daughters' safety as they tramped the streets organising protests and demonstrating against fascism

(B. J. was arrested at a huge anti-fascist protest in Bermondsey in October 1937), Sylvia was worried they were fundamentally misguided politically, as well as jeopardising their chances for social success.[248] By the early 1930s, Sheila and B. J. both worked in publishing. Sheila had a position with Victor Gollancz, heavily involved in running the Left Book Club, while B. J. worked at Peter Davies, then later at William Heinemann. Both were also card-carrying members of the Communist Party of Great Britain (founded 1920). This was not an untypical move for young middle-class intellectuals of the time, outraged by the visible suffering of the national Hunger Marches during The Great Depression, and frustrated by Labour's decision to align with Conservatives and Liberals in a National Government in 1931 that forced through cuts to unemployment benefit via the Means Test; in an influential study on *British Writers of the Thirties*, Valentine Cunningham dubbed this trend as 'Going Over'.[249]

B. J. – who signed up to the Party first – had, according to her mother at least, lost Bryan Guinness because of her radical politics (an engagement notice for Bryan and Elisabeth Nelson appeared in *The Times* in September 1936; Bryan had the sense to send both B. J. and Sylvia a letter in advance. His first wife, Diana Mitford, married Oswald Mosley in secret two days after Cable Street). B. J. was active at street level, defending tenants' rights and opposing evictions with her new partner, lawyer Jack Gaster. She'd fallen for Jack after being asked to spy on him when he joined the Communist Party from the Independent Labour Party in 1935 (part of a wave of resignations following the failure of mainstream parties to tackle Italian aggression in Abyssinia and the shift in Communist policy at the Third International towards forming a 'Popular Front' with moderate social and liberal groups in order to defeat fascism). Jack proposed to B. J. at a socialist summer school, and they were married in Marylebone Town Hall in October 1938.

Sheila meanwhile, appeared to Sylvia to be increasingly hard up. While her eldest had been living with David Granville – 'who has had no work since May,' Sylvia recorded furiously in her diary, 'and is blacklisted as a communist, he surmises' – 'Sheila is in rags' Sylvia observed in October 1936. 'I have had to stand her stockings and a jumper too. What will become of her?' (the previous year, Sheila had apparently returned vast quantities of new underclothes to John Lewis, protesting against her mother's excessive 'pauperisation rather than present-giving').[250] Her daughters' fates, Sylvia realised, were for her mixed-up in a wider sense of socio-political calamity. 'But indeed', Sylvia acknowledged in the same diary entry, 'There is certainly going to be a new war soon and heaven knows what will happen to all of us.'

Sylvia's anxiety for Sheila and B. J., as well as for her own name and reputation, clearly seeped into her reading of Rosamond Lehmann's *The Weather in the Streets* for the club. Lehmann was a commercial and critically successful author, taken seriously by both the Bloomsbury group and the book clubs. Her first three novels were bestsellers on either side of the Atlantic and she was hugely popular in Europe, especially in France. Lehmann wrote lyrical prose that powerfully captured women's interior lives and was widely seen as a more readable Virginia Woolf. Sylvia was a huge fan.

The Weather in the Streets was Lehmann's fourth novel, much darker than *A Note in Music*, her previous Book Society choice in August 1930. Developing the story of Olivia Curtis (Lehmann's protagonist from her third novel, *Invitation to the Waltz*), *The Weather in the Streets* begins with Olivia ten years older and now separated but not divorced from her husband, living in London with a cousin, working (without much interest) as a photographer's assistant. Clearly musing on Sheila and B. J., Sylvia remarked in her club review that Olivia 'seems to typify all the charming, vulnerable, independent young women whom the last twenty years have set drifting through life'. And, as she pointed out for good measure, she 'smokes far too many cigarettes.'

When Olivia embarks on an affair with the charming Rollo Spencer – an acquaintance from childhood, now also married unsuccessfully, with a toxic mixture of good looks, inherited wealth, and upper-class style – we know it is likely to end badly. This inevitability is not missed by Olivia either but she, rather like the narrator, is swept up in the thrill. But Sylvia's more critical reading found Olivia's desire and behaviour unnerving, while she rebuked the protagonist's unwillingness to settle down. The affair is a 'modern rake's progress through obscure country inns and the lesser London restaurants,' Sylvia argued in her review, refusing to glamorise a liaison that ends up in the 'abortionist's terrifying parlour' (*The Weather in the Streets* was one of the earliest treatments of abortion in modern fiction). 'The whole sinister side of life is unfolded for Olivia,' Sylvia added, 'the tender, disinterested soul whose lot it is not to be lucky'. Tellingly, she contrasts Olivia unfavourably to Kate, her 'brilliant and lovely elder sister'. Kate is dissatisfied by domesticity and motherhood and the sensible match she has made. But 'if life has disappointed her,' Sylvia counselled Book Society readers, 'she has the sense and courage not to say so'.

***

On 10 December 1936, King Edward VIII gave up the British throne. The Lynds had known about his affair with Mrs Simpson since the beginning of the year. At a dinner party at Rose Macaulay's in January, for instance, Sylvia reflected that conversation had been 'blasphemous, scandalous, disloyal and obscene' as they discussed Lady Sibyl Colefax who had had the nous to make friends with a Mr and Mrs Simpson 'in whom his new majesty takes a special interest'. In October, while Mrs Simpson's second divorce case was going through court, Robert had come home from the office with the 'stunning news' that the King was prepared to abdicate if he could not marry her. Sylvia thought this decision brave if tragi-comic. 'We all thought I think it particularly nice if not particularly necessary for him to want to marry her,' she wrote in her diary. Aunt Tatushka summed up the views of the public at large. 'She thinks he will regret it & hopes he will. She feels that he has preferred Mrs. Simpson to his loyal subjects including herself & she is very much annoyed.'

Considering the question of private pleasure versus public duty again, now under the glare of the abdication crisis, Sylvia reaffirmed her position. Writing for the *Sunday Times* Christmas book supplement, Sylvia spotlighted two novels from the autumn season: Margaret Kennedy's *Together and Apart* and Kate O'Brien's *Mary Lavelle*.[251] Both writers she knew personally from the *Prix Femina*. Margaret Kennedy (Mrs David Davies) was a friend, part of the Hampstead circle and a regular at Sylvia's parties. Her *Together and Apart* was dedicated to Sylvia's best friend Rose Macaulay and was Book Society choice for December 1936 (Kennedy had two further novels chosen by the club in the 1950s). Sylvia had long admired Irish writer Kate O'Brien, meanwhile. *Mary Lavelle*, O'Brien's third book, featured in the Book Society's recommended lists for November.

Together and Apart and *Mary Lavelle* were serious, enjoyable books that showed 'considered views of conduct' in romantic affairs, Sylvia summarised. But they came down on opposite sides of the current debate. Like *The Weather in the Streets*, *Mary Lavelle* seemed to celebrate the 'wild', 'extreme' of passion, according to Sylvia: 'The dazzling moment is worth whatever engulfing darkness may follow' (This was not an uncommon reading. The book was banned in Ireland and Spain, where the story was set). For Margaret Kennedy on the other hand, whose *Together and Apart* explored the pain and fallout of divorce, passion was something 'to be sacrificed, if need be, to the general good'. Kennedy 'writes for mature readers, for those who have lived to see the end of many stories,' Sylvia made plain. The moral would have struck home to readers that Christmas, still processing the shock of the abdication crisis.

But few would have guessed how much personal anguish was tied up in Sylvia's Christmas message to put passion and momentary happiness aside in favour of public responsibility, duty, and sticking it out. Earlier that year, 'on a morning of brilliant sun and frost' as Sylvia recorded in her diary, Gordon Campbell had turned up at her house unexpectedly. 'The day of the miracle' she thought she had longed for over the last six years.[252] They had just a moment together at the doorstep before Robert came down. Gordon was going grey, she'd noticed, and was 'very charming just in his old way,' full of a recent holiday to Sweden and the doings of his eldest son Patrick (Paddy). He was 'evidently quite happy,' Sylvia noted bitterly in her diary afterwards, 'while pretending not to be'. She and Robert had their difficulties, she realised, but they'd forged a successful, working partnership despite the odds, and would endeavour to see each other through. There was value in the strength and humility needed to sustain a loving relationship long-term, Sylvia felt. No matter how much she disapproved of her daughters' current choices, she hoped they'd find a similar degree of stability through marriage, communist or otherwise.

1935

79	October	*Here Lies a Most Beautiful Lady*, Richard Blaker
80	November	*Gaudy Night*, Dorothy L. Sayers
81	December	*Antony, A Record of Youth*, Lord Lyyton

1936

82	January	*See How They Run*, Jerrard Tickell
83	February	*The Son of Marietta*, Johan Fabricus, trans. by Irene Clephane and David Hallett
84	March	*South Riding*, Winifred Holtby
85	April	*The Thinking Reed*, Rebecca West
86	May	*The African Witch*, Joyce Cary
87	June	*Saint Joan of Arc*, Vita Sackville-West
88	July	*The Weather in the Streets*, Rosamond Lehmann
89	August	*News from Tartary*, Peter Fleming
90	September	*But Beauty Vanishes*, Richard Blaker
91	October	*August Folly*, Angela Thirkell
92	November	*Desert Encounter. An Adventurous Journey through Italian Africa*, Knud Holmboe, trans. by Helga Holbek
93	December	*Together and Apart*, Margaret Kennedy

Chapter 5. CDL, 1937-8

Battle of the books

I

Cecil Day-Lewis by Howard Coster
half-plate film negative, 1937 © National Portrait Gallery, London

In April 1937, Cecil Day-Lewis joined the Book Society. Julian Huxley had handed his notice in at the start of the year – overworked, suffering with lumbago, and frustrated by the number of proofs he received from the club each month – and the selection committee judged Day-Lewis 'exactly the man for the job'. 'We need badly someone to represent the younger generation,' Walpole wrote to him in a fulsome invitation, 'and that object is not quite so strong in the Committee as it once was.' They'd improved their processes, Hugh reassured him, with an initial sifting now done by 'a very efficient staff,' making the job less onerous than it once was, and Day-Lewis would have read many of the novels anyway for his reviews for the *Telegraph*. 'The influence you would have and the help you would give to young writers make it really worth while,' Hugh wrote persuasively. 'From the human side it is I think by far the nicest and pleasantest Committee I've ever been on. Do say yes.'[253]

On the face of it, Day-Lewis was a surprising addition to the club, and news of his appointment caused some excitement in the press. 'I wonder if this means a more revolutionary note in the operations of the Society,' asked the *Sheffield Independent*, 'for Mr Lewis believes that culture will be revived only when the working-classes seize power.'[254] Next door to the Lynds' house, where poet Geoffrey Grigson and his wife Frances ran *New Verse*, a small but influential literary magazine, the news was met with malicious delight. 'Day-Lewis joins up' screamed their May 1937 issue; not to aid Spain, as some of the contemporary writers he was associated with had done, but he'd 'taken the bribe' as they said in the '30s.[255] He'd sold out. 'The Book Society is a Limited Company pimping to the mass bourgeois mind,' Grigson declared, as usual pulling no punches. Joining 'Mrs. Book Society Lynd' on the selection committee, Day-Lewis apparently signalled 'Change, Revolution, Youth, the Rising Generation.'[256] But at the same time, according to a purist like Grigson, he became 'the Underworld Man, the yesterday's newspaper, the grease in the sink-pipe of letters who has been posing for ten years as spring water'. 'Mr Day-Lewis and his Legend are now liquidated,' Grigson concluded with a flourish, 'the liquid has flowed to its oily shape and low level in the old sardine tin of Respectability.'

Perhaps Day-Lewis was taking a risk in joining the club, but he knew and respected Edmund Blunden (although only eight years older, Edmund seemed a generation apart because of the war), and had become fond of Hugh after praising the latter's support for young writers in a piece for the *Telegraph* (their correspondence developed quickly into a straight-talking friendship whereby Hugh could tell Day-Lewis that he didn't like the whole last quarter of his 1936 novel, *The Friendly Tree*). The Communist Party approved Day-Lewis's instinct to accept Walpole's invitation. The world was in crisis, and it was 'too late to be romantic rebels', as Day-Lewis wrote to his ally, poet Stephen Spender (a temporary neighbour of Hugh's in the Lakes the previous year).[257] The Book Society meant reaching a wider, mainstream demographic than Day-Lewis could access ordinarily through the left-wing press. Sharing progressive books with more readers was worth a little name-calling.

Cecil Day-Lewis was certainly a catch for the club. Tall, Anglo-Irish, 'almost handsome,' as Sylvia acknowledged in her diary, Day-Lewis was only thirty-three that April 1937, and already famous as a spokesman for the 'Popular Front' against war and fascism (a wide alliance of Left-wing groupings), and a leading member of the International Association of Writers for the Defence of Culture.[258] Known to broadcasters and journalists as 'Red Cecil' (he hated seeing his first name in print and dropped the hyphen in his surname for most of his career), Day-Lewis was part of the famous 'Auden gang', later known simply as 'The Thirties Poets' who defined a generation of post-war, political commitment.[259] 'We did not know we were a Movement until the critics told us we were,' Day-Lewis wrote in his autobiography, stating that he, Auden and Spender (the central players) were not together in one place until after the war (others associated with the group included Day-Lewis's student housemate and best man, Rex Warner, as well as Louis MacNeice, Edward Upward, and Christopher Isherwood).[260] But they socialised, corresponded, and reviewed each other's writing, reinforcing one another's influence and ideas from a 'leaning tower', as Virginia Woolf framed the group in a lecture to the Workers' Educational Association in Brighton in 1940. This was still a privileged tower built on 'middle-class birth and expensive education,' she acknowledged, but leaning leftwards 'under the influence of change, under the threat of war'.[261]

In his first poetry collection, published when he was twenty-one, Day-Lewis had followed the pastoral 'Georgian' style that dominated British taste in the 1910s and early 20s (the last of the bestselling *Georgian Poetry* anthologies, in which Edmund Blunden was a mainstay, was published in 1922). But after his first two volumes, and with his move to the Hogarth Press in 1929, Day-Lewis became radicalised, glimpsing revolution as 'victims / Of a run-down machine, who can bear it no longer' preserved 'The nerve for action, the spark of indignation –.'[262] This was partly down to the influence of Auden. But it also reflected Day-Lewis's increased social awareness from seeing the hardships facing miners in Edwinstowe, his father's Nottinghamshire parish, where Cecil lived, an unhappy only child, with his father and stepmother (his mother died when he was four) during school holidays from boarding school and, later, university.

Day-Lewis had been dazzled by Auden when they met in 1926 during Day-Lewis's last year as an undergraduate reading Classics at Oxford. Both worked for the TUC during the General Strike and after Day-Lewis graduated they collaborated on the Preface to *Oxford Poetry 1927*, crafting a joint statement in which they famously argued that poetry must synthesise public and private worlds. Confronting a society in crisis, they believed the poet needed to go beyond scaffolding, as T. S. Eliot had done in his apocalyptic 'The Waste Land' a generation earlier. 'We obscurely felt the need to do more with the fragments' Day-Lewis spelt out, 'than shoring them against our ruin.'[263] The Auden group's radical verse of pylons, train tracks, and night mail signalled a shift in poetic form and language, compelled by the poet's 'positive sense of engagement' with the world around them, as Day-Lewis explained, 'when it seemed possible to hope, to choose, to act, as individuals but for a common end'.[264] In his bestselling manifesto, *A Hope for Poetry* (first published in 1934, it appeared in eight editions over thirteen years), Day-Lewis argued that the younger poets were 'learning to communicate through a new kind of power'. Poetry was 'everyone's business,' he would declare in the 1936 postscript: it should be accessible, engaged, and 'rooted in common and garden life'.[265]

If Day-Lewis's decision to join the Book Society raised eyebrows in certain quarters, it showed the reality of trying to make a living from writing full-time without the cushion of private means. At the start of 1937, aged thirty-two, Day-Lewis was supporting his wife Mary and young sons (Sean, aged five, born 1931, and Nicholas, aged three, born 1934) while living in Box Cottage, Charlton Kings, a pretty village on the outskirts of Cheltenham. Twelve months previously, at Christmas 1935, he'd quit his job as a prep school teacher at Cheltenham College 'to be a literary hack,' as he told Stephen Spender (the governors had also made clear that he couldn't be a member of the Communist Party or give talks to the Friends of the Soviet Union and teach schoolboys).[266] Since then, he'd eked out a living as a professional poet and writer, combining serious literary fiction for Jonathan Cape with popular detective novels under a pseudonym, Nicholas Blake, published in Collin's crime club. He wrote an unpaid monthly column for *Left Review* (the British section of the Communist-run Writers' International) and well-paid reviews for the *Telegraph*.

The success of Nicholas Blake enabled him, as he later put it, 'to put butter on the bread provided by poetry'.[267] But the politics he was known for shone through. In the first of his Nigel Strangeway mysteries, *A Question of Proof* (1935, recently reissued), the protagonist is a dissatisfied teacher in a prep school, regarded as 'something of a Bolshie' by colleagues, who is angered by the affluent society the school patronises. 'The spectacle of all this painted, feathered, complacent, chattering flock made him feel sick inside,' the narrator observes of the parents attending a school sports day. 'It was to maintain this portentous scum that millions sweated or starved beneath the surface.'[268]

Writing full-time, in 1936 Day-Lewis had three book-length works out: a novel; his second Nicholas Blake story; and a long prose poem, *Noah and the Waters*, which dramatised the crisis faced by committed individuals in a 'country that needs cleansing' and opened with an extract predicting 'the disintegration of the ruling class' from *The Communist Manifesto*.[269] He also clarified his views on Spain. In a pamphlet for *Left Review* written with Rex Warner, *We're not going to do nothing. A reply to Aldous Huxley's "what are you going to do about it?"*, Day-Lewis called for 'a People's front in this country on the same lines as that recently set up in France,' whose 'backbone should be the Labour Movement'. Contradicting Huxley's pacifist statement (written for Dick Sheppard's Peace Pledge Union) that war was inherently wrong, Day-Lewis argued that direct action against the current fascist threat was necessary. 'The recent events in Spain show us the lengths to which the reactionary elements in a country will go when faced by a democratically elected government pledged to the task of social reform,' he pointed out.[270] Watching Auden, Spender, Orwell, and other writers join what became the 'world's "civil" war' (Day-Lewis co-edited a memorial volume for Ralph Fox, killed at the Spanish Front in December 1936), he'd contemplated going out of course.[271] But Day-Lewis had a young family to support and, as he wrote simply of the International Brigade much later in his autobiography: 'I believed I ought to volunteer for it, but I lacked the courage to do so.'[272] His first selection committee meeting was dominated by the shocking news of the bombing of Guernica, the Basque capital, destroyed by Nazi

Germany's Luftwaffe and Italian fascists (Franco's allies) on 26 April 1937 in an unprecedented display of modern air warfare targeting civilians.

During 1937 there was another novel for Cape, a third Nicholas Blake, and a collection of edited essays addressing *The Mind in Chains: Socialism and the Cultural Revolution*. He'd worked on the latter at the start of the year, just before joining the club. The volume discussed the fate of culture under fascism alongside education, literature, and the arts, representing 'the whole range of left politics' according to Cecil, indicating 'what a firm theoretical basis for the "Popular Front" is already in existence'.[273] His own introduction showed him at the height of his communist sympathies. He had joined the Party only the previous year after a long period of hesitation, worn down eventually by Party officials hot-footing it to Box Cottage, keen for a literary celebrity in the ranks. Cecil knew that his contribution to the movement was best done on paper. 'I am a writer and no speaker,' he wrote to the Birmingham branch declining an invitation, 'I can lecture, take part in discussions, that kind of thing, but I've no experience of straight propaganda-speaking, nor the voice for open-air work.'[274] In his introduction to *The Mind in Chains*, Day-Lewis looked to the destruction of culture in the fascist countries and argued that 'the quality of intellectual production is inevitably debased under monopoly-capitalism'. In the Soviet Union they'd got it right, he perceived. 'Under socialism alone will the warping, obstructive, anarchic profit-principle cease to falsify' writers' and artists work, he went on. 'We can only realise our strength by joining forces with the millions of workers who have nothing to lose but their chains and have a world to win.'[275] The Book Society and its readers were navigating a world in crisis. Bringing Day-Lewis onto the selection committee marked their desire to get a grip on the times.

II

A wave of new readers turned to organised book clubs in the late 1930s to try and make sense of the rise of far-left and far-right. In May 1936, Victor Gollancz (assisted by Sylvia's daughter, Sheila) had launched the Left Book Club, a mass movement in the fight against fascism which, according to Victor, aimed to 'be a sort of reading "Popular Front"'.[276] By 1939, the

Left Book Club had over 57,000 members receiving progressive cut-price non-fiction each month (ranging across philosophy, politics, education: famous LBC titles included George Orwell's *The Road to Wigan Pier* (1937) and Labour MP Ellen Wilkinson's *The Town That Was Murdered: The Life Story of Jarrow* (1939)). As well as providing access to cheap books at half-a-crown (two shillings and sixpence, rather than seven to twelve shillings and sixpence, like the Book Society), the Left Book Club had a cultural and social agenda, organising a newsletter, weekend schools, local discussion meetings, and rallies. The following year, in April 1937, Foyle's bookshop established the Right Book Club, reprinting conservative titles in politics and current affairs to try and counteract what Christina Foyle described as 'an hysterical swing to the left' (by the end of 1937 they had around half of the LBC's membership, but they did outlast it, going on until the 1950s).[277] Both dwarfed the size of the Book Society, which by 1939 had stabilised at around 10,000 subscribers. A glut of other specialist book clubs followed suit (there were clubs on liberalism, peace, religion, travel, art) in what *The Times* dubbed 'the battle of the books'.[278] Many of these new clubs of the late 1930s took the lead from the Book Society's methods of advertisement and reader engagement, but sent out cheaper, specially produced 'book club' editions or pamphlets, often reprints of already-successful titles, and not the publisher's first, potentially collectable, full price edition like the Book Society.

The Book Society had to tread carefully. Subscribers had not signed up to a political book club, and the judges were mindful of choosing anything too controversial that risked being sent back in its thousands. But while some voices deplored the politicisation of the contemporary book trade, the Book Society saw an opening. At the National Book Fair in London in November 1937, for instance, Winston Churchill criticised the 'deliberate publication of books of a uniform political tendency to an organised mass of reader'; readers who were not able to speak to, nor try and understand, each other.[279] But this was the value of belonging to the Book Society. For in addition to its monthly choices, the club recommended a dozen or so titles in the *Book Society News* as alternatives, potentially highlighting a wide range of views. The recommended titles could push boundaries in style and content and were generally split between fiction and non-fiction. Often these lists were a consolation, where the judges' bruised egos could be soothed and books that might otherwise be overlooked were defended. But in a wider 'battle of the books' for hearts and minds, this is where the club could offer a diverse steer to an anxious, increasingly polemical society.

In accepting Sir Hugh's invitation (Walpole was knighted in the Coronation honours list in June 1937), Day-Lewis knew he was unlikely to get many Popular Front titles chosen as book of the month. But by the end of his first year, in April 1938, he'd recommended a range of works on Spain, Soviet Russia, and Nazi Germany, as well as topical books on 'proletarian' or working-class life including Ralph Bates's *Rainbow Fish* (follow up to his better-known Spanish novel, *The Olive Field*), and Jim Phelan's prison autobiography, *Lifer*. In the recommended pages of the *Book Society News*, Day-Lewis pressed for the younger generation of writers he was associated with – Rex Warner, Christopher Isherwood, John Lehmann – and brought a touch of American machismo to the lists by highlighting the work of John Steinbeck and Ernest Hemingway (the latter's *To Have and Have Not* 'will shock some readers and irritate others', Day-Lewis wrote in his review. 'It will not do for those who want a soothing syrup or a mild pipedream; but those who can take it will like it.') He was sensitive to western portraits of other cultures. 'Can any European write a novel of India?' he asked in February 1938, introducing American-born Louis Bromfield's *The Rains Came* to the club (Cecil judged this a positive attempt, more E. M. Forster than Kipling). A Marxist take on fiction was also clear in some of his reviews, where collective solidarity trumps the solitary hero. This is evident in his dig at C. S. Forester's ever-popular Hornblower in his review of *A Ship of the Line* (recommended in April 1938), with its 'preoccupation with a single character' comprising both 'the strength and weakness of the book'. The shift from the club's general avoidance of political engagement in the early 1930s was striking.

A couple of Australian novels were sent to readers that summer. Choice number one hundred, Leonard Mann's *A Murder in Sydney*, was billed as part of a new, contemporary Australian literature ('hitherto Australian writers have naturally dealt with pioneering times' explained the dust jacket) while Helen Simpson's *Under Capricorn* (her second Book Society choice) explored the mix of settlers and former convicts in the historical development of Sydney. Australian-born Simpson had been educated in Europe from the age of sixteen and was a collaborator with Clemence Dane, both founder members of The Detection Club in 1930, a group of writers which included Agatha Christie and Dorothy L. Sayers (author of *Gaudy Night*, Book Society choice number eighty). Prompted by their publisher, Simpson and Dane had collaborated on a trilogy of detective novels set in the world of Arts and theatre: *Enter Sir John* (1928), *Printer's Devil* (1930), and *Re-enter Sir John* (1932). *Printer's Devil* (title *Author Unknown* in the US), was an unusual story centred upon 'London's first and only woman publisher' (possibly based on Dane's agent, Nancy Pearn), killed by one of her authors for rejecting his memoir.

In August 1937, the selection committee backed Auden and MacNeice's unusual travel spoof, *Letters from Iceland*, to be their one hundredth Book Society choice. This was a rambling mix of letters and lists – 'morsels of thought' or perhaps 'un-thought', as MacNeice pointed out – written in verse and prose, spliced by apparently random photographs, mainly taken by Auden.[280] The book satirised the serious poetic concerns of Eliot and Pound, post WWI, mocking a 'chromium-plated future' that ignored tenements, mills and the huge economic divisions fracturing modern British life. Auden and MacNeice were travelling in Iceland – an island on the edge of Europe – when the Spanish Civil War broke out in July 1936. The distance gave them an ironic perspective on a continent hurtling towards war once again, driven (perhaps) by Marxist historical necessity towards military crisis. 'The truth is', they wrote, 'we are both only really happy living among lunatics.'[281] Clemence Dane agreed to take this one on. She was resigning that autumn to pursue her screenwriting career in America, and, in one of her last reviews for the club, she admitted that she couldn't get her head around *Letters from Iceland*. 'It is a strong cup', she counselled readers, 'I have read it twice through – and dipped into it on and off for a fortnight, and I still do not know quite what I think about it as a whole.'

III

In December 1937, *Left Review* published *Authors take sides on the Spanish War*. The pamphlet was organised by poet Nancy Cunard and came out of the PEN International organisation's annual meeting in Paris that June (PEN, founded in London in 1921, stood for Poets, Essayists, Novelists. It remains an international writers' organisation fighting for human rights and freedom of expression). The pamphlet printed the responses of one hundred and forty-eight writers asked which of the two sides fighting in Spain they supported. The vast majority (one hundred and twenty-seven) were 'against Franco,' as Rose Macaulay put it succinctly, in support of the democratically elected Republican government. Sixteen of the respondents were neutral, including pacifists Vera Brittain and Malachi Whitaker, as well as some prominent authors (T. S. Eliot, Ezra Pound, H. G. Wells) who disdained the questionnaire mentality (George Orwell, still recovering from the fighting, spoilt his ballot). Only five writers voiced the minority viewpoint, coming out against the Spanish government. And one of these was Day-Lewis's colleague on the Book Society: Edmund Blunden.

Day-Lewis had not attended the PEN meeting in France that summer, but as a spokesperson for the Popular Front his answer to Cunard was clear. 'I am bound to help in the fight against Fascism,' he replied, 'which means certain destruction or living death for humanity.' Less clear was Edmund Blunden's view, who responded to PEN's questionnaire initially with diffidence. 'I know too little about affairs in Spain to make a confident answer,' Edmund began his reply. 'Memories of 1914-18 perhaps do not allow me to see some incidents you mention in the isolated and flamboyant way the manifesto has them.' But then he went further, rejecting not only the popular, Left-wing take on Franco but also the wider evidence by 1937 of the actions of the fascist dictators. 'To my mind (subject to that first reservation),' Edmund wrote:

> it was necessary that somebody like Franco should arise, and although England may not profit by his victory I think Spain will. The ideas of Germany, Italy etc., in your document do not square with those I have formed *upon the whole* of the recent history of those countries.

The reservation was based upon personal experience and printed in italics, but it captured Blunden's fundamental ambivalence. He maintained this precarious attitude, hovering between hatred of war, denial, and rejection of what he perceived as scaremongering, up into the 1940s.

***

In June 1937, when the international writers of PEN were meeting in France to discuss Spain and solidarity with writers persecuted under fascism, Edmund was attending an alternative authors' congress in Germany. He'd been invited by Dr Hans Grimm, poet, Anglophile, and author of the best-selling nationalist novel, *Volk ohne Raum* [people without space], a slogan politicised by the Nazis to justify German expansion. Grimm's annual literary gathering met in the village of Lippoldsberg in central Germany where, over a long and pleasant weekend, the assembled writers read aloud in the Grimms' beautiful walled garden, entertaining schoolchildren and troops from local depots. Many of the German writers attending had first met on the Western Front and made important contributions to WWI literature, some of which was known to readers in England (Blunden particularly admired Hans Carossa, Rudolf Binding, Edwin Dwinger, and Paul Alverdes - shot through the throat in 1915). As Edmund wrote afterwards in an essay on 'The Klosterhaus Readings' for the journal *German Life and Letters*, he valued the conversation and friendship with these 'gifted men of Germany' and saw his participation as a contribution to 'the cause of Anglo-German understanding and friendship'.[282] He would attend Lippoldsberg again, despite the gathering war clouds, in August 1939.

Blunden had met Grimm two months earlier, in April 1937, when he and his wife, Sylva, were on another 'good-will' visit to Germany.[283] Staying with academic friends and enjoying his German hosts' hospitality, Blunden spoke to enthusiastic audiences in Göttingen, Marburg and Heidelberg. His lecture was topical, considering 'The Englishman's Discovery of War' as portrayed by writers through the centuries: from Shakespeare, through Milton, coming to the present day and his personal discoveries in 1914, namely, as Sylva put it in her report of the tour, 'that the man on the other side of No Man's Land was not the enemy'. Afterwards, they'd find themselves fielding anxious questions from students about Britain's attitude to Germany which they found difficult to answer. For 'how can we come to Germany with words of reassurance', Sylva asked herself in her diary, 'other than our tiny personal ones?' She blamed the press, 'or a good part of it,' 'for diffusing an ignorant hostility' about National Socialism and twisting Hitler's words 'to prove his bad intentions'.[284] 'Germany was a very pleasant experience and a sad one,' Edmund wrote Rupert Hart-Davis after their August 1939 tour, 'for everyone, Nazi or not, is so decent, so fair, and even now so inclined to treat an Englishman with special kindness. I am afraid I can't admire our public mood and manners towards that country,' he went on, 'nor can I rejoice that encirclement political and commercial has caused them any difficulties in their ordinary life.'[285] Always Edmund's stress was on the fate of politics and political decision-making on the lives of ordinary people, whether they be English or German.

What Edmund thought privately about life in Nazi Germany on these trips is not clear (no diary from this period survives and they do not feature in his letters to Sassoon), but his wife Sylva, at least, admired some of what she saw, including the 'invigorating' music of the military band in Marburg that woke them at 6.30am, and the more sensible attitude to alcohol demonstrated by their German hosts compared to the excesses of Oxford academic life. She was critical of one of their hosts in Heidelberg, 'a small dictator,' she noted in her diary, who micro-managed their visit and 'overdoes the no-smoking, no-drinking ideal of the Nazi regime'; 'This was the man we had been warned (even by Germans),' she recorded, 'was so ardent a Nazi.' But she was nevertheless willing to absorb racist, antisemitic explanations of the re-appointments taking place in German universities under Hitler. 'The fact that Hitler once dismissed the Jews we must leave as a feature of internal politics,' Sylva wrote in private. 'Do we imagine the Jews will be wiped out?' Neither she nor Edmund made antisemitic comments in public, but Sylva's diary and her letters suggest that such sentiments – common at the time – may have been shared between them in private, helping to justify maintaining their German associations. By the summer of 1939, Sylva had volunteered for the Women's Auxiliary Territorial Service (formed 1938), and would confide in Edmund what she couldn't say about Poland at the camp: 'how obviously we have taken the wrong course and are now at the mercy of this excitable jumpy little nation (shan't dare to talk of this when I get to camp so am blowing it off now).' Early August 1939, she signed off a personal letter to him with the fateful words: 'Heil Hitler, and lots of love, Sylva.'[286]

In Göttingen during their spring tour of 1937, the Blundens had to field rumours that Oxford might refuse to send official delegates to the university's bicentenary, something they feared 'would mean a breach between English and German universities that would be hard to lessen'.287 After this was confirmed when they got home, Edmund wrote a public letter to *The Times* in protest, warning that a 'temporary gulf' in academia should not be 'deliberately widened' by English 'aloofness'.[288] He'd found a 'generous atmosphere' of debate, learning, and discussion in Germany that spring, he tried to reassure readers. Predictably, his intervention caused outrage, prompting 'the wrath of strange and dreary correspondents from most parts of Europe,' as Edmund confessed in a letter to the novelist Enid Bagnold, plus giving him and Sylva 'the private intimidation game' to deal with. 'Both my wife and myself have been addressed and spoken of as Nazis,' Edmund revealed to Bagnold.[289] It was the beginning of a suspicion that would stay with them for years.

* * *

Edmund's recommendations to the club regarding international relations during the late 1930s preached caution, seeking to move away from what he called the 'one-way observation' of the time.[290] He remained committed to peace and efforts to avoid military conflict and thought Cecil and the Popular Front's call for direct action against fascism was naive. In April 1937, Edmund recommended Captain Liddell Hart's *Europe in Arms* to the Book Society. Hart was a fellow survivor of the Somme and a famous critic of the WWI generals' disastrous military strategy. Hart was passionately against the introduction of conscription to fight the new fascist threat and by the late '30s, with a hand in Chamberlain's government, he argued that if Britain were ever to fight in another European war, it should be air and naval forces who took the strain, not ground troops. Blunden thought Hart's pragmatism debatable but recommended *Europe in Arms* to readers as a serious, 'temperate' study of the likely course and effects of another great war, written from the perspective of one who had been there. Always scathing of warmongers, Blunden quotes Hart on the tragic consequences of fear and ignorance:

> If fear be the predisposing cause of war, ignorance is the most potent of the factors that nourish it. The fear of the unknown breaks down armies in wartime; in peace time it drives nations, like the Gadarene swine, down to the abyss.

So, while tensions on the global stage worsened, the club ran its own version of 'authors take sides', encouraging readers to see for and against Chamberlain's strategy of appeasement. Edmund worked against Day-Lewis and Sylvia to bring more right-wing choices onto the lists, often aligning with selections from Christina Foyle's Right Book Club. In February 1938 for instance, he reviewed a study of Japanese militarism – *Japan over Asia* – by journalist William Chamberlain and concluded that 'At a time when hasty judgements are being formed', the book's perspective gave 'reasons for thinking beyond present passions'. He reviewed Arnold Wilson's *Thoughts and Talks, 1935-7: The Diary of a Member of Parliament*, and Ernest Hambloch's *British Consul: Memories of Thirty Years' Service in Europe and Brazil.* Wilson was an outspoken supporter of Franco and applauded the dictatorships of Germany and Italy; Hambloch's discussion of the new fascist dictatorship in Brazil left room to accuse him of admiring it. Blunden took away an insightful moral from Hambloch that the author's:

> attitude of disfavour towards some of our rivals and their determined organisations does not prevent him from offering a little candid advice to us, to try and see ourselves as the foreigner sees us. The illusion he believes we have helped to create 'is that we are too proud to want to be understood'.[291]

Sylvia was furious with Edmund for recommending books that could be seen as sympathetic to the far right and protested to Hugh that Hambloch and Wilson were 'both thoroughly bad books apart from other objections'.[292] Her review of G. L. Steer's *The Tree of Gernika* was placed next to Edmund's on *Japan over Asia* in the *Book Society News*. Steer had arrived in the Basque capital a few hours after the fascists' air bombardment, while the city was still burning, and was a 'first-rate war correspondent', Sylvia observed, 'who can make his readers look on at battles as if with their own eyes'. His account of one of the most terrible episodes of the Spanish Civil War emphasised 'the horror of war,' she wrote, bringing home how 'the finest things are destroyed by it'. Edmund was in absolute agreement.

IV

The question of how to prevent another global conflict animated the Book Society's lists as Hitler sought to expand the Third Reich. After the Anschluss of March 1938 (when Germany annexed Austria), the club magazine began a section on contemporary affairs; by November, after the Munich crisis, this was titled 'European affairs.' In the summer of 1938, Sylvia recommended two books asking what women could do to prevent war in Europe. Virginia Woolf's *Three Guineas* (recommended in June) and Eric Linklater's *The Impregnable Women* (July choice) were seemingly chalk and cheese. *Three Guineas*, Sylvia acknowledged in her review with reverence, was a 'fine, elegant' essay that offered a feminist take on the patriarchal roots of fascism, in which Hitler and Mussolini became extreme examples of the sexist bigot at home. Written partly in response to the death of her nephew, Julian Bell, in the Spanish Civil War, it was according to Woolf only by transforming sexual and economic relations – distributing work equally, paying women a real wage for mothering children, educating women equal to men – that the warped, hyper-masculine ideologies of Hitler and Mussolini could be prevented from triumphing: 'the public and private worlds are inseparably connected,' Woolf wrote, 'the tyrannies and servilities of the one are the tyrannies and servilities of the other'.[293] 'The only unsatisfactory thing, from a practical point of view,' Sylvia lamented (as did many others), was Woolf's suggestion that educated women should dispense with leagues, conferences, and campaigns to form a 'Society of Outsiders' fighting for liberty, peace, and equality in 'new words' with 'new methods'.[294] Woolf was frustrated with the public debate on pacifism and thought women would do better by resisting the Hitlerism in their own families and society. But Sylvia had stood inside Albert Hall during the Black Shirts' fascist rallies. She lived and breathed agendas and committee meetings. Woolf's radical, feminist-pacificist idea that women should stand outside of society to better critique patriarchy, militarism, and nationalism did not easily square.

Eric Linklater's *The Impregnable Women*, sent to Book Society readers the following month, was – as Sylvia pointed out in the club magazine – like a 'ribald comment' on *Three Guineas*. *The Impregnable Women* imagined the Next War around the corner, where Britain and Germany were allies, and the enemy was France. Linklater's satirical take on women's role in the peace effort went back to Aristophanes' Greek comedy *Lysistrata*, where an international sex-strike is organised by Lady Lysistrata to stop the war. It was 'very masculine humour', Sylvia acknowledged, and she did her best to read it with a straight face. But the book was more than a sexist fantasia, serious in its critique of the stupidity of war and the uneasy peace. The opening of the book captured the world much as it was at present, Sylvia noted: 'There had been, as it happened, no less than three successive crises in as many weeks, and the papers, according to their several tempers, were either desperately calm or hysterically agitated.' Linklater's satire of the 'prudent expediency' and self-interest of British foreign policy was merciless: 'Britain's careful avoidance of trouble, its cautious belief that honesty was not always the best foreign policy, its sensible perception that where honour conflicted with self-interest, honour was the lesser sacrifice.'[295] Anticipating readers' enjoyment, the July *Book Society News* ran a members' competition asking for sensational headlines to be used by the popular press if events in *The Impregnable Women* ever occurred. The winners were announced in October 1938. But by that point, the moment had passed. It was not felt wise to publish headlines about a legendary war of tomorrow when, as the club acknowledged, 'the wings of real war have since brushed us all so nearly'.[296]

V

The Munich Crisis of September 1938 brought tensions between the judges to a head. On September 30, the Prime Minister Neville Chamberlain flew back to Britain, announcing 'peace for our time' after signing with Hitler an agreement that ceded the Sudetenland (western Czechoslovakia) to the Nazis. Six days later, with the threat of war subsiding and a big vote of confidence in Chamberlain from MPs, the Book Society selection committee met in Hugh's flat. Day-Lewis and Sylvia Lynd were vehemently against the agreement (known by the Czechs and Slovaks as the 'Munich betrayal'), arguing it pandered to Hitler and only delayed the inevitable. Sylvia was still furious. 'What an abject surrender', she'd written to her father, and she didn't hold back with the judges, attacking Edmund for defending Chamberlain's continued efforts to avoid war.[297] Hugh sat back guiltily, as he admitted later in his diary, appalled by Sylvia's 'hysterical, anti-Chamberlain' position, but in general sympathy with her views. Afterwards he wrote to Edmund, intending to apologise for not speaking up for him, at the same time making his own views plain. 'I didn't want to speak of politics the other day but I loathe all their hatred. I think Hitler and his four friends may reach a point when they must be stopped by the whole world.'[298]

Edmund disagreed, and the front-page of that Saturday's *TLS* featured his celebratory poem on Munich, 'Exorcized'. The poem imagined the grim spectre of WWI – 'That giant enemy of sleep, that ghost which summed the worst they knew' – being 'exorcized' by 'The meeting of four men as friends':

Back to your madhouse, child of hell: too many of us know you well;
Infest our sleep, if thence we keep some record of your eyeless eyes.
But trespass not in the face of day. You find you cannot prowl this way;
Your very foulness forearmed those who now have checked your matinee,
The generous, selfless, wise.

The following week, on October 15, 1938, a Latin translation of Blunden's poem in the *TLS* further graced the occasion. He and his wife Sylva had delighted at 'The Good News', as Sylva wrote to him, which put a pause to some of the war preparations already happening around them: gas masks at Oxford Town Hall, pictures at the Ashmolean being packed up ready to be sent away. 'I am almost laughing at ARP & kindred organisations as we did formally,' Sylva wrote Edmund happily, signing off with a 'Peace Kiss.'[299] Edmund was grateful to Chamberlain, Hitler, Mussolini, and Daladier for avoiding war. 'The Merton fieldmouse' – as Geoffrey Grigson had him down – would not put aside the fate of ordinary people when their future was in the balance.[300]

* * *

In October 1938, the Book Society selected Elizabeth Bowen's sixth novel, *The Death of the Heart*. Chosen late summer, as the Sudeten crisis unfolded, *The Death of the Heart* captured a sense of the times. Bowen's central character, sixteen-year-old Portia, has suffered a difficult, rootless, childhood, brought up in a series of continental hotels in the shadow of shame and divorce (her father leaves his first wife and child after a fling with Portia's mother). When Portia is thrust into respectable, upper middle-class society after her parents' early deaths, she finds London cold, and her relatives – her elder, half-brother Thomas and his wife Anna, who are compelled to take Portia in – emotionally barren. Their vivacious townhouse, 'all mirrors and polish,' has 'no past' and no memories, 'no place where shadows lodged, no point where feeling could thicken'. The shadow of appeasement and the inevitability of a future war haunts the characters' desperate actions. Talking to Portia in his study, Thomas concedes a sense of malaise where history is 'Bunk, misfires, and graft' and they 'go round in rings'. 'And also there was a future' back in the past, he tells her. 'You can't get up any pace when you feel you're right at the edge.'[301]

Reviewing *The Death of the Heart* for the club, Day-Lewis emphasised Bowen's central theme of the 'tragedy of innocence' and compared it to Chekhov. People who had seen director Michel Saint-Denis's recent production of *The Three Sisters* at the Queen's Theatre, Day-Lewis noted, would appreciate the nod to the book's wit, characterisation, and 'charming air of inconsequence and ruthlessness'. Impressed, Bowen wrote to thank Day-Lewis for 'a grand and most understanding' review.[302] The reference to Chekhov underlined for Day-Lewis the class-based moral emptiness behind the novel's portrait of a society on the brink. By the following year, the topical relevance of *The Death of the Heart* could be named more explicitly when, early in 1939, V. S. Pritchett reviewed Bowen's family drama as foretelling the death of civilisation from approaching war.

In October 1938, Day-Lewis's ninth collection of poetry was published. *Overtures to Death* had been written during the Spanish Civil War and policy of appeasement, as well as the unexpected death of his father in July 1937 and Day-Lewis' gradual rejection of Soviet communism. Dedicated to E. M. Forster, the collection was marked by doom, destruction, and a helpless sense of foreboding. It was also popular, the bestselling of all Day-Lewis's volumes of poetry in the 1930s, resonating with the anxious mood of the times. Conflict was inevitable 'For us', a post-war generation 'born into a world / Of fledged, instinctive trees, / Of lengthening days, snowfall at Christmas,' the opening poem declared. 'We are here in the shrouded drawing-room,' waiting for the grim reaper's 'first, your final knock'.[303]

The resignation in much of the volume was offset by reminders, as Forster wrote Day-Lewis in appreciation, of 'the possibility of heroic action, and many will be satisfied by that; but not you nor I'.[304] A long narrative poem, 'The Nabara', based on G. L. Steer's eye-witness account of the destruction of Guernica and the heroism of Basque fishermen during the Spanish Civil War, was a timely reminder of the importance of standing up to fascism, 'When madmen play the piper / And knaves call the tune.'[305] But Day-Lewis could find no easy answers, and his political identity was in crisis.

Earlier that summer, while on stage with fellow writers against fascism at the Queen's Hall in London, Day-Lewis was overwhelmed by the need to step back from campaigning, revulsed, as he later put it, 'not from Communism but from the self which political activity had fostered'.[306] Overworked and increasingly doubtful of Soviet Russia's cultural policies, he was like many others (as Sylvia put it in a review for the club of Eugene Lyons's *Assignment in Utopia*), 'still a believer in socialism,' but 'no longer believes that it is to be found in Russia'. After the Queen's Hall event, Cecil and Mary started to look for a house in the country, 'partly because in a remote village I hoped to be able to cut myself off from meetings, committees and the day-to-day work of the Party,' as Day-Lewis explained in his autobiography. They found it in Brimclose, 'quarter of a mile from the village of Musbury' on the Devon border with Dorset: 'two cottages knocked into one, with white-washed cob walls, a deep thatch roof, an orchard, a pleasant small garden, and an overgrown tennis court on which the previous occupants had kept goats'.[307] Shortly before the publication of *Overtures to Death*, the Day-Lewis family had left Cheltenham and moved in.

On the Book Society selection committee, Day-Lewis respected Blunden's war experience and determined, quietly spoken pacifism. They had been friends since Edmund had agreed to visit him and give a talk in Cheltenham in 1935. But Day-Lewis nevertheless disagreed with Edmund fundamentally on what had been achieved in Munich that autumn:

> Your politicians pray silence
> For the ribald trumpeter,
> The falsetto crook, the twitching
> Unappeasable dictator.
> For any else you should be pleased
> To hold your tongue: but Satan
> Himself would disown his teaching
> And turn to spit on these.
> ('Self-Criticism and Answer')

On the 11 November 1938, *The Times* reported on 'A Black Day for Germany' after the horrific pogrom of 9-10 November; what became known as *Kristallnacht*, or the Night of Broken Glass. 'No foreign propagandist bent upon blackening Germany before the world could outdo the tale of burnings and beatings, of blackguardly assaults upon defenceless and innocent people, which disgraced that country yesterday', *The Times* declared.[308] As news of the orchestrated antisemitic violence across Nazi Germany, Austria, and the Sudetenland shocked the world, with images of burning synagogues and looted homes and businesses consuming news reels, to many the necessity for action finally seemed clear. In response, that same month the club shared a poem from Day-Lewis's new collection in the *Book Society News*. 'The Volunteers' was a muted, patriotic poem, where future war was necessary to save a greater good. Its publication clarified where most of the judges stood by now, reinforcing the views of many of their readers:

> Tell them in England, if they ask
> What brought us to these wars,
> To this plateau beneath the night's
> Grave manifold of stars –
>
> It was not fraud or foolishness,
> Glory, revenge or pay:
> We came because our open eyes
> Could see no other way.
>
> There was no other way to keep
> Man's flickering truth alight:
> These stars will witness that our course
> Burned briefer, not less bright.
>
> […]
>
> Here in a parched and stranger place
> We fight for England free,
> The good our fathers won for her,
> The land they hoped to see.
> ('The Volunteer')[309]

In the 1936 postscript for *A Hope for Poetry*, Day-Lewis had warned 'today the shadows are getting longer. Death refuses to stay upstage. And it is not so much the death of you and me: it is the death of civilisation which threatens.'[310] Nothing he, nor any of the other judges, could recommend for the Book Society would avoid the coming crisis.

1937

94	January	*The Stranger Prince. The Story of Rupert of the Rhine*, Margaret Irwin
95	February	*The Happy Return*, C. S. Forester
96	March	*Present Indicative*, Noel Coward, or *Something of Myself*, Rudyard Kipling (Special Alternative Book)
97	April	*Man of December. A Story of Napoleon III & the Fall of the 2nd Empire*, Alfred Neuman, trans. by Eden and Cedar Paul
98	May	*And So–Victoria*, Vaughan Wilkins
99	June	*Sugar in the Air*, E. C. Large
100	July	*A Murder in Sydney*, Leonard Mann
101	August	*Letters from Iceland*, W. H. Auden and Louis MacNeice
102	September	*Under Capricorn*, Helen Simpson
103	October	*The Turning Wheels*, Stuart Cloete
104	November	*Enchanter's Nightshade*, Ann Bridge
105	December	*Portrait of a Village*, Francis Brett Young, or *The Pasquier Chronicles*, Georges Duhamel, trans. by Beatrice de Holthoir

1938

106	January	*Northwest Passage*, Kenneth Roberts
107	February	*The Rains Came. A Novel of Modern India*, Louis Bromfield
108	March	*South Latitude*, F. D. Ommanney
109	April	*Count Belisarius*, Robert Graves
110	May	*Scoop. A Novel about Journalists*, Evelyn Waugh
111	June	*Crippled Splendour*, Evan John
112	July	*The Impregnable Women*, Eric Linklater
113	August	*Rebecca*, Daphne du Maurier
114	September	*Testament*, R. C. Hutchinson
115	October	*The Death of the Heart*, Elizabeth Bowen
116	November	*Flying Colours*, C. S. Forester
117	December	*Edgar Wallace. A Biography*, Margaret Lane

Chapter 6. Sylvia, 1939

Rooks and aeroplane engines

I

Tillies Cottage, Forest Green

Sylvia Lynd fell for Tillies Cottage at first sight. Situated in a quiet country lane encircling the village green, Tillies is the oldest building in the rural hamlet of Forest Green, near Ockley in Surrey. A layer of Virginia creeper covers the fifteenth-century brickwork and timber, weaving its way around tiny, irregular windowpanes and a double-breasted chimney. To its front, the cottage looks out onto a bowling-green and small hammer pond, a relic of Surrey's ancient ironmaking industry. Behind rise the forested slopes of Leith Hill, one of the highest points in southeast England. Nightingales nested at the local garage and at the seventeenth-century Parrot inn just down the road. Sylvia and Robert could get away from London and drive to Forest Green in an hour and twenty-five minutes on a good day. It was the perfect break from Hampstead, Fleet Street, and the tiresome demands of literary celebrity.

Sylvia had turned fifty in September 1938 and needed a change of pace. The committees and rounds of parties ('I seem to be the only person left in the world who gives dinner parties – oh wish I could stop', she exclaimed in her diary), alongside Robert's weekly deadlines, were taking their toll. A few years earlier, Clifford Sharp, one of their oldest *New Statesman* friends, had died 'literally of whiskey,' according to Sylvia: 'he drank two bottles on the day he died,' she mourned, 'but he was dying for years before then'.[311] Seeing Tillies, Sylvia dreamed she 'might work down there and help Robert to live sensibly again'. She asked her father to buy the cottage for them and arranged to pay him rent. They had a lot to do, haemorrhaging money on mending the ancient pump and cesspit. Sylvia built a little writing desk for herself in the alcove behind the stairs and planted fruit trees out the back, a row of cox's orange pippins. Sheila, now 'tired of David' (she would marry fellow party member Peter Wheeler before the war) came down to help and gardened vigorously. 'The cottage with its lit windows' was 'looking like Paradise,' Sylvia wrote with relish mid-April.[312]

But it was spring 1939, and war was looming. When Hitler occupied Prague in March, Chamberlain announced the end of appeasement and the need to step up domestic planning for war, and Forest Green swung into action. Early February, as Sylvia nursed a temperature in bed, counting the number of birds visiting the lump of fat at her window and listening to the sounds of ducks and cowbells coming off the green, she did her reviews for *Harper's* magazine and the Book Society, then filled out a form for the number of refugees they could house at Tillies. With immediate family only - cousin Greta who was staying with them, plus her husband Derek and daughter Veronica, 'our two selves, the daughters & Pater' (Sylvia 'restrained' herself from including the girls' husbands, though realised that if things got too bad they would have to sleep down in Forest Green with them) - they were already three over quota. She signed up as a volunteer to help in the evacuation of London ('my district will be St Pancras, if the moment comes') and had the car lights dimmed and painted according to regulations.[313] It was a struggle to make the old house properly dark at night unless they veiled the inside lights as well as the windows. Walking back from the Parrot inn with Robert late one evening, they realised the black-out in Forest Green was far from perfect. 'Robert said it was foolish of Forest Green to make itself look like the middle of London,' Sylvia noted.

One afternoon mid-April, as springtime finally sprung, Sylvia and Robert took a walk together up Leith Hill. The plum and pear trees were coming into blossom and the garden was bright with flowers. The blackthorn – quite tall trees in this part of Surrey – smelled sweet and the hawthorn was everywhere bright green. They walked back down the hill slowly, listening out for nightingales 'but heard only a willow-wren. Or perhaps a garden warbler.'[314] It was a beautiful day, though their thoughts were ominous. The news from Spain of Franco's victory at the start of that month was depressing, marking the beginning of his dictatorship with mass reprisals against the defeated Republican forces. The seeming inevitability of a second world war left Sylvia feeling trapped and prematurely aged. Most of all, she worried about air-raids. She and Robert had protected the girls through WWI when they were children, taking them to live in the countryside, but they couldn't do that for them now. Sheila and B. J. were already busy up in London. Sheila was leaving Victor Gollancz and the Left Book Club to be an Air Warden, refusing to relocate to Brimpton, Victor's country home near Newbury, to run the LBC groups with him there as he'd suggested. Sheila had reprimanded Victor, telling him 'we think that in wartime it is more important to *display* courage than common sense,' and that she resented being treated as an 'office boy' rather than an officer: 'for you have shown that you don't want a political assistant, but a short-hand typist to type your letters to the Groups'.[315] 'She is splendidly brave,' Sylvia acknowledged in her diary. She was equally proud of and terrified for her daughters.

At the end of June 1939, Sylvia was unseated by news of her friend Mark Gertler's suicide. She had been reading his autobiography, offering advice as he went along, and had already pitched the project to publisher Norman Collins. 'So it had become part of my future as well as his,' she acknowledged in grief, 'Besides it would have been a brilliant book & I should have loved to read it.' Mark had visited her, distressed, the week before gassing himself in his studio – traumatised by antisemitism and the threat of war, caught in a financial crisis as he separated from his wife – and Sylvia wished that she had 'taken charge of him for a little while. Brought him to No 5 or here.' Mark Gertler symbolised an early connection to her love for Gordon Campbell and she painfully felt the severance from her past. 'I did not know before how much he had become part of my life,' she mourned in her diary. She observed on the willow by the pond 'a single magpie, sign of sorrow'. 'The future is not to be thought about really, for war is impending.' All she could do was hold on to work, family, and the comforts of daily routine. 'Now I must get lunch, cut some flowers & go back to town.'[316]

***

The new club rooms in Book Society House, Grosvenor Place

The Book Society celebrated its tenth birthday that April. 'Soon we shall be strutting around in long trousers, flaunting our first cricket-bat,' Alan Bott told readers in the *Book Society News*. Hugh offered a reflection on the club's first decade, admitting that he had 'on several occasions tried to break away,' underlining the differences in tastes among the judges and the variety of choices they offered, while stressing what he saw as their 'real business' in promoting young, debut authors. Some of the changes in bookselling and book buying he had anticipated when the club was first mooted had finally occurred, Hugh recognised, 'but more slowly than I then thought it would,' with the mass book clubs that followed after them and the beginning of cheap paperbacks. 'But the problems have now, by 1939, moved away from us to the whole question of cheap books,' Hugh asserted. 'I am certain that we shall in the next five years, see quite a revolution in bookselling.'[317]

The club had come a long way in ten years. After the Great Depression, membership had settled at around the 10,000 mark and, according to manager Alan Bott 'included five Queens, one notable author who had attacked the society, and residents in thirty-three countries'. Looking back over what they'd achieved, Alan shared some of his favourite readers' letters. 'I hate you so much that I am beginning to like you' came from Anon. And there was a gem from a member in Robin Hood's Bay, Yorkshire, which spoke to the bookish community of reading and collecting the club had achieved:

> I look ahead, say in five years time. I shall have sixty or more books, keenly chosen, approved by myself. Each book will have coloured a month in a member's life. I wonder how many of us could show a like record from any five years of our own haphazard reading.[318]

Physically, the club had also moved up in the world. Two years earlier, during the summer of 1937, the Book Society had relocated from 10 Buckingham Palace Gardens to more spacious headquarters in Grosvenor Place. Book Society House (as it was called in the magazine) was a large, dignified building off the back of Buckingham Palace gardens, close to Hyde Park Corner and easily accessible from all parts of London, as the club assured readers. In the *Book Society News*, subscribers were invited to use the club room facilities whenever they were 'up' in town: 'members may read, write, telephone and meet friends at leisure,' they advertised.[319] How many took advantage of this offer we don't know, but London clubs in this period were an expensive luxury (and often male only): opening a plush club room for men and women of whatever trade or background – the only stipulation being that you were able to afford twelve new books a year – was a nudge for democracy.

Alongside the special birthday issue of the journal, members received a facsimile reproduction of Royal Academy artist Henry Rushbury's 'View From a balcony: Hyde Park Corner.' Rushbury had sketched the impressive view from the first-floor balcony of Book Society House during a recent visit to the Print Society, which was about to publish a signed, limited-edition etching. His image captured the stately bustle of Hyde Park Corner with people, buses, and motorcars dwarfed by the symbols of royal London and the triumphal Wellington Arch (built, along with Marble Arch, to commemorate Wellington's victories in the Napoleonic Wars). On the right, the bronze sculpture of 'Peace descending on the Quadriga of War' sits atop the Wellington Arch, the Angel's laurel of peace held aloft. As a special offer, members could have the print mounted and framed cut-price through the club if they wished: 'thus securing a hand-made article at a mass-production price'.[320] From the late '30s, the *Book Society News* regularly advertised the Print Society, which aimed to make contemporary artwork affordable, alongside another sister company, Sequana, the French Book-of-the-Month Club (Book Society members could receive the latter's illustrated magazine without charge as an extra service, and subscriptions could be sent in via the Book Society).[321] But Rushbury's 'Hyde Park Corner' was the only reproduction the club shared with members direct. It was a view of tradition and dignity of life in the capital to hold onto as they contemplated a second world war.

Henry Rushbury R.A., 'View From a balcony: Hyde Park Corner', Print Society, 1939

* * *

For many writers, the threat of war numbed creativity, and the number of proofs the judges had to select from was starting to dwindle. At the judges' meeting that April, Sylvia found the selection committee 'Gay to begin with but afterwards rather melancholy. Hugh cross because the non-fiction books were so poor & inclined to scold poor Colin de la Mare to all our embarrassment.'[322] As an author, Hugh was aware of the difficulties in keeping going and tried to stick to the writing schedule he had maintained all his life. But for many, the 'war of nerves' after the Munich crisis – a time of 'incalculable catastrophe, in which the whole of western civilisation and half oriental civilisation may go down' as E. M. Forster described 'The 1939 State' in an essay that June – was simply paralysing.[323] Geoffrey Faber, President of the Publishers Association, would observe later that year that:

> Ever since Munich the atmosphere of Europe has grown more and more unfavourable to creative literary work…'How can I write with the world in this state?' is a cry I have heard more than once in the past few months.[324]

Yet despite challenges in the wider book trade, the club endeavoured to guide readers through the anxiety and try to keep track of events. Consequently, international authors and stories combining 'contemporary interest with literary merit and "human" appeal' were high up the 1939 lists.[325] In January, the judges chose bestselling novelist Pamela Frankau's *The Devil We Know*, a dramatic novel about a young Jewish filmmaker fighting persecution. There were countries in Europe where the book could not have been published, Day-Lewis pointed out, and while Frankau (at thirty, already the author of nineteen books) wasn't a political writer by trade, this was 'a good book to read just now,' Day-Lewis noted, given 'wings by the potential nobility of this theme'.[326] Work by Stefan Zweig – among the best-known of the German and Austrian writers currently in exile – was recommended, while other club selections explored international affairs. This included American writer Pearl Buck's *The Patriot*, selected by both British and American book-of-the-month clubs. The previous year, Buck had been awarded the Nobel Prize for Literature for her sympathetic portrayal of Chinese peasants, and while the Sino-Japanese war informed *The Patriot*, Day-Lewis observed in his review that there was 'A refusal to allow the simple pattern of the book to be blurred, over-complicated, or in any way stampeded by the violence which is latent in its subject.'

In February 1939, the Book Society selected H. G. Wells's novel, *The Holy Terror*. This was a futuristic account of dictatorship in which an English dictator, Rudie, sets up a Party of the Common Man to fight for a worldwide English-speaking union. The seventy-three-year-old Wells articulated a profound feeling of crisis for humanity and the planet, while his depiction of the 'Frightened Thirties', taking in the rise of populist movements and the ability of demagogues to leverage social and economic fears, was profound:

> Then had come, not formal war, all declared and set, but a gradual decline into warlike violence and destruction all over the world; Abyssinia, Spain, China and Japan, Macedonia, Syria [...] Everywhere there appeared the same phenomenon of unemployed and discontented masses of young people milling about in revolutionary movements; everywhere demagogues rose to exploit them [...] The formulae of the gangsters varied from extreme leftism to extreme rightism, but the material facts were everywhere the same. Governments everywhere were afraid to declare war definitely or to restore an effective peace.
> Civilisation as he knew it, was going to pieces.[327]

Hugh Walpole abused chair's privilege to affirm a religious, national patriotism in his club review of *The Holy Terror* that would have been antithetical to Wells himself, arguing that Wells 'has never understood why men will die for their country or that it is possible to love your country and be just to other countries as well'. Hugh believed it was an ideological war they were fighting which could only be won 'by the people who most profoundly, energetically, and to the death believed in the absolute necessity of their idea prevailing'.[328]

In the press, there was debate as to whether Well's dictator was modelled on Hitler or Stalin. Six months later, when the 'staggering news' of the Nazi-Soviet Pact of Non-Aggression signed in Moscow shocked the world, the ruthlessness of both men was made clear.[329] For many 'fellow travellers' on the Left, this nullified their hopes in Soviet communism. Like many others,

Day-Lewis had resigned from the Party the previous year while some, including Sylvia's daughters, held out. 'Rose tells me BJ & Jack still believe in Kind Joe Stalin, alas,' Sylvia wrote in her diary that September (Sheila meanwhile would join a later wave of resignations after the Soviet Union's crushing of the Hungarian Uprising in 1956).[330] But Sylvia already knew where she stood. 'Mussolini called on the Devil & Hitler appeared,' she recorded in her diary after hearing news of the Pact, which made Germany's ambitions to invade Poland more likely. 'Hitler called on the Devil & Stalin appeared.'[331]

For the first time in its history, the club broke precedent that June by sending out a choice that was not newly published but nevertheless timely and important (members were compensated with a fine edition at the price of an ordinary one). Nora Waln's *Reaching for the Stars*, published the previous month, was an eye-witness account of life in Germany during the Hitler era, widely praised as coming 'nearer to solving the psychological riddle of Nazi Germany than any other book', according to at least one reviewer's endorsement on the cover. For Hugh, it seemed to answer 'what we all want to know. Where is the Germany we have loved and trusted and found so much in common with?' 'She says that the future of the world must depend on the preservation of that love' for the people of Germany, Hugh continued. Again, he used reviewer's prerogative in the *Book Society News* to sum up the duty he felt the Allied nations were now honour-bound to pursue:

> Because a future of hatred and distrust is hopeless and desperate for mankind. Somehow I feel we must do as Miss Waln has done; preserve our love, and at the same time fight to the very last ditch for the principles of freedom and justice and tolerance in which we believe.

II

When it finally came in September 1939 the outbreak of war split the selection committee. For George, Hugh, and Sylvia, the turn to decisive action was in some ways a relief.

George Gordon had been busy preparing the University of Oxford for war since becoming Vice-Chancellor in October the previous year: negotiating with Ministries over plans for undergraduates, pooling University and College buildings, deciding what could be requisitioned or rented and what should be kept for academics. After Hitler's invasion of Poland on Friday 1 September, George was ready for the government's announcement at 11am on the Sunday that Britain was finally at war. 'An intolerable situation has at last acquired the awful explicitness of war,' he addressed colleagues and students. 'At any rate all the sham is off,' he added privately, 'and the world knows, what's what.'[332] George's two eldest sons, Tony and John, were conscripted in June 1939 under the first wave of compulsory military training (this was initially aimed at single men aged between twenty and twenty-two), due to be sent overseas after Christmas following a period of six months training.[333] But at Oxford, George planned to keep a steady ship running and he rebuked impatient dons for worrying government departments about getting commissions. He remained determined to keep Oxford open 'with whatever dwindling of its activities' for undergraduates who did go (even if only for a couple of terms) before being called up.[334]

Hugh was also relieved that they had finally stood up to Nazi Germany. Despite the 'black days' of August and the gravity of Hitler's brinksmanship, Hugh felt that people were much calmer in September 1939 than during the Munich Crisis the previous year. 'Determined not to give in to Hitler ever again' he wrote in his diary on returning to London at the end of August after holidaying with his siblings in Scotland. Hugh spent Britain's first day at war in his flat, supervising his servant John packing up his pictures, before going to Hampstead to be with the Cheevers. After dinner, he walked out with Harold to see the guns on the Heath and stayed with the family overnight. At three, they were woken up by the confusion of an air-raid warning. Two hours later, at five in the morning, Hugh and Harold set off with sixteen pictures in the car for the Lakes. They were at the cottage by lunchtime, 'everything perfect and hopeful', Hugh noted, and hung the artwork up for safe keeping.[335]

The following week – 'Warsaw still holding out', Hugh recorded in his diary – they did a return trip and spent another afternoon packing up pictures (Hugh made a half-hearted promise to stop collecting for a while).[336] The cottage at Brackenburn was an 'abode of Peace' Hugh realised, but he refused to hide out there while the world turned on its head ('heard Russia had invaded Poland', he wrote on September 17. 'So that's the horrifying end of poor Poles.') All his life, Hugh's ambition and a sense of duty had drawn him to the centre of events, and this second world war was no exception. Besides there was Harold down in London with Ethel and the children. Hugh acknowledged in his journal that he could 'look at my White Wall Utrillo, my Bellini, my Manet drawing, my Cezanne water colours with a rushing protective love.' 'Nothing must destroy you, no matter if I go – you must remain,' he went on, 'They are certainly more important than I.' But he knew where his heart lay. 'I would sacrifice the whole lot for Harold's little finger.'[337]

Sylvia Lynd's start to the war was also busy. On both Friday and Sunday she'd dashed up to town to help with the evacuation of London; finding an empty school hall in Haverstock (on Sunday, only seven mothers and children had been in), she picked up her father and compelled him to return with her to Surrey. 'Meantime the whole of the defence forces of London had turned out,' she noted, 'the streets were full of "tin hats" & balloons tethered close to the ground in unexpected places. Everyone looking very cheerful & I had a conviction the Germans would be over the moment the ultimatum expired.'[338] On the way back to Forest Green they were caught in an early air raid warning on the Kingston Road and were advised by an air-warden to take cover, so they pulled off to shelter in a pub for a while. That evening, back safely in Tillies, Sylvia had a sense of being out-of-time as an old world passed and a new one began. 'We listened to the King's speech, to Mr Chamberlain's & to all the news - & cheered when we heard that Winston Churchill is back at the Admirality' she recorded in her diary. 'We all feel that now black is black & white is white again & that the Nazi regime is going to be demolished.'[339] A few days later the cottage was invaded by Greta and the children, so that 'to our usual muddle at Tillies of cigarette packets, & newspapers, has now been added shoes & toys & sugarsticks & all sorts of things'. Sylvia bought a dozen vests 'for the distributed army of refugee children' who were sent out to Surrey from London, 'many of them have no warm clothes with them'.[340] She feared the sky down in Surrey on the flightpath to London 'full of rooks & aeroplane engines'; 'To the West something that sounds like gunfire & distant explosions.'[341] But the move to some form of action was at least a relief. 'The loss of our apple-pie picturesque no longer troubles me at all' she confessed in her diary.

***

For Edmund Blunden meanwhile, Britain's declaration of war against Germany was a long-awaited catastrophe. Like Hugh, Edmund started a new diary on Sunday 3 September, 1939. But whereas Hugh was full of the present, Edmund was drawn back to the past. Like most of his diary entries following the trauma of WWI, Edmund marked the start of the Second World War with an anniversary that still felt like yesterday. 'The twenty-third anniversary of our disastrous attack on the German trenches north of the River Ancre' his WWII journal begins, 'the same sort of day, fine blue skies, but a breeze blowing.'

That weekend, Edmund had to face some hard facts. His desperate attempts to maintain dialogue with Germany through visits and lecture tours had come to nothing, and the international crisis could no longer be averted. On the Sunday he awoke 'with some faint hope left, but heard that the Government had sent an ultimatum at 9 demanding an acceptance by 11, and that faint hope became still smaller'. From the first syllables of Chamberlain's broadcast it was 'clear that the news was bad', Edmund recorded in his diary, while rumour started up immediately. Sylva heard from Wolvercote signal box that four German planes had raided London – three were supposedly down - and Edmund felt sick. 'We shall have lots more of this stuff,' he despaired to his diary, 'the same and from the same sources as have worked us into the horrible present situation.' Unsure what to do with himself, he took a long walk through Port Meadow and back past Binsy and Godstow, stunned by the difference between the beauty of the Thames – the aspens shining, the wild hops thick in the hedges - and knowledge of the carnage to come. He and Sylva had been due a fortnight's holiday before term started, after their annual pilgrimage to Flanders and France for the Imperial War Graves Commission (Edmund had accepted the position of literary advisor very reluctantly, antithetical to the views of his predecessor, Kipling, and not wanting to glorify the dead. 'O for a Commission for the living,' he wrote in his diary, 'and half even of the efficiency with which these pathetic cemeteries are maintained!')[342] Instead, Sylva was busy packing and making arrangements, expecting to be called up by the Women's Auxiliary

Corps. Later that night, after struggling to get off to sleep and thinking about Klosterhaus, Edmund had a strange dream about a woman with his mother's features 'but taller, and a little German' who he interrogated about the distinction between Nazi leaders and ordinary German citizens. He woke to an overcast morning, still livid at a warmongering, indiscriminate press. 'I am baffled by the fate of such indifference to common people,' he despaired:

> A few years ago everyone was intensely moved by the miseries and futilities exemplified in 'Journey's End.' But that and other appeals to the ruling class have failed. The war cemeteries, and the hard truth which they enunciate (oh those endless endless graves of mere boys) have not been visioned for a second by the 'war-worshippers'.[343]

Later that evening, after going into college to collect some of their belongings (he and Sylva were moving out to stay with a family on Boars Hill, three miles outside Oxford), Edmund received a telegram from D. L. Murray, editor of the *TLS*, asking 'Have you any poem?' They'd published his verses in honour of Munich a year ago but now Edmund was wary. The pieces he'd written at Klosterhaus that summer were all too 'sane' to be published right now, Sylva cautioned. Dodging a reprimand from the Air Warden who warned they'd get a fine if they didn't do better with the black-out, Edmund worked on the poems again. 'My wish to serve Germany as well as the rest of us may not be regarded as disloyal' he reflected in his diary. They would 'not wrangle about political tradition, they merely offer a picture of German life'.[344]

***

As the nights began to lengthen that autumn, Edmund's asthma got worse, and he struggled to do anything productive or to get on with his new book on Thomas Hardy. He was worried about his German sister-in-law, Annie, as well as his parents down in Kent, plus Aki Hayashi living alone 'on the edge of Hampstead Heath, in a top floor room' (she could 'retreat at need into the basement', he reassured himself). At home and at work, life turned on its head. Edmund's college rooms at Merton were requisitioned by the Home Office, meaning most of September was spent moving personal possessions and books to another room in Fellows Quad. Despite George Gordon's caution as Vice Chancellor, Edmund didn't expect to be teaching there long – perhaps a few months – until his old commanding officer found him a job. At home, Sylva's Armenian parents moved in and his mother-in-law quickly took over, creating more stress. Out on Boars Hill they could hear aeroplanes circling daily, flying ominously low over the woods and houses into the night. 'Big devils some of them,' Edmund shuddered as he wrote late one night in his diary. 'Their noise suggests what a full-dress air offensive with its gunfire and machine guns must sound like.'[345]

Above all, Edmund wanted peace and to preserve a sense of the decency of ordinary Germans. 'My one real concern with the war now – for I do not stand with those who think Hitler is the sole cause of human happiness or otherwise', he wrote in his diary on September 6, 'is to see it end.' Later that month, he received a telegram from the Peace Pledge Union asking him to speak at a rally planned in Manchester for October 7, but Edmund was unsure how to respond. 'The arrival of the war makes conscientious objection unreal, so far as I am concerned,' he felt, 'I won't attack those who think otherwise – and I am reluctant to get into any position which would not be quite mine.'[346] Instead, in desperation on Tuesday 12 September, Edmund toyed with the unthinkable, drafting a letter to Sir Oswald Mosley asking him to lead a coalition for 'the peaceable,' feeling that Mosley might give voice to those who felt unrepresented by current policies and the mainstream press. 'I venture to appeal that you would stand for peace, or peace negotiations wherever possible' he tried out, 'as a spokesman beyond party boundaries.' 'With party politics I have never had any connection,' Edmund went on, 'but when I was in Germany during August I was struck by the ray of hope that lit up people's faces, here and there, on the mention of your name.' What the Book Society judges, never mind the wider public, would have thought if this letter had been sent or made public, Edmund well knew. It remains loose in his personal papers in Texas. Drafted, but unsent.

III

The first weeks then months of waiting for war to take hold in Britain were strange and disconcerting. At the start of September 1939, most people put leisure and cultural life on hold. Theatres, cinemas, and library reading rooms were immediately closed when war was declared, readers returned library books, and many Book Society members asked to suspend their membership. But when little happened in Britain during those first weeks and then months of what became known as the Phoney War, entertainment venues re-opened. The bookstalls on Farringdon Road were 'open but not lively,' Edmund noted during a brief trip to London on September 15, and 'A. Hayashi is pleased that the British Museum will be accessible to readers.' Before long, the Book Society soon found members coming back to the club. After the anxious build-up, feelings were oddly deflated. 'No arrival yet of the Germans in force' Sylvia recorded in her diary on Sunday 12 November, 'though we all expected them yesterday.'

On October 3 1939, the judges met in Hugh's Piccadilly flat as usual. 'Publishing is semi-stagnant,' Rupert Hart-Davis, still at Cape's, confirmed to Edmund, 'though I suppose people will be driven to reading as the blackout hours lengthen.'[347] Members of the club were receiving Richard Llewelyn's *How Green Was My Valley* that month, a steely novel of life in the South Wales mining valleys, destined to steer readers through a time of national danger. *How Green Was My Valley* was 'The great novel of Wales,' according to *The Bookseller*, 'as good as bread, this book' (it was still selling a thousand copies a week six months later, making it a transatlantic bestseller for the first year of war).[348]

Along with Llewelyn's future classic, that month the *Book Society News* set out the club's wartime agenda. In a long essay titled 'Books Will Go On,' penned by Alan Bott, the club reassured readers that they would vary choices and recommendations between books of topical interest and those 'bridging the gulf between to-day's madness and the dainty that lives in fine imagination'. Though WWII would go on for much longer and affect the club and its judges more profoundly than any one of them could imagine, the diversity of the wartime lists generally bore out this intention.

A predictable theme in the club's response to war was the necessity and consolation of reading more books in wartime. 'Thus far, all the news has been most of the reading' Alan Bott judged in his essay, 'but before long people will turn to books as the best comfort, the greatest recreation in an anxious, darkened world.' This had happened during WWI, when millions of new readers had been made, and the possibilities of reading through the black-out to pass dull evenings stuck at home or in shelters quickly became publishing mantra. 'More time for reading!' was 'one black-out benefit!', ran an ad to join Boots Book-lovers' Library. Books could stave off boredom and help fill blacked-out evenings with pleasure and forgetfulness, Alan counselled, while membership still represented good value for money. 'The book costs less than a few sandbags at the profiteers' price,' he advised, 'or a bottle of evaporating scent, or a stall in the peace-time theatre.' 'Books may become more necessary than gas-masks.'[349]

If books were important to civilians, they were seen to be even more crucial for the troops. The War Office had been planning how to get books out to those on active service since the start of conscription in June 1939, and the Book Society was quick off the mark. The October 1939 club magazine included a list of cheap, cloth-bound reprints that members could choose from and have sent out to any war address – 'the front, the back of the front, the base camps and training camps' – with a personalised greeting card included. These were valuable services for those stationed away in wartime, giving also perhaps a small measure of comfort to the gift-giver at home. Many who had suspended their membership came back to the club in November 1939, while a rush of new enrolments provided the second largest boost to the club's numbers in any month since its formation a decade earlier.

***

The last two selection committees of 1939 were tense. None of the judges had been approached immediately for their services to the country as writers. Hugh, probably the best connected, had made overtures to friends at the Ministry of Information, suggesting he might form a committee of authors useful for cultural propaganda, but had so far been rebuffed; later, in November, he was invited by the Lord Mayor to chair a books and manuscripts fund-raising sale for the Red Cross, work he could throw himself into. Edmund worried that he hadn't heard 'of any of us war authors – Mottram, Sheriff, Aldington, Tomlinson, Guy Chapman, Sassoon – being called for any expression.' 'But probably the Ministry's functions are not such as require the abilities and experience of these men,' he realised; 'yet what functions are they?'[350]

For Cecil Day-Lewis meanwhile, as the youngest member of the selection committee, the question of war service was urgent. Petitioning Hugh, on Alan Bott's advice, about what work writers could best do in wartime, Day-Lewis admitted he was 'no good at languages, which I imagine puts me out of the running for a good many jobs'. 'I am inclined to join up in one of the ordinary war-services,' he added in a desperate letter as the conflict broke out.[351] Fortunately, it would take some time for the war to be felt in the Day-Lewis's new home in rural Musbury. 'September, 1939, passed,' Day-Lewis reflected later in his autobiography, 'We were at war, but nothing had altered in the quiet village.'[352] In fact, it was not until March 1941 that, following medical examination, Day-Lewis was recommended for the Armoured Corps and called-up to join the army 'at some god-forsaken place in Yorkshire'. He served one day before being recalled to London ('Conduct during Period of Service, Good' stated his certificate of temporary discharge), saved by the Ministry of Information, which had finally decided to employ him that month.[353]

In the meantime, as 1939 ended, what could the judges do but continue with the club? The supply of literature seemed 'poorish' to some of them, Edmund especially, but they resolved to do their best – personal constrictions, travel disruption, and publishing crises notwithstanding – to try and maintain access to new books, along with their promotion, while circumstances allowed. 'We have yet to see whether all this array of critical energy can keep readers going under the strain of our war administration,' Edmund noted drily in his diary.[354] Sylvia was excited by a page-turner she'd found for November 1939, published under the pseudonym Ethel Vance. *Escape* was a dramatic thriller about an actress condemned to death and imprisoned in a concentration camp, duly rescued. 'It's quite incredibly good,' Sylvia enthused in her diary, '& I keep wondering who, really, can have written it' (the publishers capitalised upon this speculation, asking on the dust jacket 'Who is "Ethel Vance?"' and questioning why they wanted to keep their identity hidden from the Nazis? *Escape* was later revealed to be the work of American novelist Grace Zaring Stone, who had adopted a pseudonym to protect her daughter, then living in pro-Fascist Hungary).[355] But when talk at the Book Society turned to the Phoney War and the language of boredom – some people were even looking forward to an air raid on London to see how things worked out, according to Hugh – Sylvia found herself fuming. 'I preferred it to be boring' Sylvia told them. 'All properly brought up people know how to endure boredom. What I don't want is to be frightened or hurt – either of them.' Unlike her best friend Rose Macaulay, who had signed up as an ambulance driver and was to be 'splendidly intrepid,' Sylvia's war work had so far involved knitting covers for hot water bottles at First Aid posts and navigating petty tensions between the Red Cross and St John's Ambulance Services. When she came up to town she was shocked by how quickly London had changed. 'Hampstead is full of empty bankrupt shops – two dress shops, a stationers, a green grocers, a home decorators' she noted in her diary, and most women were wearing trousers, without hat or scarf. But Sylvia would go on being smart 'in my motley clothes,' she confessed, 'pretending as hard as I could that everything is as used to be.'[356] *Escape* made compulsive reading and was widely compared to *Gone with the Wind* in the press. Like Enid Bagnold's *National Velvet* and Stuart Cloete's South African debut, *Turning Wheels*, it was one of the rarer books chosen as book-of-the-month on both sides of the Atlantic. It had all the excitement Sylvia needed.

Towards the end of that year, Edmund and Hugh had a major falling out. Edmund was generally fond of Hugh and admired much of his early writing, regarding him, as he observed in his diary, the 'kindest as well as most emotional of disputants, still magnificent in his bowler hat and massive overcoat'.[357] But when, during the discussion of *Escape*, Hugh broke 'into violent invective against the whole German race' (Day-Lewis's words), Edmund, normally so diffident, 'launch[ed] at him a steely counter-attack'. 'I was carried back to that earlier war,' Day-Lewis wrote in one of his few references to the club in his autobiography, 'when the civilian blindly hated, but the front-line solider, if he lived long enough, learnt respect for the enemy and felt a kinship with him; and for all my detestation of Nazism, it was Edmund I sided with now.'[358]

The following month, Hugh contemplated a wartime Christmas and 'A terrible year for the world' ('but I must confess a grand one for me', he added in the privacy of his diary: 'Great success of *Sea Tower* and *Herries Chronicle*. Excellent health. Friendship with HC.') For his annual essay in the club's Christmas issue, Hugh selected the theme of 'Re-reading in Wartime.' 'We are living at present (we may not be by Christmas)' he began, 'in a sort of ghost-world, where all the sounds are muffled and voices whispering.' Hugh was to live in London during the winter, he told readers, separated from most of his book collection up in the Lakes. But 'this strange war offers a perfect time for re-reading' he counselled, and he looked to books around him that could sustain his courage through an air-raid.

Remembering George Gordon's BBC talks on 'companionable books,' Hugh mulled over his 'unfailing re-readable friends and timeless companions'. 'I frankly cannot conceive any world situation in which the Odyssey, *Pride and Prejudice*, Wordsworth or Keats's poems would fade into nothingness' Hugh wrote. 'I could, I believe, read *Pride and Prejudice* seated in the middle of the air-raid-ruined remnants of the Athenaeum club.'[359] It was an ominous, prophetic piece, linking books, continuity, and friendship. 'What makes a book live for you?', he asked readers. 'Friendship simply,' came the reply. 'And a friendship on both sides.'

1939

118	January	*The Devil We Know*, Pamela Frankau
119	February	*The Holy Terror*, H. G. Wells
120	March	*Dynasty of Death*, Taylor Caldwell
121	April	*The Patriot*, Pearl Buck
122	May	*The Open Sky*, L. A. G Strong
123	June	*Reaching for the Stars*, Nora Waln
124	July	*The Priory*, Dorothy Whipple
125	August	*Love in the Sun*, Leo Walmsley
126	September	*One Way of Living*, James Bridie
127	October	*How Green Was My Valley*, Richard Llewellyn
128	November	*Escape*, Ethel Vance
129	December	*My American*, Stella Gibbons

Chapter 7. Cecil, 1940

Watching Post

I

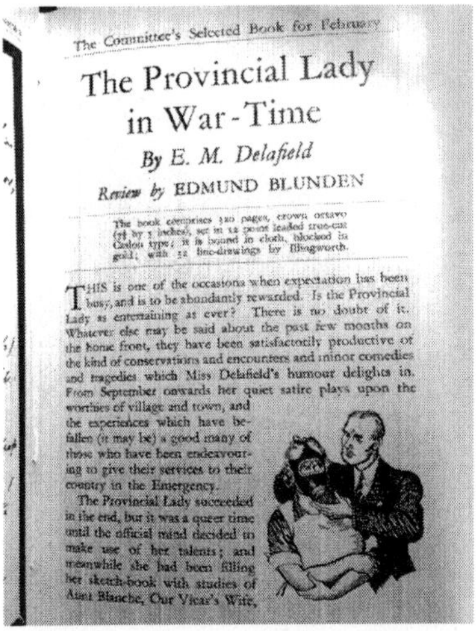

The Committee's Selected Book for February

The Provincial Lady in War-Time

By E. M. Delafield

Review by EDMUND BLUNDEN

The book comprises 320 pages, crown octavo (7½ by 5 inches), set in 12 point leaded true-cut Caslon type; it is bound in cloth, blocked in gold; with 32 line-drawings by Illingworth.

THIS is one of the occasions when expectation has been busy, and is to be abundantly rewarded. Is the Provincial Lady as entertaining as ever? There is no doubt of it. Whatever else may be said about the past few months on the home front, they have been satisfactorily productive of the kind of conservations and encounters and minor comedies and tragedies which Miss Delafield's humour delights in. From September onwards her quiet satire plays upon the worthies of village and town, and the experiences which have befallen (it may be) a good many of those who have been endeavouring to give their services to their country in the Emergency.

The Provincial Lady succeeded in the end, but it was a queer time until the official mind decided to make use of her talents; and meanwhile she had been filling her sketch-book with studies of Aunt Blanche, Our Vicar's Wife,

Book Society News, February 1940

The club saw in the New Year of 1940 with two established authors. January Choice, *The Valiant Heart*, was by publisher and journalist George Blake, an old friend of Hugh's and author of earlier choice, *The Shipbuilders. The Valiant Heart* was the second instalment of his 'Garvel' series set in Scotland, this one encompassing WWI and the conflicts between family and patriotic duty. For February, the judges chose E. M. Delafield's fourth book in her series about a provincial lady. Blake and Delafield were familiar names in the club's lists and their books made reassuring reading. Both Hugh and

Sylvia were missing from the meeting in January and there was little insight on government policy. 'War secrets very scarce just now even with Alan Bott,' Edmund observed.[360]

Everything else was on edge, confused and uncertain. War economy was hitting the book trade, with production costs rising due to higher prices for printing and binding, and imports of the wood-pulp needed to make paper disrupted by war in Finland and the torpedoing of cargoes from Sweden. Some of these costs had to be passed onto readers and Blake's novel was the first Book Society choice to be sold at the new standard novel war-price of eight shillings and threepence, up nine pence from usual. Worried that subscribers would pull out, the club reminded members to keep exchanging books they didn't like, even in wartime. The in-person offer in the members' club room at Grosvenor Place was enhanced with a new bargain table selling recent books at cut price. With demand for books increasing while publishers' materials were being rationed, new books were likely to have smaller print runs and sell out faster, even when sold at a higher price. For many subscribers, the idea of a trip to London was no doubt impossible, but the offer was there, and encouraging members to work through the club's backlist made good war economy.

The number of new books the judges had to choose from that January was the smallest they could remember, but 'Miss Delafield has let her Provincial Lady out afresh over the home front,' as Edmund noted after the meeting in his diary, 'and we decided to choose this book for all reasons.' Taking a light-hearted look at gas masks and evacuees, *The Provincial Lady in War-Time* was guaranteed to be popular during the 'vast gloom and insistent enigma' of waiting and emergency measures, Edmund acknowledged in his review for club readers. 'We may as well make the best of all the opportunities for cheerfulness and the pleasantly absurd while we can.'

In his personal life, Edmund was practising what he preached. Sylva had been away at the army base at Tidworth since late September 1939, and Edmund struggled with depression, ill-health, and loneliness through the cold winter months, unable to work or put his pen to anything productive. But he'd found a silver lining. Claire Poynting was a twenty-one-year-old undergraduate at St Hilda's, originally from Manchester, bright, ambitious, and determined. Claire had fallen for Edmund in tutorials, impressed by his quiet wit and charm, and – with Sylva gone that winter – she made herself at home: calling by Edmund's rooms with a friend initially, then by herself, dropping in for lunch unexpectedly, accompanying Edmund on his walks across the meadows and around town. Claire shared Edmund's passion for poetry and cricket and was happy to talk with him endlessly about Milton and John Clare and Keats.

In February 1940, Claire sent Edmund a Valentines and when later that month he lay ill in bed, caught out by an attack of pleurisy, she came over to nurse him (Sylva, worried about his ability to look after himself, had offered to request leave from the army by reporting him sick, but Edmund had refused). 'I am twice her age, but we do not seem to be working to that time scheme,' Edmund confessed. He justified the large age gap to himself (Claire was only two years older than his own daughter) through the vague sense that he had been half-dead since WWI and this new love was a bridge to his twenty-year old self. 'Claire is to me a complete reward for my former desperate years' he wrote in the privacy of his diary, 'it is as if I came straight out of the trenches at *Ferme du Bois* in 1916 to find her smiling and expectant at the exit of the communication trench.'[361] His 'Clarissima' was a 'nymph' and, to jaded eyes, a godsend. She restored Edmund's ability to write and helped him find hope in the world.

By the end of February 1940, Edmund had told Sylva about the affair. Busy with the army, she was disappointed but not surprised and assumed it would blow over. 'Luckily for me,' Edmund observed in his diary, 'Sylva is not inclined to dominate my emotional life, and I allow her an equal ease; let whoever reads this, for some may, perceive that we do not live by mutual tyranny.'[362] In March, Edmund introduced Claire to Aki Hayashi in London. It was the second time in their now fifteen-year relationship that Aki had been compelled to accept a new and younger woman by Edmund's side. Thankfully for her at least, Claire would be the last.

In public affairs, Edmund was still hoping for reconciliation. That March, he signed a controversial letter asking the British government to sue Hitler for peace, and, as the Nazis began their march across Europe, Edmund went up to Manchester with Claire, having agreed to speak at a large meeting of the Peace Pledge Union. They combined the trip with a visit to Claire's friends and family and took her mother out to lunch where, to Edmund's relief, his future mother-in-law was 'courageous enough' to welcome him without too much alarm.[363] When he got back to Oxford, Edmund wrote to the editor of *The Times* arguing against the bombing of civilians in German cities. Realising that 'This moment indeed may not be the most convenient,' he pointed out that everything the Allies were fighting for depended upon treating the German population in wartime with decency.[364] His college friend, professor H. W. Garrod, 'mildly reproves me,' Edmund noted in his diary, 'saying that such a letter will appear abroad as showing want of trust in our Government... No doubt there'll be a righteous howl from those who have their picture of a set of cherubim as their leaders in Whitehall,' he added wryly.[365]

At the Book Society, the selection committee that March 1940 was reduced to Hugh, Edmund, and Alan Bott. Paper rationing had just been introduced, reducing publishers' paper stock to sixty percent of what they had used in the three months between March and June the previous year, and the meeting was a struggle, degenerating into fierce argument. Hugh and Alan were against all talk of peace by negotiation ('Bott says that "the millionaries" are for a negotiated peace,' Edmund observed), perceiving Edmund 'pro-German,' as Hugh reflected afterwards in his diary: 'and I feel it difficult to sit in the same room with him!'[366] Alan meanwhile was 'ironical, informed, based on the last war' Edmund noted, 'still a flying man who sees the world in a rapid panorama,' and when he piled on the tension by saying that the war was likely to go on for years, Hugh flew off the handle, denouncing Alan 'as a dangerous pessimist'.[367] Appalled by the 'nerves and nonsense' bred in London, Edmund beat a retreat, upset by the impact of gossip and war hysteria upon Hugh especially. 'The brawl perhaps continued after I said my little piece in mediation & goodbye,' he observed in his quiet study in Oxford. Edmund had marking and examiners boards to be getting on with, and there were welcome signs of life in the college with young men on leave coming to stay and enlivening the atmosphere. Spring was arriving, and Edmund was rediscovering poetic inspiration through Claire. 'John Clare's weather,' he noted in his diary mid-March, 'whitethorn in flower, beeches budding'; 'I have only to go to the door opening on the Library lawn to behold a miracle.'

'I am in love' he wrote simply the next day. 'I come to life again.'[368]

II

The Nazi offensive of spring 1940 marked an end to months of waiting and preparation in Western Europe. German forces overran Denmark and Norway in April, then in May invaded France through Holland and Belgium. The reality of war was getting nearer for Britain. George Gordon's son, John, was wounded in Flanders (a 'straightforward bullet wound,' George reported to Tony, his eldest) but got home before the port of Boulogne was defeated.[369] Tony meanwhile was in the Allies chaotic retreat from Dunkirk, evacuated along with 338,000 others from the beaches of Northern France between 26 May and 4 June.

The speed of Hitler's advance through France was shocking, and as news spread that British forces were hurrying for the Channel ports, Edmund observed sadly that 'The war map of 1916 comes into use again, a frightful recurrence – so all my dreams were, in the main theme, true soothsaying.' With fears mid-May that the Germans might be in England within a month, Edmund expressed some guarded admiration for Hitler's forces. 'It is impossible to overstate the genius of the Fuhrer in these sorts of matters' he wrote in his diary, 'He seems to have inspired his men with his own rapidity. The fall of the Western front defence scheme, prepared so long, in a few hours is like magic.'[370] Facing the threat of imminent invasion, Edmund and Sylva agreed that the English and French should seek an armistice 'since the continuation of hostilities can only increase casualties without saving the situation'.

On the home front, domestic life took on a new form as Edmund found himself spending more time with both Sylva and Claire. Sylva was back in Oxford having left the army (she had some paid hours at the Bodleian, giving her more time for writing) while Claire was busy preparing for exams. Playing cricket at Queens' College one afternoon, Edmund was cheered on by both women together and took them out for drinks. 'I must be an old soak,' he confided in his diary, 'I gave Sylva a glass of cider at the Apollo inn, and after hall and bowls in the Fellows Garden I gathered Claire in for a dreamy lounging at the Port Mahon.' Claire had found herself 'under inquisition' by the college authorities, while Edmund's daughter, Clare (also at Oxford) begged her father not to cause a scandal. But desperate times licensed desperate measures. 'If these pages ever come to the eyes of someone who has not met any of us involved in the record,' he cautioned, 'I trust that the mystery of events and experiences will prevent any virulent and commonplace readings "of life" as it chanced to us.'[371]

For Hugh meanwhile, 'The Terrible Week' of 17 to 24 May 1940, when the Nazis swept across France and invasion seemed imminent, was spent in a state of fear and panic. 'For a whole week I did not sleep (an astonishing thing for me!)' he wrote later in an *Open Letter of an Optimist*, addressed, appropriately, to Alan Bott:

> I saw [...] myself beaten in a Concentration Camp, [...] and saw, not only France, not only Britain, but the whole world conquered by an evil, foul doctrine of cruelty, plunder, greed, savagery.[372]

Ploughing away to finish his latest book, *The Blind Man's House*, Hugh marked black news days during May and June 1940 in his diary with doodles of skull and crossbones. Like Edmund, he was staggered by the success of Hitler's Blitzkrieg: 'Most serious position Britain has been in for 1000 years' Hugh wrote as Hitler's troops reached Boulogne on 23 May. 'France seems to have lost her head altogether. Heaven knows what may happen. Everyone waiting.' Hugh had the bolthole of Brackenburn to fall back on, but he didn't want to desert the capital. On 16 June 1940, as the French government collapsed and the pro-Armistice Pétain took over, confirming the French army's surrender to the Nazis the next day, Hugh acknowledged in his diary: 'I have a strange detached sense that I must be "in" at the bombing, destruction, occupation of London as it may be.' By the end of the month, as he started his next book, *The Killer and the Slain*, he was 'waiting like everyone for Invasion this week'.[373]

As France fell to the Nazis, members of the club received Jules Romain's *Verdun* [The Battle], translated by Gerard Manley Hopkins. This was the sixteenth volume of the French writer's epic saga of French life, *Les Hommes de bonne volonté* [Men of Good Will], which had started to appear in 1932 (Hugh had abandoned it somewhere about the fifth volume, he admitted to Book Society readers). But *Verdun* recounted the huge loss of life at one of the bloodiest battles in WWI and was comparable to *War and Peace* or Zola's *Debacle* in its importance, Hugh argued in a review with Churchillian echoes. 'That is why it is not a depressing novel, and why it is so extraordinarily pertinent to the present occasion,' Hugh counselled, because it put the terrible subject of war into human perspective: 'The smells, explosions, the easy life of a general, the heroism of the common man, the futility and the glory, all are here.'

After Dunkirk, Churchill had addressed parliament on 4 June with the rallying cry: 'We shall fight on the beaches, we shall fight on the landing grounds, we shall fight in the fields and in the streets, we shall fight in the hills; we shall never surrender.' Aware of Edmund's views and some of the public calls for Armistice as civilian morale collapsed, Hugh followed Churchill and used his review of *Verdun* to dig in. 'The pacifists, the peace-at-any price hysterics, miss so completely the importance of the present conflict' Hugh warned Book Society readers. The real battle was not the minutiae of the field, he reminded his audience, but the bigger fight for freedom, and that fight was 'glorious, even though it is cruel, stupid, muddled – yes, and endless,' Hugh wrote, with a nod at Alan's realism.

Verdun was already available as part of the publisher's series (Hugh claimed the judges had not received the proofs due to an oversight) so the club issued a special edition 'bound in fine buckram with a red label stamped in real gold-leaf' that was also slightly cheaper in price (nine shillings sixpence instead of ten shillings sixpence, the standard amount for a longer novel, biography or history). The *Book Society News* reaffirmed its commitment to its ally, reminding readers that subscriptions for the French Book Club (chosen in Paris, for readers outside France) could be sent in via themselves. 'French books are best read in the original,' the club noted in its 'Members room' page, 'and there has never been a time when contact with the thought and language of the nation nearest to us was as useful as it is today.'[374]

The Fall of France further impacted the book trade by disrupting the importation of esparto grass (used in papermaking) from North Africa, and the club magazine cut back on its paper usage that month by adopting a smaller typeface (Times rather than Garamond), altering its lay-out, and asking the judges to write shorter reviews. Club choices would be less affected by paper rationing, they tried to reassure members, as even though the paper drain would inevitably affect book production, the best of what was published would still come to the club. In fact, the total number of new books published in 1940, including reprints and new editions, was 11,053 as compared to 14,904 in 1939; in 1941 this figure would drop to 7,581.[375] 'We shall continue our service unless and until we are bombed, parachuted or expropriated out of existence' was the public affirmation to members.[376]

But behind the scenes, the selection committee were aware of another kind of pressure starting to weigh upon their operations that spring. Assessing the books submitted from publishers before publication as usual, they felt the hand of the Ministry of Information. The MoI, set up by the government at the outset of WWII, was responsible for controlling official news and running publicity campaigns, producing patriotic war books and pamphlets for domestic and overseas markets. But in addition to their in-house publications (Day-Lewis would join the Publications Division in 1941), the MoI worked covertly with commercial publishers by supplying up to half the necessary paper for books 'that it wished to encourage'.[377] Unlike radio or film, books were seen as a relatively stable medium for propaganda purposes, with broadcasting subject to jamming and being cut off for security reasons, and overseas broadcasting limited by the number of transmitters available.[378] Internal documents at the MoI reveal how 'The Ministry considers that under present conditions books can play a considerable part in maintaining public morale, while the long term propaganda value of books in the empire and in foreign countries is an important factor in the presentation of the British case.'[379]

Edmund reported in his diary in March 1940 that the MoI were 'pushing N. Henderson's account of his dealing with the rulers of Germany' onto the club.[380] *Failure of a Mission: Berlin 1937-1939*, published by G. P. Putnam's & Sons, explored Henderson's dealings with Nazi Germany as the last British ambassador in Berlin. It was the 'story of his attempt, and his failure, to avert the calamity of European war,' as the American BOMC put it, providing 'first-hand confirmation' of 'the shifts of influence in Germany which made a war inevitable'.[381] Edmund found the book depressing and agreed with Hugh that as a diplomat Henderson was '('his word') stupid, & Scotch stupid'. 'The neutral reader will easily see,' Edmund observed in his diary, 'that this man was kindly used in Germany, liked it all, had no genius for his official task, and is now full of wonder at his being God's instrument at such a period of history.'[382] The club would assist the MoI in getting the book an audience, he noted resignedly, 'but what does it matter'. *Failure of a Mission: Berlin 1937-1939* was duly offered as an alternative non-fiction choice for May 1940, with Edmund predicting that most subscribers would keep the fiction choice, Frederick Niven's *Mine Inheritance* instead. This was a dramatic historical novel about 'the first important British settlement in the Canadian West' (from the dust jacket), following a group of Scottish Highlanders compelled to migrate following the enclosure of common lands and forced evictions in eighteenth and nineteenth-century Britain. 'This book should be a permanent possession for every Canadian (or Scotsman or Englishman) who cares about his Empire's history,' Sylvia declared in the *Book Society News*. Edmund declined to put his name to either choice on offer that month, sticking instead to reviews of serious non-fiction.

III

In May 1940, the Local Defence Volunteers (renamed the Home Guard in July on Churchill's orders) was established to defend Britain during the anticipated invasion. Men aged between seventeen and sixty-five not in regular military service were encouraged to volunteer, and one and a half million signed up. Duties were split between preparing to defend key routes from attack and getting ready to obstruct German invaders by force. For many, the members of the Home Guard seemed to live, as Hugh put it, 'a life that recalls the early romances of Conan Doyle and Rider Haggard. They are forever rising at three in the morning to confront imaginary parachutists, and half their work is as mysterious and secret as free-masonry.'[383]

As distinguished WWI veterans, now pushing fifty and sixty, Alan Bott and George Gordon joined their local units. George told his son Tony that he was 'hop[ing] to pop a parachutist before the business ends'.[384] His wife Mary, with two children at the Front, was 'green with envy', according to George. 'There is no one in the British Isles who would kill a German with holier satisfaction than she.'[385]

On the outskirts of Musbury on the Devon/Dorset border, Day-Lewis also joined his local Home Guard. Unlike George or Edmund, whose children were older, Day-Lewis didn't have to worry about his sons joining up, and as he was not required for war work as a writer nor had yet received his military call-up (for what would turn out to be one day of service), he threw himself into the work of his local platoon. Quickly appointed Assistant Commander, Day-Lewis was known for winding up operations early enough to make closing time at the pub. But there were times of genuine fear, as in early September 1940 during the Battle of Britain when the Germans were expected to land on Seaton beach and the Musbury defenders – 'Roadmen, farm labourers, masons, turned to another trade' – were ordered to 'Stand-To' for thirty-six hours. Day-Lewis would honour the individual men and incongruity of war in two poems published later that year with Cape in his *Poems in Wartime*:

> Since last night may be the last night all thirty men go home,
> I write this verse to record the men who have watched with me
> –
> Spot who is good at darts, Squibby at repartee,
> Mark and Cyril, the dead shots, Ralph with a ploughman's gait,
> Gibson, Harris and Long, old hands for the barricade,
> Whiller the lorry-driver, Francis and Rattlesnake
> ('The Stand-To')

'Watching Post', written in July 1940, stressed the camaraderie of local patrol, with farmer and poet united by the timeless rhythms of agriculture and the force of the natural world:

> A hill flank overlooking the Axe valley.
> Among the stubble a farmer and I keep watch
> For whatever may come to injure our countryside –
> Light-signals, parachutes, bombs, or sea-invaders.
>
> The farmer and I talk for a while of invaders:
> But soon we turn to crops – the annual hope,
> Making of cider, prizes for ewes. Tonight
> How many hearts along this war-mazed valley
> Dream of a day when at peace they may work and watch
> The small sufficient wonders of the countryside.
>
> Image or fact, we both in the countryside
> Have found our natural law, and until invaders
> Come will answer its need: for both of us, hope

Means a harvest from small beginnings, who this night
While the moon sorts out into shadow and shape our valley,
A farmer and a poet, are keeping watch
('Watching Post')[386]

In his autobiography, *The Buried Day*, Day-Lewis perceived that the move before the war from Cheltenham to Musbury had enabled him to grasp a 'simpler world where wood and iron, grass and flowers and windy skies could renew a mind dulled by abstractions'. Rural life suited him. After writing about the working-classes for so long, he enjoyed banter with the farm-labourers and locals in the pub, playing games in the Red Lion of an evening, as well as indulging in an affair with a fellow village newcomer, Billie Currall (she would have his baby, another son, in September 1940). 'I felt not only settled, rooted here, but even proprietorial' he acknowledged in his autobiography. 'I who had never much desired to possess anything.' During the first year of war, Day-Lewis was commissioned to write a Nicholas Blake play for BBC radio (MI5 warned that because of his communist past he was not to get near a microphone), and he began to translate Virgil's Latin *Georgics*, a classical poem of agriculture and rural labour. 'I began work, my imagination quickened and enriched by all that I had come to love here,' he later wrote, 'the places and the people – and by a sense that this work might be a valediction to them.'[387]

For some commentators, the retreat of the 'Thirties Poets' in wartime provoked anger. Auden and Isherwood suffered a public backlash after emigrating to America (they left Britain in January 1939 before war broke out, but when they stayed away they were dubbed deserters, with questions even asked in parliament as to whether their citizenship should be revoked). Seen as part of the group, Day-Lewis inevitably came under fire during the fallout. 'The phrase I used about the fire-eating poet and the Ministry of Information was given to me and I reproduced it as it stood,' Jack Priestley explained to him after receiving a wounded letter from Day-Lewis for mocking Auden and Isherwood on the radio (Priestley said he had not intended to include Day-Lewis in the attack, but was unrepentant in his views on Auden and Isherwood).[388] At the Book Society, there was an angry scene when Hugh lashed out at Day-Lewis for 'playing at soldiers' (Day-Lewis's words) in the Home Guard. As Edmund recalled:

> C. D. L. was sitting peacefully enough beside me [...], but Hugh was full of wrath incited by somebody's latest poems. The wrath fell on C. D. L. 'You poets', Hugh declared, biting his pipe, 'you piped us all onto the parade ground, and now the show begins you are somewhere else'. C. D. L., whose silences are worth *watching*, had his eyes on the agenda paper, and said nothing.[389]

Aware of his critics, Day-Lewis tried to still the noise when *The Georgics of Virgil* was published later that year, writing in a dedication to Stephen Spender that he had been 'taking a leaf from Virgil's laurel' by singing 'in time of war the arts of peace':

> Where are the war poets? The fools inquire.
> [...]
> We were at war, while they still played with fire
> And rigged the market for the ruin of man:
> Spain was a death to us, Munich a mourning.
> No wonder then if, like the pelican,
> We have turned inward for our iron ration
> ('Dedicatory Stanzas to Stephen Spender')

***

During the height of invasion fever that June, it became clear that Edmund and his family were of interest to the authorities. At Annie's house in Tonbridge the police spent hours going through Edmund's old library, removing some private letters of Annie's (as a German, now an enemy alien) and Sylva's to him. When the police returned at the start of July, looking it seemed for documents concealed within the pages of books, Edmund's suspicion that he was in fact the object of the search, rather than Annie, was confirmed. 'I must be ready for any construction to be placed, and action taken, upon my (& Sylva's) desires to help in averting war with Germany and on our friendships and visits there,' he acknowledged. High-profile figures were being detained for their German sympathies: Oswald Mosley and his wife Diana Mitford were imprisoned in May 1940; Admiral Barry Domvile (of the Royal Navy) and his mistress Olive Baker were arrested in June. 'If the posse concerned has worked through the Mosleys and Domviles,' Edmund realised, 'then less notable figures will become targets.'[390]

After the heady days of romance in spring, by summer Edmund found himself suddenly alone. Claire had left Oxford after Finals and returned to Manchester, and was thinking of joining the WAF. Sylva meanwhile was busy in a canteen and working on a farm. The quietness of college in summertime was disconcerting, making Edmund feel vulnerable, and by Tuesday 9 July he was sufficiently anxious to stop writing his diary and post it to Claire in Manchester for safekeeping. He had begun writing it in response to international events, but it had become a private love story. 'Some things in it do not concern the national safety,' he noted, and while his room at Merton was 'at the mercy of any pickers and stealers' he didn't want it read 'in the interests of Freedom, by some Churchillians spy-maker.'

The following day, Edmund was hauled in by the Warden of Merton to discuss police reports of his questionable patriotism. Thankfully, he could affirm that he'd written to his old commanding officer for a commission, and the following week he was given a post as map-reading instructor with Oxford Officer's Training Corps. Edmund's lectures on the geography of France and Flanders over the next four years were full of literary anecdotes and entertaining diversions on maps and their makers. There was a depressing circularity to his return to uniform. 'Strange that once again I should be making use of experiences before I reached my 21st birthday.'[391]

1940

130	January	*The Valiant Heart*, George Blake
131	February	*The Provincial Lady in War-Time*, E. M. Delafield
132	March	*The Thirties. 1930-1940 in Great Britain*, Malcolm Muggeridge
133	April	*Verdun*, Jules Romains, trans. by Gerard Manley Hopkins
134	May	*Mine Inheritance*, Frederick Niven
135	June	*The Mixture as Before*, Somerset Maugham
136	July	*The Near and the Far*, L. H. Myers
137	August	*Night in Bombay*, Louis Bromfield

he Love of the
oolish Angel
by
n Beauclerk
Author of
reen Lacquer Pavilion"
ecorations by
und Dulac

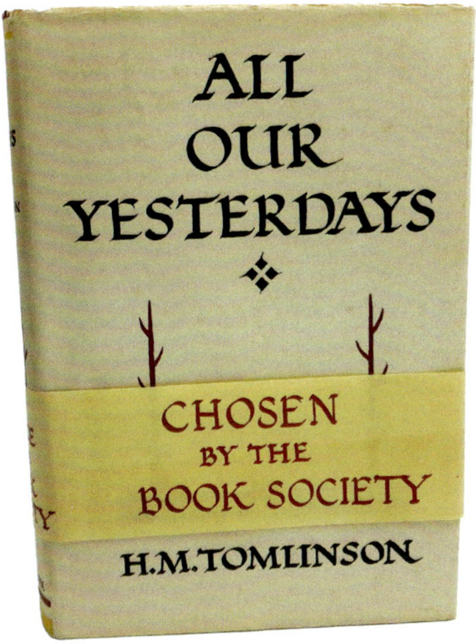
ALL OUR YESTERDAYS
CHOSEN BY THE BOOK SOCIETY
H.M.TOMLINSON

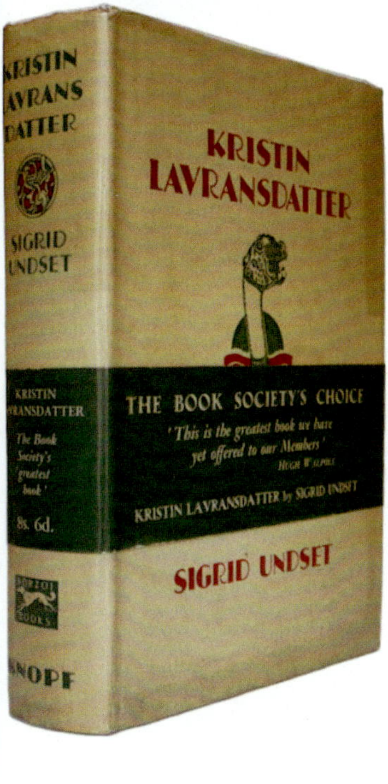
KRISTIN LAVRANSDATTER
SIGRID UNDSET
THE BOOK SOCIETY'S CHOICE
'This is the greatest book we have yet offered to our Members'
HUGH WALPOLE
KRISTIN LAVRANSDATTER by SIGRID UNDSET
'The Book Society's greatest book'
8s. 6d.
SIGRID UNDSET

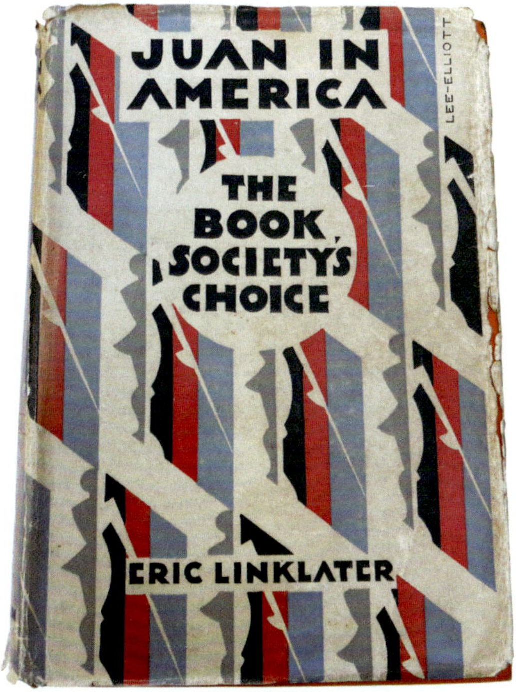
JUAN IN AMERICA
LEE-ELLIOTT
THE BOOK SOCIETY'S CHOICE
ERIC LINKLATER

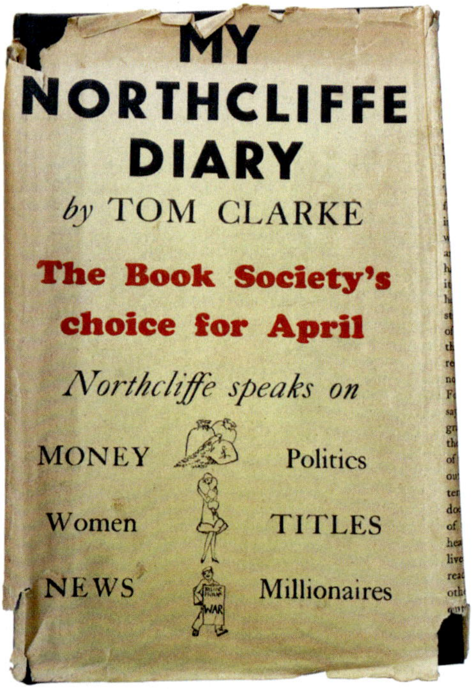
MY
NORTHCLIFFE
DIARY
by TOM CLARKE
The Book Society's
choice for April
Northcliffe speaks on
MONEY
Politics
Women
TITLES
NEWS
Millionaires
WAR

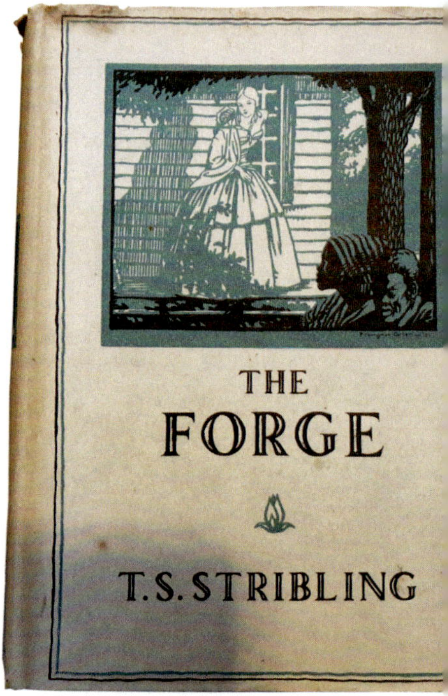
THE
FORGE
T.S. STRIBLING

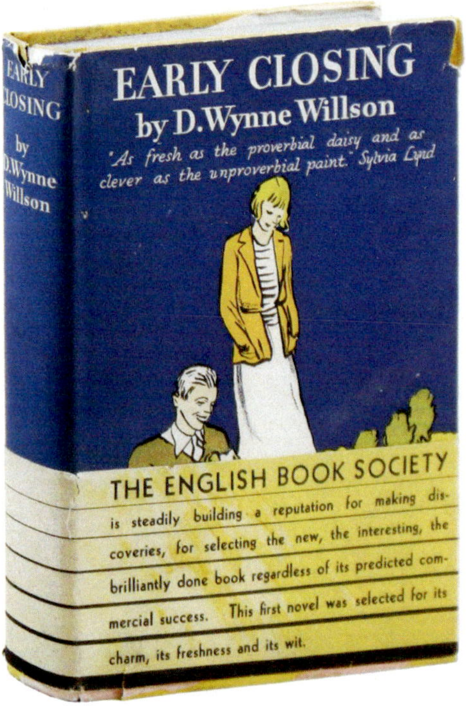
EARLY CLOSING
by D. Wynne Willson
"As fresh as the proverbial daisy and as clever as the unproverbial paint." Sylvia Lynd
EARLY CLOSING by D. Wynne Willson
THE ENGLISH BOOK SOCIETY
is steadily building a reputation for making discoveries, for selecting the new, the interesting, the brilliantly done book regardless of its predicted commercial success. This first novel was selected for its charm, its freshness and its wit.

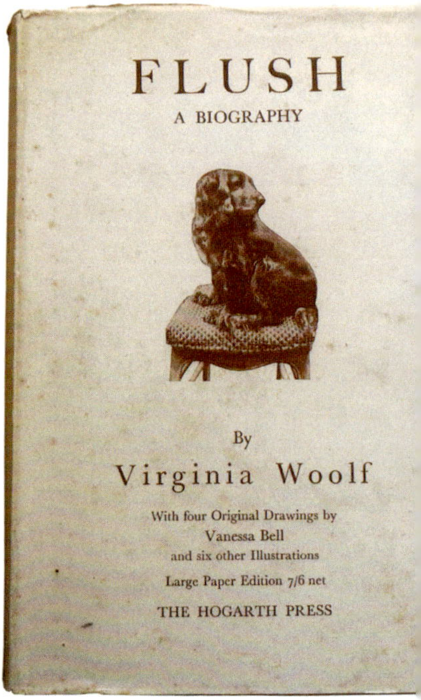
FLUSH
A BIOGRAPHY
By
Virginia Woolf
With four Original Drawings by
Vanessa Bell
and six other Illustrations
Large Paper Edition 7/6 net
THE HOGARTH PRESS

THE
SHIPBUILDERS
A Novel By
George Blake

ILLYRIAN SPRING
ANN BRIDGE
AUTHOR OF "PEKING PICNIC"
CHATTO & WINDUS
ILLYRIAN SPRING
ANN BRIDGE
AUTHOR OF "PEKING PICNIC"

SOUTH
RIDING
WINIFRED
HOLTBY

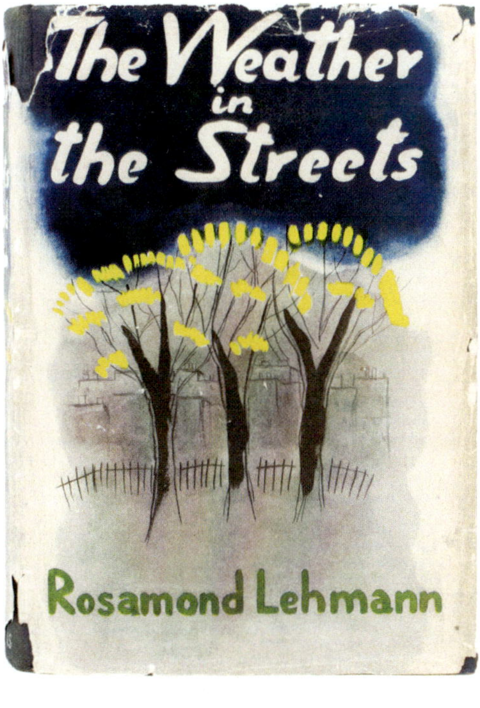
The Weather in the Streets
Rosamond Lehmann

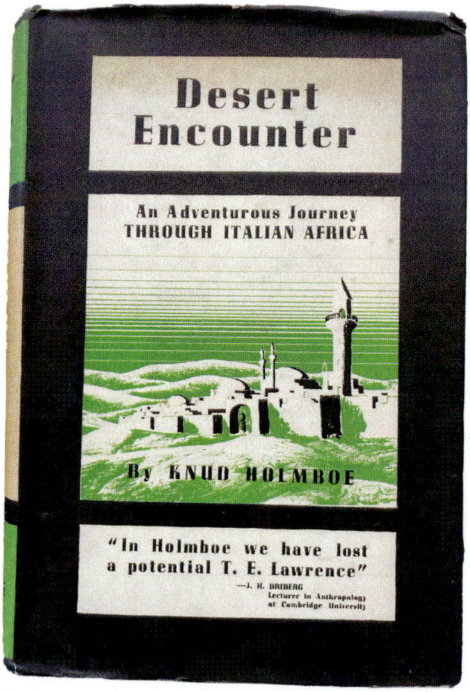
Desert Encounter
An Adventurous Journey
THROUGH ITALIAN AFRICA
By KNUD HOLMBOE
"In Holmboe we have lost a potential T. E. Lawrence"
—J. H. DRIBERG
Lecturer in Anthropology at Cambridge University

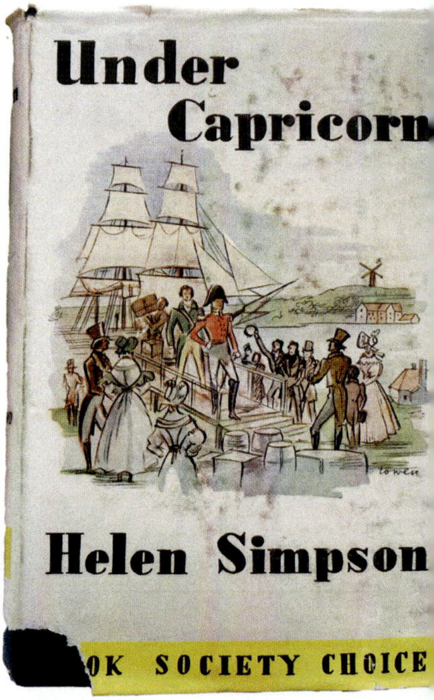
Under Capricorn
Helen Simpson
OK SOCIETY CHOICE

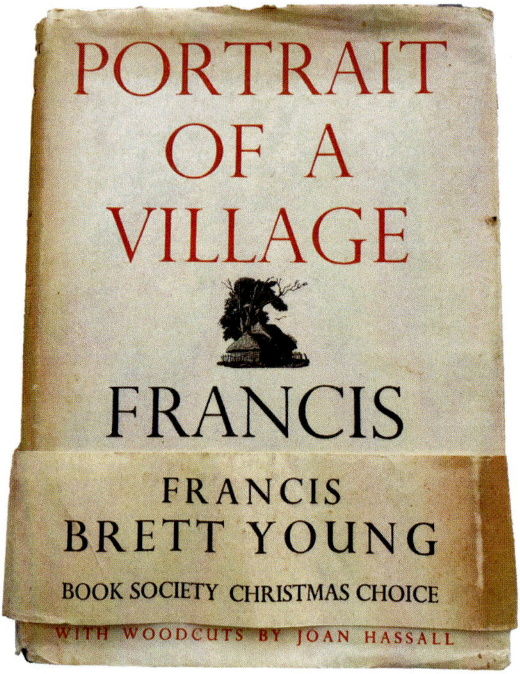
PORTRAIT OF A VILLAGE
FRANCIS
FRANCIS BRETT YOUNG
BOOK SOCIETY CHRISTMAS CHOICE
WITH WOODCUTS BY JOAN HASSALL

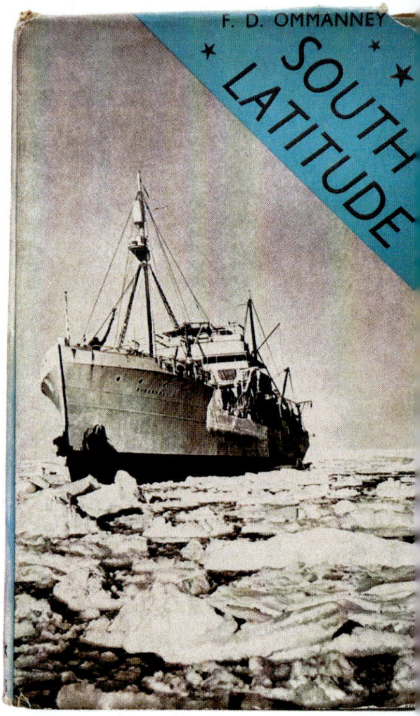
F. D. OMMANNEY
SOUTH LATITUDE

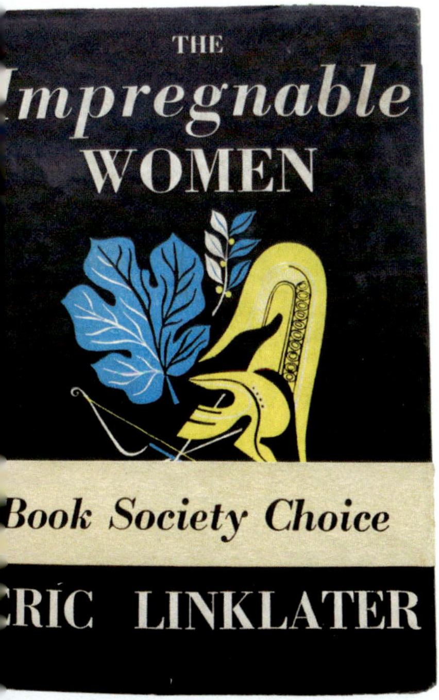
THE
Impregnable
WOMEN
Book Society Choice
RIC LINKLATER

BY DAPHNE DU MAURIER
REBECCA
8/6
net
GOLLANCZ
DAPHNE
DU MAURIER
a new novel
REBECCA
a new novel
DAPHNE
DU MAURIER

REACHING
FOR
THE STARS
Chosen by
THE BOOK SOCIETY

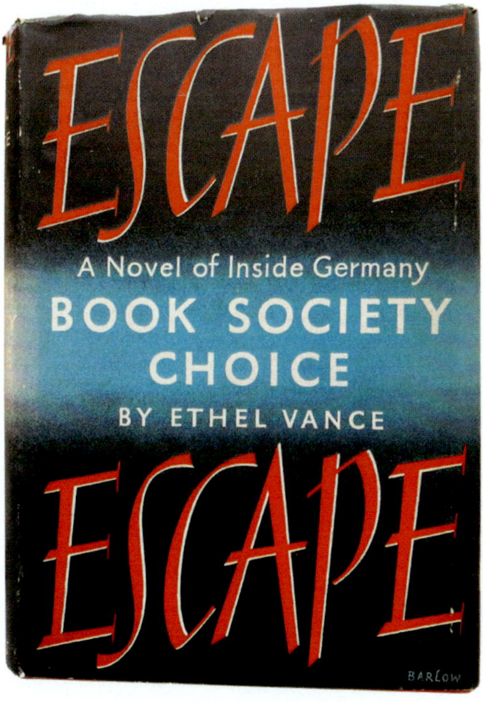
ESCAPE
A Novel of Inside Germany
BOOK SOCIETY
CHOICE
BY ETHEL VANCE
ESCAPE
BARLOW

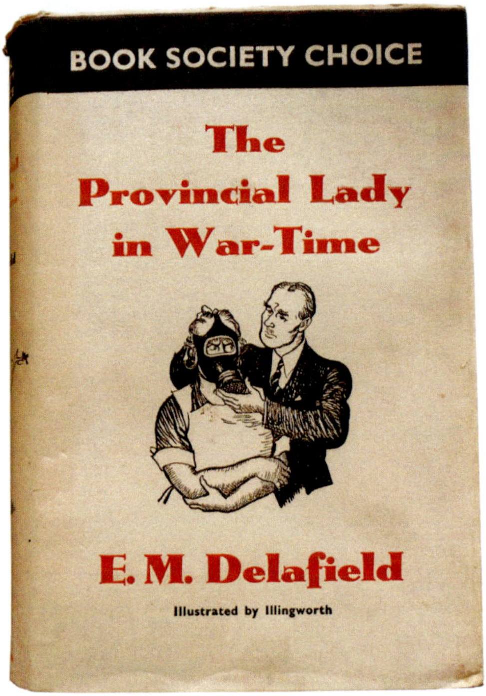
BOOK SOCIETY CHOICE
The Provincial Lady in War-Time
E. M. Delafield
Illustrated by Illingworth

VERDUN
BOOK SOCIETY CHO
JULES ROMAIN

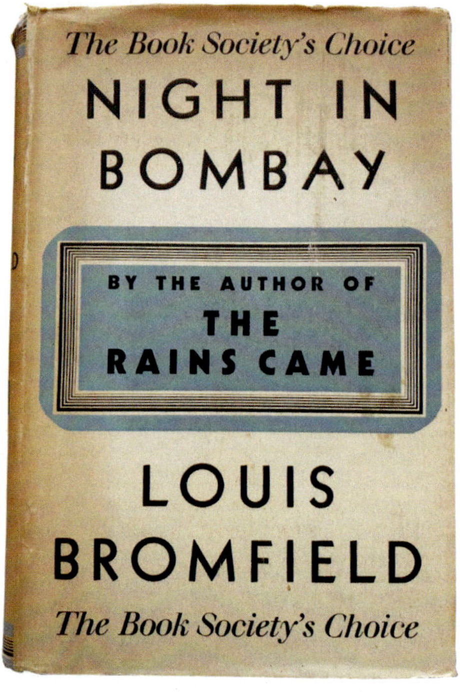
The Book Society's Choice
NIGHT IN BOMBAY
BY THE AUTHOR OF THE RAINS CAME
LOUIS BROMFIELD
The Book Society's Choice

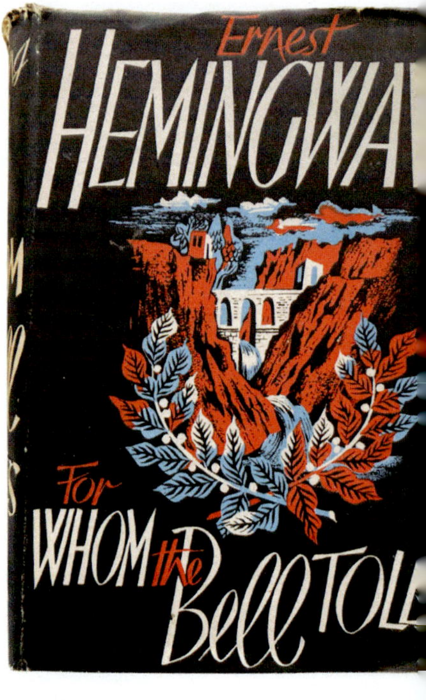
Ernest
HEMINGWA
For WHOM the Bell TOLL

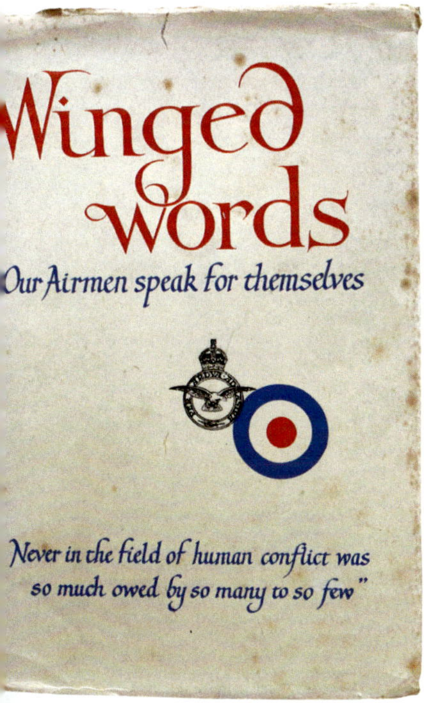
Winged words
Our Airmen speak for themselves
Never in the field of human conflict was so much owed by so many to so few"

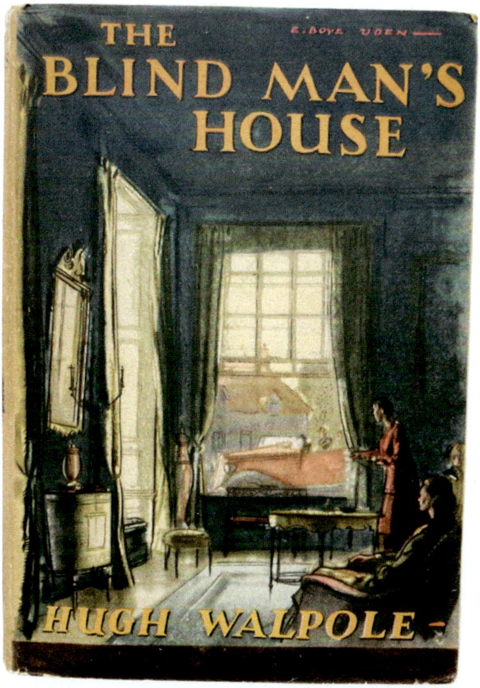
THE BLIND MAN'S HOUSE
HUGH WALPOLE

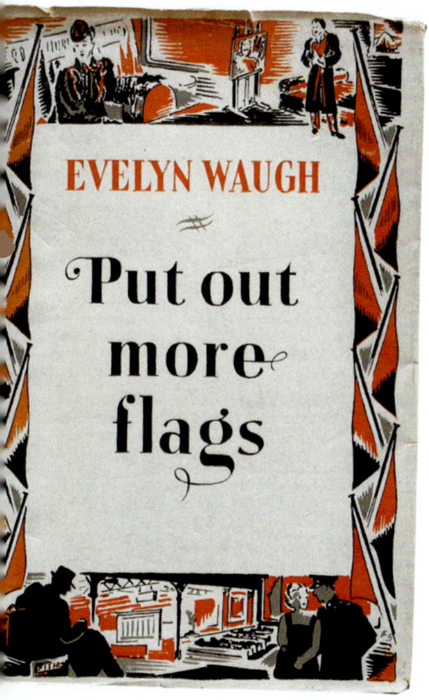
EVELYN WAUGH
Put out more flags

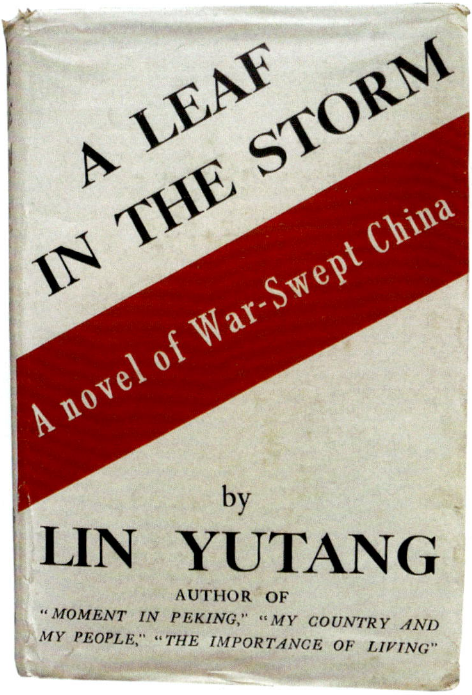
A LEAF IN THE STORM
A novel of War-Swept China
by
LIN YUTANG
AUTHOR OF
"MOMENT IN PEKING," "MY COUNTRY AND MY PEOPLE," "THE IMPORTANCE OF LIVING"

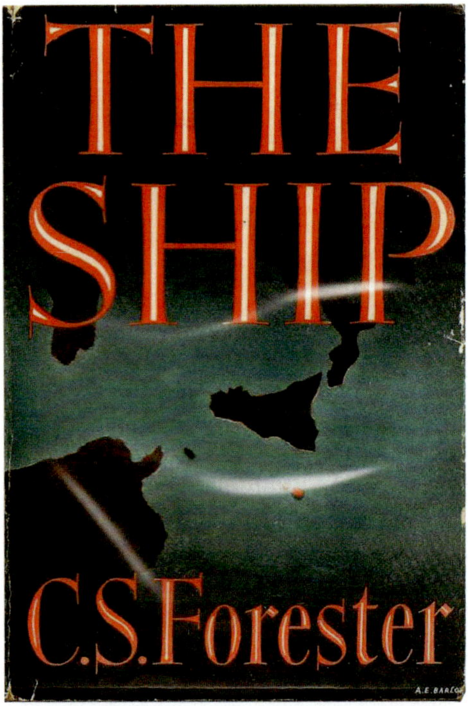
THE
SHIP
C.S.Forester

ANNA KARENINA
LEO TOLSTOY

STORM JAMESON
CLOUDLESS
MAY

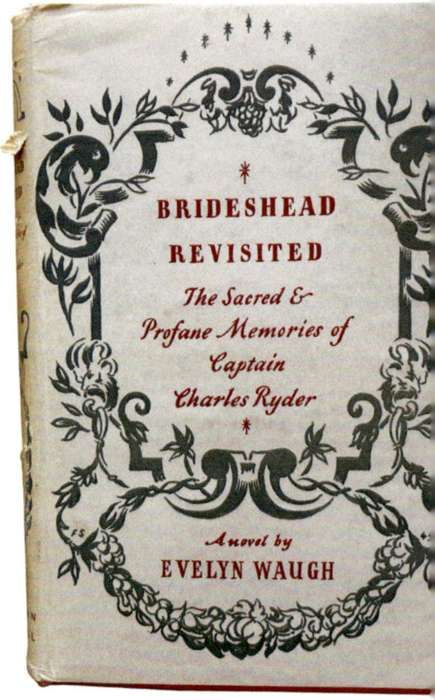
BRIDESHEAD
REVISITED
The Sacred &
Profane Memories of
Captain
Charles Ryder
A novel by
EVELYN WAUGH

Chapter 8. Hugh 1940-41

Battle dress

I

THE "VICTORY ROLL"
A British fighter-pilot doing the " Victory Roll " in his Hurricane—one of many illustrations from a short but informative book on British Fighter Planes, by C. G. Grey (Faber, 5/-). Winged Words, *The Book Society June Choice, records deeds by our victorious airmen, told by themselves.*

Book Society News, June 1941. From Edmund Blunden's review of *Winged Words. Our Airmen Speak for Themselves*, Book Society Choice for June

The devastating air warfare that Sylvia had feared since reading about the destruction of Guernica in the Spanish Civil War was finally unleashed upon Britain in September 1940. Following air raids in July and August as the

Luftwaffe sought to aid a seaborne invasion, the Blitz that began over the London docks on 7 September became a prolonged aerial bombardment of the city. Over the next nine months, many British towns and cities would suffer the terrible effects of the Blitz, with two million houses damaged or destroyed, over 50,000 people injured, and more than 43,600 civilian deaths.

As these raids on the capital began, the Book Society announced that they were complying with the advice of their ARP squad to take down the eighteenth-century French chandelier in Grosvenor Place, to prevent it being smashed into pieces. They would also cut down further on paper usage by reducing the statement-form for orders and exchanges to half its former size. Disruptions to supply, with postal delays and last-minute price increases, were increasingly likely; some members did not receive the October 1940 choice until the end of the month. 'The fault was not ours' the club explained, 'it was just one of those things that happen in wartime', when the railways were sometimes late with non-war material, including in this case the printed sheets of Charles Morgan's *The Voyage*.[392]

For November 1940 the judges selected a comforting read with Mazo de la Roche's *Whiteoak Heritage*. This was a prequel to the Whiteoaks saga and 'a piece of the modern world that is yet remote enough from everyday life to have the glow of romance upon it', Sylvia counselled. For December, after three hard months of the Blitz (London faced fifty-seven consecutive nights of attack) and a Christmas that for most would mean 'quiet days at home, of letter-writing and attempts at telephoning between scattered families', they chose conservative historian Arthur Bryant's *English Saga (1840-1940)*, a patriotic panorama that showed England as an island fortress. According to Hugh's review, Bryant's history revealed 'above all the humanity of our story. We are as fallible as any people can be, but a remarkable toughness and self-respect is central in our character.'[393]

Despite the turmoil, it could also be 'a Christmas of books', the club assured readers, thanks to the ruling that books and newspapers were to be exempt from the new purchase tax being imposed by the Treasury, preventing a so-called tax on knowledge. Since June 1940, the Publishers Association had orchestrated a high-profile campaign to exclude books from the new tax, stressing the economic and propaganda value of publishers' export trade (in a survey, the export business – much of it done with the Dominions and USA – was found to equal around one-third of most publishers' total revenue).

Alongside this was the moral value of reading and the perceived effect on public morale, as well as wider forms of education. Hugh had presided over a packed industry meeting at Stationers' Hall earlier that year where he had warned that, if the tax were enforced, 'it might very easily make the whole of contemporary literature silent and invisible'.[394] So 'At a time when the price of everything else has soared, that of books is approximately what it was at Christmas 1938,' the *Book Society News* celebrated. It was some blessing for a Christmas dinner of 'expensive turkeys or rationed joints, followed by Christmas puds without the unobtainable raisins', the club pointed out, when 'the bombs, surely, will fall as usual'.[395]

***

The Book Society judges were all affected by the bombing. Down in rural Sussex, Sylvia lived in the capital's flightpath and heard the bombers overhead day and night with 'terrible faint thudding' to the North, and frequent bombing not far away in Guildford. Over Christmas 1940, she and Robert dug a shelter in the garden, for even in the relative safety of Forest Green they weren't immune from the Blitz. One morning the cottage that Max Beerbohm and his wife Florence were living in, higher up on Abinger Common, was wrecked along with the spire of Abinger church above it; on another tragic occasion they heard 'the wretched crew of the German bomber screaming as it fell'.[396] Aged fifty-two in September 1940, Sylvia became a grandmother that summer when Lucy – B. J. and Jack's first's daughter – was born in July.[397] According to Sylvia's diary, Robert's drinking worsened through the war and she took on more of his work for him, occasionally writing his reviews for the literary pages of the *News Chronicle* and obituaries published under his name.

For Edmund in Oxford, the air raid sirens sounded between seven and midnight each night as heavy bombers passed overhead, attacking nearby Abingdon or flying northwards to Birmingham and other towns (in his diary, which he felt safe enough to start up again mid-October, Edmund speculated that the city must be used as a mark of direction). While the city centre itself was spared, evidence of the bombing was all around. Out walking one night, he and Sylva watched flashes on the eastern horizon followed by a vast explosion. 'A queer thing', Edmund wrote afterwards at home, 'this walking ordinary roads with that monstrous performance happening a bit away'. A week later, during a visit from Claire (she was back at home in Manchester, training to be a teacher), he and Claire walked north of Oxford from Begbroke to Bladon and 'came on a great hole made by a bomb, with heavy slabs of clay tossed out all round, another a few yards from some houses'. Claire's reports of the violent, repeated attacks on Liverpool and Manchester, hushed up in the press, were alarming. They 'must haunt the memory of any one who endured them', Edmund realised.[398] In November, they watched flashes high into the northward sky as Coventry came under heavy attack, leaving one thousand casualties and damaging the cathedral. Edmund had updates from Annie about the daylight raids on London – she, like Sylvia, being in the flight path – and learnt that Hawstead, the farmhouse where he had lived with her and his brother in the early 1930s near Bury St Edmunds, had suffered bomb damage.

He was also concerned about Aki Hayashi, vulnerable in her top floor room on the edge of Hampstead Heath. Aki was struggling with the overcrowded conditions in the shelters, 'Oh! What a time I'm having!! Thanks God, I am alive' she wrote him September 1940, 'I never spend nights in my house, I've to go to a public underground shelter, full up: no sleep for 7 nights except a few hours in the morning after coming back here.'[399] She considered moving up to Oxford or Durham to escape the raids, but couldn't bring herself to leave the city she'd lived in for over ten years. Nevertheless, she pleaded with Edmund against travel. 'I think you do not realise how dreadful it is in London. Please wait until it is better.' Despite her concern, Edmund continued to visit London throughout the Blitz as the selection committee kept up monthly meetings in the capital. Edmund tried to see Aki around them, mindful of the problems in getting about, noting in his diary the 'fragments' of remaining buildings around the Farringdon Road bookstalls. She meanwhile found sustenance in her work at the British Museum, barring frequent disruption and closures, making her corresponding address c/o the British Newspaper Library at Colindale for the war's duration.

But of them all, the Blitz affected Hugh the most. Taken on by the BBC in the summer of 1940 to make occasional broadcasts and compelled by a sense of duty to the capital, Hugh endured the stress of daylight raids and the sirens and bombs of the Blitz, on his knees by his bedside each night praying to get through the shelling. Six days in ('Natural History Museum damaged' Hugh recorded in his diary, 'awful scenes in East End' [...], 'Bomb in Bond Street: Buckingham Palace. Piccadilly Circus roped off'), Hugh moved out of Piccadilly to stay with the Cheevers in Hampstead after a bomb fell so close to the flat that the whole building shook, leaving cracks in the walls.[400] He moved back and forth between central London and Hampstead for as long as he could, occasionally still sleeping in the flat, broadcasting during air raids, working on a new novel *The Killer and the Slain*, seeking occasional relief with a trip to the pictures with Ethel Cheevers. But Hampstead was still in the firing line. There were deaths from anti-aircraft fire in Keats Grove late September, and on Sunday 19 October, while Hugh was alone in the house with Ethel, reading *War and Peace*, a bomb hit the Cheevers' home: 'The window behind me blew in. I heard a rush of falling glass. Ethel was coming downstairs and I thought she was killed. [...] Main damage to pantry, where part of the bomb had penetrated. Windows smashed, doors blown in.'[401] The house opposite was completely wrecked, and Hugh took refuge with the Cheevers in Brackenburn for much of the end of the year, still travelling up and down to London for radio broadcasts, risking blacked-out trains and London's glass topped railway stations. He was not the same man after the near miss, Harold would later recall.[402]

On 15 November the Piccadilly flat was hit and when Hugh went round to inspect the damage the next day, he found John and Mary, the two servants, 'wearing tin helmets and hoovering a small space in the middle of the debris'.[403] At Christmas 1940, he visited Edinburgh to be with his brother and sister as usual and drew a line under the end of a horrible year. 'End of 1940. Thank God' he wrote in his journal. He returned to Brackenburn on the morning of 31 December to see in the new year with the Cheevers. Harold gave him a five-year diary inscribed with a message of love and hope:

> 'Dearest Hugh. Here is a book in which to record our Victory, and the days of happiness and peace to follow. Love from Harold.'

Such days would follow, but Hugh would not be there to share them.

Brackenburn, looking down from Cat Bells, with Derwentwater.

II

On 29 December 1940, London's book trade took an enormous hit when Paternoster Row, off St Paul's cathedral, was attacked in what became known as the Second Great Fire of London. That night, as St Paul's was illuminated by flames, the premises of seventeen publishers and over a million books were destroyed, along with the offices of trade magazine *The Bookseller* and the warehouse of Simpkin Marshall, the largest book wholesaler of the time. 'Once basements full of stock,' *The Bookseller* reported on 2 January 1941, were 'now the crematories of the City's book world.'[404] The devastation put further pressure on book supply and permanently shifted the geography of London's book trade westwards, away from its traditional printing centre and towards Holborn and the area around the British Museum.

For the club the December 1940 choice, *English Saga*, ushered in more topical non-fiction through the first half of 1941 as the Blitz continued across Britain. The most important title was *Into Battle: Speeches by the Rt. Hon. Winston S. Churchill*, a bestseller that became one of the club's most popular choices of the war, with a large initial print order as guaranteed by the Book Society swelled to a further eleven print runs before the war's end. *Into Battle* was also a transatlantic bestseller and selected by the American Book-of-the-Month Club. Bringing together Churchill's major speeches between May 1938 and November 1940, compiled by his son Randoph S. Churchill, this was not only fine prose but 'history itself' as the *Observer* pointed out. 'Not the book of the week. Nor yet of the month or the year', James Agate exclaimed in the *Daily Express*, but 'a book for all time'. In the Book Society January 1941 magazine, George Gordon underlined its significance. 'This book takes easy and just precedence of anything published in this country, or indeed in any country, since the war began' he wrote in a review that criticised appeasement, no doubt irking Edmund Blunden.[405] 'It grows more difficult every day, and posterity will hardly make the attempt', George wrote for the Book Society, 'to forgive the complacent blindness of our pre-war Governments, or the monstrous docility of the House of Commons.' For any reader living through it, this was a classic book to have on the shelf and the Book Society leveraged its role as a key distributor to boost membership, reporting in March that the fourth large printing was nearly sold out. A few copies would be set aside, they confirmed in the *Book Society News*, for any new members enrolling that month.

In May 1941 the club announced that the magazine would go into 'battle dress' by shedding its outside cover, and for June they selected another war book. *Winged Words. Our Airmen Speak for Themselves* was a documentary account of the Battle of Britain compiled from BBC broadcasts by the RAF and WAAF transmitted between December 1939 and February 1941. With Churchill's words from his 'magnificent speech' of 20 August 1940 emblazoned on the cover – 'Never in the field of human conflict was so much owed by so many to so few' – the book, published by Heinemann, aimed to raise money for the Royal Air Force.[406] Though this was, like *Into Battle*, obviously designed to capitalise on war fever and raise morale, Edmund chose to stress the nuance of the volume's content in his club review. There was a powerful description of an electrical storm, the work of the maintenance crews, or the occasion when a wing-commander looked into the eyes of an Italian driver and did not fire on his goods train. Recalling his own *Undertones of War*, the testimony of the serving airmen revealed 'the many-sided picture of air war', he pointed out, and was 'not necessarily always something of a combatant kind'.

***

1941 began well enough for Hugh. He felt in relatively good health and enjoyed the bright winter sunshine and snowfall around Brackenburn, and the sight of the lake frozen over. He had a new love interest (Dick, an actor he'd first seen on the stage, soon-to-be called up as an airman), and early in January he finished *The Killer and the Slain*. This was his fifty-sixth book, a macabre story that had poured out of him, the closest thing to automatic writing he'd ever done. The Cheevers returned to their patched-up house in Hampstead and in late February Hugh, missing HC 'quite horribly', followed them back down to London.[407] The Piccadilly flat, still looked after by John, was now 'all mended, looks quite miraculous' and with a brief lull in the air raids, Hugh put pictures back up on the walls. He began some new stories, *The City Under Fire*, while anxiously following news of the Allies campaign against Italy in East Africa.

In March, as the raids started up 'quite like the old style', as he put it, Hugh turned fifty-seven and agreed to do a weekly series of overseas broadcasts for the BBC. By April, he was committed to long hours (recording late evening, all morning), broadcasting several days a week.[408] 'Hugh Walpole Talking' was propaganda for the 'Blitz spirit' aiming to boost civilian morale. Positive conditions in the shelters were stressed – 'one that I visited the other day has almost all the amenities of a first-class hotel', Hugh reported – alongside friendship, international collaboration, and tolerance towards Allied refugees.[409] Drawing on his public persona as 'Man in the Street', Hugh affirmed public desire for a new form of society after the war, calling attention in his talks to the so-called 'New Order people, who are in a terrible state of excitement about what we are going to do when we have won the war' (the 1941 Committee, chaired by Jack Priestley, put forward various socially democratic proposals that would lay the foundations of the Welfare State). Arguing that 'the snobbery of class difference', something he'd despised since his schooldays, would be a prime casualty of the Blitz,

Hugh underlined the need to turn Britain 'into a real democracy'. 'It has needed the Blitz of the last six months to bring the consciousness of the creation of the new world into our hearts,' he argued, 'this second war will complete the awakening of the social conscience, that ever since the Reform Bill of 1832 has been stirring.'[410]

'Hugh Walpole Talking' was animated by personal stories of the war's impact on Hugh and 'two or three of my very close friends'. Harold Cheevers appeared as 'my brave secretary' (later disguised as 'Frank'), an embodiment of 'sound common-sense' whom Hitler would never conquer: 'He is over fifty, so that he can't do all the things he'd like to. But he is by far the best ARP warden in our district.' Ethel featured as a stoical housewife coping with rationing and two sons, the eldest 'in Egypt or in Greece, she doesn't know which'. 'She has been nearly killed in blitzes three times now,' Hugh declared 'and has never turned a hair in any of them.'[411]

Hugh also used Ethel to offer guidance on reading, casting her as the typical novel reader who was missing new fiction as supply was retracting. Prior to the war, Ethel liked to have at least two new novels a week, Hugh told listeners, and was now trying to read them more slowly, as well as having a go at the classics. 'She reads them with some interest, but not a great deal,' he admitted, emphasising the variety of tastes and reading pleasures as he would in the *Book Society News*. 'They don't take her mind off the war, she says. The new ones do.'

In a survey for Mass Observation, *Books and the Public*, published the following year and estimated to be based on the reading habits of near 10,000 people, the hunger for all kinds of books was made clear. This included fun and escapist titles that 'take my mind off the war' as well as a general increase 'in intelligent and serious reading'.[412] Several of the Book Society's pre-war fiction choices remained favourite reads and were among the most-often borrowed books from libraries (this included Daphne du Maurier's *Rebecca*, Louis Bromfield's *The Rains Came*, and Richard Llewellyn's *How Green Was My Valley*). In other contemporary surveys, newspapers and fiction came out as the most popular genres for war-time readers in the UK. And as war wore on, the club would increasingly invest in fiction as the main choice.

***

Early April 1941, Hugh was devasted to learn of Virginia Woolf's death, 'a terrible tragic loss to her friends', as he said on the radio, 'and a real catastrophe for contemporary English letters'.[413] Two weeks later, on the night of Wednesday 16 April, he had what he called 'one of the oddest days and nights of my life' when London endured one of its worst raids of the Blitz. After a trip to the Palladium with Harold and Ethel, they were listening to the nine o'clock news in Hugh's flat when the alarm sounded. 'I don't know why', Hugh revealed in a dramatic account broadcast a few days later, 'but I realised at once that this was going to be a bad raid. I fancied that ever since I heard that the Berlin Opera House and Unter Den Linden had been hit, I knew there would be a recoil.' Harold drove them out to Hampstead 'through a chaos of noise and flashing lights', but the noise of the bombing and the constant roar of the guns and the planes that night was unbearable. Hugh couldn't sleep at all. 'Lying in my bed, it really seemed to me that they were flying straight into the room,' he recalled afterwards on the radio, and the devastation when they came back to the flat the next day, even after living through months of bombardment, was shocking. St. James's was 'a sight. Every window smashed', Hugh observed in his diary, and from Leicester Square to Holborn it was the same, he was told. He took a walk through the debris of streets and shops he had often written about, sharing a picture of a city under siege. 'Nearly 35 years ago,' as he said on the BBC's Eastern Service:

> I described them myself for the first time in a novel called *Fortitude*, and I remember how, then, a very young man, I went down a certain fashionable street, with a little penny notebook, and wrote down the names of certain shops and hotels so that I might be realistically accurate. On this morning, four of those places were gone. The sunlight was gay above the pearl-grey houses that I had known all my life. One famous street had in the middle of it a crater big enough to contain a cart and four horses. One famous provision shop was gaping with glassless windows; and on the windowsill of one of them three very smart ladies, with elegant little hats, were seated swinging their heels.[414]

Concerned, Sylvia wrote him from Forest Green: 'I hope you are still safe after these last two nights...Piccadilly I'm told caught badly this time, I hope not your flat again.'[415] Hugh and the flat had survived physically, but the trauma was beginning to show.

After reliving the horrendous experience on air and mulling over his unfinished article on Woolf, the next day, Sunday 20 April, Hugh suffered what he called 'a crisis of nerves' and, after snapping at Harold, stormed out of the Cheevers'. He caught a bus into town, calling in at a cinema and the Athenaeum, then wandered aimlessly about the suburbs the next day. HC was 'a complete angel', Hugh reflected afterwards, but the breakdown shook him, underlining the acute strain of the last eight months of the Blitz. 'In four months time, [...] we will have had two years of it', Hugh acknowledged on 26 April. It would be one of his final radio broadcasts.

Hugh's last meeting with the Book Society fell the following week on Tuesday 29 April 1941. There was hectic discussion over Auden's complex new volume, *New Year Letter* (this was published to generally negative reviews) and, as ever, Hugh enjoyed the judges' company. A few days later he travelled back up to the Lakes. Bombs were dropping on Carlisle but at Brackenburn, compared to London, Hugh found 'perfect peace'. On 17 May he led a march through Keswick for War Weapons Week (a charity drive to raise funds) and took to bed a few days later, complaining of bad indigestion. When Harold returned on the 21st from Saltash, where he'd been looking after his parents, full of horrifying stories about the raids on Plymouth, he found Hugh seriously ill, agonising over news of the German attack on Crete where the Cheevers' eldest boy was caught up (he went missing and was found as a Prisoner of War in Germany later that year). On 23 May, Hugh wrote a last diary entry. HC was 'a blessing', he recorded, while the international situation was dire; the Battle of Crete likely 'a fine rehearsal for our own Invasion'. A few days later, Hugh slipped briefly into a diabetic coma and a heart specialist diagnosed a coronary thrombosis, advising against any further strain and complete bedrest for the next six months. His brother and sister were sent for, and Hugh asked for a pile of Book Society manuscripts to be brought to his bed. The last choice he made was Robert Greenwood's *Mr Bunting at War*. He'd described the prequel, *Mr Bunting*, as 'the best first novel of 1940' and judged the follow-up of Greenwood's Everyman character just as appealing. Paying homage, Sylvia wrote in her review for the club that Hugh 'chose it for the justness of its character-drawing and the serenity of its spirit. Had he lived, these are the qualities he would have praised in it.'

Hugh Walpole died on the morning of 1 June 1941, holding Harold's hand. He was surrounded by the early summer beauty of Brackenburn.

Memorial seat below Cat Bells, above Brackenburn. 'To the memory of Sir Hugh Walpole OBE...erected by his friend Harold Cheevers, September 1941'.

III

Alongside news of the German bombing in Dublin and the start of food aid from the USA, the introduction of clothes rationing, and the British withdrawal from Crete, *The Times* newspaper reported on Sir Hugh Walpole's sudden death the next day. Their anonymous obituary subtitled 'A Widely Read Novelist', in which Hugh was acknowledged as 'among the most successful and popular novelists of his day', would become a notorious character assassination. Stating that Hugh was 'intensely ambitious' and determined, as well as 'not popular among his fellow-writers', Hugh was portrayed as 'a sentimental egotist', 'singularly sensitive to adverse criticism'. 'He could tell a workmanlike story in good workmanlike English', it went on: 'So prodigious was his industry that it is impossible even to mention the titles of all his books.'[416] Perhaps unsurprisingly, Hugh's work for the Book Society was also held against him, as well as recorded inaccurately. 'He saw himself as serving his profession', the writer mocked, 'but he resigned the office in 1935.'

A flurry of protests from friends and admirers over the following days, led by Jack Priestley and Alan Bott, included a letter from T. S. Eliot pointing out Hugh's 'capacity to appreciate and admire generously authors very different from himself'.[417] But the damage was done. 'He had some enemies, we see,' Edmund acknowledged in his diary, 'and I can understand it, for he could be annoying, and less attentive to the Rights of Man than he supposed himself to be.' Alan Bott (appointed with Rupert Hart-Davis as literary executor) had seen Hugh's papers and confirmed to the judges what they already suspected, that Hugh gave away a large sum annually to hard-pressed authors, 'and equally one never knew', Edmund recognised, 'when he would come over with some handsome public appreciation of one's literary attempts'. Rupert had written to Edmund that he and Alan planned to postpone the sale of Hugh's goods until after the war. 'There's a devilish lot of work about,' Rupert shared, '850 pictures & 16,000 books to be dealt with.' 'Dear old fellow, I was very fond of him, and I fancy you were too?'[418] Edmund was certainly fond but felt Hugh 'had too full a time-table to do anything excellently, as a writer', as he wrote in his own private appraisal. 'He should have been granted a retirement, to write without fuss on such enthusiasms. But he seems to have been burned to write for the moment,' Edmund perceived in a poignant note, 'either to keep up a large income & the style of one of London's leaders or else to be in the swim – and he had a pardonable fondness for being there'.[419]

In public, the club mourned Hugh's passing with more favourable memories. 'He showed always a deep, unflagging regard for the Book Society and its members,' read their announcement in July's magazine. Hugh was 'a man of immense vitality, geniality, humour, explosiveness, fair-mindedness, frank prejudice, kindness and enthusiasm,' Sylvia wrote in a rounded portrait depicting Hugh at home, 'playing the pianola in his shirtsleeves', surrounded by the art and objects of a lifetime's passionate collecting.[420] 'As a writer, his fellow-writers, for the most part, I think, under-rated him' Sylvia underlined in another obituary published in his old school magazine. 'To meet him always was to feel an increased vitality.' 'So I see him, stepping away to the latest concert or film or picture show, his bowler hat titled a little over one eye, his umbrella hooked on his arm, his carnation in his button-hole, his eyes behind his glasses twinkling a farewell.'[421] He was 'worth any two of the popular novelists of his day' she added. 'Nowhere does Hugh Walpole's death bring a greater sense of loss than to the Book Society. Every Committee meeting will be a reminder of his absence.'

***

The late June 1941 meeting, the first without Hugh, was 'very peaceful' with 'little war talk' according to Edmund. Nobody thought the Soviet Union would hold out against Germany, who had invaded a week earlier, for long, though 'one or two felt that resistance was unexpectedly good', Edmund acknowledged, '& might last three months'. Edmund had rushed to join the judges in Grosvenor Place after a hurried farewell to Claire at Victoria (she was starting as a schoolteacher in Newbury), following a short stop in town and a half-hearted scout around Farringdon Road. His anxiety and depression were mounting, colouring his impressions of the bombed-out capital. 'The plane trees in St Brides's churchyard were as pleasantly gleaming through the windows as if the church were anything but a burnt fragment' he observed in his diary. 'London not quite alive. No real talk about the peace, no unguarded gestures, no vice or virtue, only just persons getting through the hour without gusto.'[422] Later that night, back in Oxford, he had fire drill to deal with. He'd been up in the attics and knew the chances of saving Merton in an air-raid were slim: 'The old woodwork, & the rubbish of ages, would love a firebomb.' But Edmund found something distracting at least in being on watch every night, taking him out of himself and back to his youth. 'The boys on watch assembled in the vaulted cellar under the hall, and made a good show,' he noted in his diary, 'I almost wished we had all been on the old Western Front with something happening of a less sordid kind than this air bombardment.'[423]

As well as agreeing to make Hugh's next-to-last novel, *The Blind Man's House*, choice one-hundred-and-fifty when Macmillan published it in the autumn, the judges voted for Jack Priestley to rejoin the club after Hugh's death. Jack was a long-term ally, one of Hugh's closest friends, and the committee felt that his popularity as a household name would help them appeal to a wide demographic, as well as signalling their relevance through the continuing crisis. In January 1941, Jack had returned triumphantly to the BBC with a second run of his Sunday night *Postscripts*, the no-nonsense, morale-boosting broadcasts that helped define the Dunkirk spirit and were seen to have calmed the country through the threat of invasion the previous year (it was estimated that almost thirty percent of the adult population in Britain had tuned into the BBC Home Service between June and October 1940 to hear him).[424]

In Spring 1941, Jack had been bumped off the airwaves again in a BBC editorial decision underscored by political pressure from the Ministry of Information and the backbench Conservative 1922 Committee.[425] Now chair of the 1941 Committee, a broadly progressive group which included Edward Hulton (publisher of *Picture Post*), independent MP Richard Acland, Victor Gollancz, and Kingsley Martin of the *New Statesman*, only Churchill matched Jack's fame as a wartime leader at home and abroad. Jack was an old friend of Sylvia's and George Gordon, and Edmund found him 'attractive and original', in agreement with the others that he was an 'intelligent speaker, almost universally acclaimed as the best of his kind this war'.[426]

Jack was back on the selection committee by August 1941, almost ten years after his turbulent departure. Now nearing fifty, he was a stable influence second time around, becoming something of a literary statesman after the success of *An Inspector Calls* in 1946. He would stay on the committee after the war, until late 1948.

***

After the urgency of some of their wartime non-fiction at the start of the year, the judges changed tack in the summer of 1941 by choosing several long works of historical fiction. The war was shifting to the Eastern front with Germany's invasion of Russia. 'The war goes on somewhere in the heat,' Edmund wrote in his diary, 'on the Russian battlefield, Syria,' while civilians 'are mostly reclining, so to speak, on the interval between the air wars.'[417] The July choice was Taylor Caldwell's re-imagining of the reign of Genghis Khan and the thirteenth-century Crusades (Taylor Caldwell was the pen name of British-born American writer Janet Caldwell, assumed to be male by the critics). *The Earth is the Lord's* was a 'series of decorative panels', explained Sylvia, whose 'main theme is the creation of a man without pity – a theme not inapposite for the world at the present day'. This was Caldwell's second Book Society choice following her bestselling debut, *Dynasty of Death*, published in March 1939. Caldwell had started out writing thrillers for mass-market magazines and had a reputation for pulp fiction; the author was 'not a careful stylist', Sylvia warned members in her review, but while the history was not to be taken particularly seriously, that was not really the point. 'So forcefully real are his characters to him that one of his readers, at any rate, does not trouble to question it,' Sylvia acknowledged. 'Such things are less important than the pictures, glowing in colour and multitudinous in detail, which the author puts before our eyes.'

Another compulsive page-turner the club put before readers that summer was C. S. Forester's naval adventure, *The Captain from Connecticut*. Forester was a firm favourite and this was his fourth Book Society choice. Set in the Anglo-American war of 1812, the novel signalled Forester's return to form, according to George Gordon's review for the club, moving away from the more serious character study of his previous novel, *The Earthly Paradise* (chosen, nevertheless, in September 1940). *The Captain from Connecticut* would please fans of Forester's earlier naval adventures, George felt. 'It is in the true Hornblower tradition, and will be enjoyed by every adherent of that choice and manly saga.'

In September 1941, subscribers received Hugh Walpole's first posthumous novel, *The Blind Man's House*: *A Quiet Man's Story*. The book itself was sold as a form of memorial, the dust jacket asking, 'How many of these famous books have you read?' including a list of Hugh's fifty-odd titles. Hugh had written the novel during the first year of war and finished it in June 1940, waiting for news of the French government's surrender and anticipating invasion. Like his Macmillan war pamphlet, *Open Letter of an Optimist*, the book was dedicated to his long friendship with Alan Bott and his wife, Josephine.

The novel centred on Julius Cromwell, the 'Quiet Man' of the subtitle, who is a typical Walpole hero – physically strong and athletic – in this case made vulnerable after being blinded in WWI. To Hugh's friends, Julius was clearly a self-portrait, and Sylvia pointed this out in her club review. The story was set in Walpole's fictional territory of Glebeshire, the West Country county, with its cathedral city of Polchester. Here, as in Virginia Woolf's last novel, *Between the Acts*, also published a few months after the author's death in 1941 (*Between the Acts* was flagged in a review by Cecil Day-Lewis as a 'special recommendation') the emphasis on communal village life, with its gossip and power-plays, was represented as both an escape from, and a meditation upon, the destruction of WWII. Initially as the drama of village life unfolds, war feels a long way off in *The Blind Man's House* and characters can choose not to engage with the news, but by its end the threat of a Nazi victory is a possibility. It could only be upended, according to Hugh and the novel's worldview, by an appeal to creativity and brotherhood. 'I wrote the other day in this book something about the creative things being the only things that remain,' says the protagonist. 'It isn't the fearful losses at Passchendaele that now remain, but the resolve created by those losses that nothing like that shall ever happen again.'[428]

IV

As the third autumn of the war drew around with longer nights for reading, the club continued to provide long works of fiction. The October 1941 Choice, *The Sun is My Undoing* by Marguerite Steen, was a one-thousand-page epic: a romantic historical saga of eighteenth-century Bristol and the slave trade, exploring the lives of prosperous shipping families and plantation owners during the Seven Years' War (1754-63) when Britain seized French and Spanish overseas territories to become the world's preeminent colonial power. Beginning in 1760, at the start of George III's reign, the novel opens when 'Every one was tired of war news; the first solemn months the ardours of recruiting were forgotten; the dramas of departing troops, of sentimental farewells, even of victorious returns, more or less exhausted.'[429] Marguerite Steen was a familiar name to the Book Society as author of 1934 choice *Matador*, a dramatic story of a Spanish bullfighter, and for celebrating 'the spirit of romance in modern fiction' in her 1933 critical study of the novels of Hugh Walpole. *The Sun is My Undoing* was grounded in Steen's childhood memories of stories at home amongst Liverpool shipping families and based on three years of solid writing and research in Bristol libraries, as the publicity pointed out. In interviews, Steen described writing the novel as 'an act of creative defiance' in wartime. Book Society readers might be forgiven for paling at the sight of this 444,000-word saga, George Gordon counselled in his review, but they could be assured it was a good read. 'Once launched, the reader will go on', George told members. *The Sun is My Undoing* was a bestseller on both sides of the Atlantic throughout the war.

For his part, Edmund continued to prioritise non-fiction. In the October 1941 list he reviewed a humanitarian account of wartime suffering in China (Joy Hamer's *Dawn Watch in China*) alongside Arthur Koestler's memoir of the French collapse (*Scum of the Earth*) and a lighter book of anecdotes by Charles Darwin's grandson, Bernard Darwin (*Pack Clouds Away*). Wading through a fog of depression and missing Claire, he was losing interest in everyday life, unable to gather himself up for the start of a new term. 'A considerable weariness attacks me every day,' Edmund wrote in his diary on 12 October, 'This heavy feeling may be caused by the continuation of the war, which envelops everything as with a sea of mud.' His daughter Clare was postponing her third year at Oxford due to stress and he was worried about his son John, now an ordinary seaman, 'reported to have gone into the submarines'.[430] Obliged to miss the November meeting in London because of term-time duties, Edmund was determined to get away early December. Jack's presence on the committee had helped rally them after losing Hugh, and Edmund looked forward to the meetings with him. Jack's contribution to the 1941 Committee's vision for society after the war, *Out of the People*, had garnered significant attention that year. Proposing devolution as the best model to organise a postwar democracy, *Out of the People* championed local knowledge and devolving power to the trade unions, the co-operative movement, and charities. 'I go to town tomorrow', Edmund wrote on the first day of December 1941, 'which is now a rare outing, and not so joyful as it might have been. It is always lively to meet J.B.P.', he added, 'he does not accept everything that is official, but is no grumbler.'

***

On 7 December 1941, 'a date that will live in infamy', as President Roosevelt declared in an address to Congress the next day, Japanese planes and submarines attacked Pearl Harbour, the US navy's pacific base on the Hawaiian island of Oahu, causing thousands of deaths and bringing the US into the war. Trying to process the shock of the news from his rooms in Merton, Edmund perceived 'a turn of events that I could not have feared when I was with my gentle and serious students there fifteen years ago', and his first thoughts were with Aki Hayashi.[431] 'Sylva suggests', he wrote with 'affectionate blessings' on Monday 8, 'and I agree, that you might possibly offer your services, if the opportunity arises, to the British Government – for example, there would be translating of the Japanese newspapers needed I imagine.'[432] Worrying for her safety, he copied out a new poem he'd submitted to the club's Christmas annual, 'The Two Books', to enclose with his letter:

> Come, tell me: of these two books lying here,
> Which most moves mind and heart to tenderness –
> The one approaching its three-hundredth year,
> The other a recruit, fresh from the press?

'She must have felt this new explosion with as deep horror as anyone', Edmund realised in his diary, 'she has brooded over the chance of such a thing for some time'.[433]

The next day, Edmund received an urgent note from Aki asking him to 'kindly write to anybody you think best what I am, & how I love England, etc, and not to be interned or anything of that kind'?[434] Spurred into action, Edmund sent a character reference to Rupert Hart-Davis, now an officer with the Coldstream Guards, to see what he could do. Rupert replied with concern on 11 December, 'I too had been thinking of her and hoping she was all right,' stating he had added a few lines to corroborate Edmund's letter and that he could get it to the Home Office through a fellow officer who was an MP. 'Let me know at once if all is not well with Hayashi,' Rupert added. 'I do hope this will do the trick. I think it will; nor can I think of better means immediately.'[435] Aki wrote to thank Edmund, apologising for giving him 'such a bother about me while you are so busy'.[436] She had to hand over all the maps in her possession and register as an enemy alien with the police, enduring years of racist abuse from neighbours who stole milk and eggs and pried into her mail. But Edmund and Rupert's influence would ultimately protect Aki from interment by the state. After the war, in 1949 when Aki was granted British citizenship, Edmund acknowledged her long suffering, writing 'I hope it means you can now find daily life a little easier in various ways.'[437]

* * *

Like Aki, members of the Book Society received a copy of Edmund's ode to books in their *Book Society Annual* that Christmas. With serious production problems becoming more apparent and the shortage of paper and labour meaning 'the most popular new books often go out of print as soon as they appear', the club promoted itself as a saving grace, still able to get the best new work out to readers, even if there was a delay.[438] The final selection of 1941 was Margaret Irwin's *The Gay Galliard*, the author's fourth Book Society choice. This portrayed Mary Queen of Scots as a modern heroine, 'more modern than any we have yet been given', as Sylvia approved in the club magazine. Irwin and her husband had been regulars at Sylvia's Hampstead parties before the war, and Irwin was pleased that the feminist aspects of her work – not often acknowledged in Hugh's reviews – might be noticed for a change. 'Oh & please Harold,' she wrote to her publisher, delighted by news of the selection, 'can I see the notice of it in the *Book Society News*? How blessed that it can never again be Hugh Walpole's'.[439]

The selection made *The Gay Galliard* a bestseller which went into several reprints the following year, absorbing over half of the publisher's total paper allowance for 1942 when paper tonnage was again restricted, this time to 37.5 percent of publishers' consumption of the last twelve months immediately prior to the war. It was an impossible balancing act for most businesses. As Irwin's publisher, Harold Raymond of Chatto and Windus, explained:

> It grows more and more difficult to keep within this quota because as time goes on we come to the end of our pre-war stocks of books, and consequently find that an increasing number of titles are clamouring to be reprinted and so are competing with new titles for that right.

'Whether I make the best use of my ration,' Raymond went on, 'I don't know; it is so very difficult to assess fairly the rival claims of the author, the reading public and the firm, whose chief consideration is to remain in being and to be ready to get into full swing again as soon as possible after the war. I have so far managed to avoid the biggest terror of all', he confessed 'Which is to have to say to an author "That new book of yours has been galloping along, but it has now got to stop, for I haven't a scrap of paper on which to print it".'[440]

The book industry was in crisis and the club would work more closely with publishers through the rest of the war, producing Book Society editions in collaboration with the trade that changed the club's remit as it took on a new, frontline, wartime service.

1940

138 September *The Earthly Paradise*, C. S. Forester
139 October *The Voyage*, Charles Morgan
140 November *Whiteoak Heritage*, Mazo de la Roche
141 December *English Saga (1840-1940)*, Arthur Bryant

1941

142 January *Kings' Masque*, Evan John
143 February *Into Battle: Winston Churchill's War Speeches*, Winston Churchill
144 March *For Whom the Bell Tolls*, Ernest Hemingway
145 April *The Story of J. M. B. (Sir James Barrie)*, Denis Mackail
146 May *The Bay*, L. A. G. Strong
147 June *Winged Words. Our Airmen Speak for Themselves*
148 July *The Earth is the Lords*, Taylor Caldwell
149 August *The Captain from Connecticut*, C. S. Forester
150 September *The Blind Man's House*, Hugh Walpole
151 October *The Sun is My Undoing*, Marguerite Steen
152 November *Mr Bunting at War*, Robert Greenwood
153 December *The Gay Galliard. The Love Story of Mary Queen of Scots*, Margaret Irwin

Chapter 9. CDL, 1942-43

Anna Karenina and the Ministry of Information

I

The symbol of 'Book Production War Economy Standard', designed by R. A. Maynard of George Harrap & Co.

The Book Production War Economy Agreement, designed to address the Ministry of Supply's demand for a forty percent cut in the book trade's consumption of resources, came into force on 1 January 1942. Establishing rules to reduce waste and usage of raw materials, it changed the feel and appearance of books produced in Britain for the rest of the war. Austerity books, so-called, bore the mark of the British lion and adhered to a minimum number of words per page, agreed sizes for margins and lay-outs, and a maximum weight for paper and binding boards. They were not popular. Some readers complained that the type was too small to read comfortably, while publishers exporting abroad feared the competitive advantage of American publishing houses, not facing the same kind of prohibitions. But the agreement answered some of the immediate supply problems facing the book trade: having to do more with less and keep up with demand.

By 1942 the number of new books being printed was less than half of what was published annually in the late 1930s, with reprints and new editions of existing books down almost one fifth. National labour shortages in printing, publishing, and bookbinding were disrupting schedules, leading to long delays at the print works and in warehouse packing departments. Millions of books had been destroyed in the bombing of Paternoster Row during the Blitz and, three years on, major book shortages ran nationwide, especially for the classics, with printers forced to salvage stereotypes and metal printing blocks (normally kept on hand for reprints and new editions) so zinc and copper rations were not reduced further.

In the national consciousness, the materials for bookmaking took on different meanings in wartime. According to the government, over eighty-five percent of paper usage nationally contributed to the war effort, either directly in industrial processes such as packing ammunition or insulating electric cables, or indirectly as in food packaging.[441] But the war machine needed more and a series of national salvage schemes for rags, bones, and paper galvanised the public to collect books and wastepaper for the war effort. Salvaged paper could make concrete runways, bomb washers, or cartridge boxes – 'Hurl your books at the foe' ran one official slogan.[442] In September 1942, alarmed by the indiscriminate pulping, the Publishers Association introduced a scheme to separate books for pulping from rare or re-usable ones better suited for redistribution to the forces, hospitals, or war-damaged public libraries. How many Book Society collections were donated for salvage in a spirit of patriotic duty, we'll never know.

In view of the challenges facing the industry, a Publishers' Advisory Committee to the government on 'special allocations of paper' was established in 1942 to try and keep books regarded as crucial to the war effort in print. Chaired by Sir Walter Moberly, trade publishers could appeal to this committee for additional paper from the Ministry's own supplies. Over half of requests were turned down: in the first six months of 1942 for instance, 154 requests were granted out of 384 applications.[443] The largest paper allocations made by the Moberly committee during the war went to keep technical and educational books in print, supporting titles like *Mathematics for the Million*, *Radio Handbook*, and *Vegetable Garden Displayed*, alongside dictionaries including *Cassell's English and German* and *English and French*, and medical and surgical titles *Gray's Anatomy*, *St. John Nursing Manual*, and *Surgery of Modern Warfare*. The war's bestsellers were technical and instructional books: 'books about engineering, and patching old clothes and making the most of your rations,' as Cecil Day-Lewis summarised in a 1944 review, 'books which help people practically to get more efficient at their work or adapt themselves to war conditions'.[444] In fiction, J. M. Dent's popular Everyman's Library (a cheap series reprinting world classics) benefited most from the Moberly pool. In one report, the only fiction title given paper was Dent's reprint of Gogol's *Dead Souls*, a comic satire critiquing serfdom in nineteenth-century Russia, said 'to reveal the Russian temperament so accurately that it produced an uproar in Russia when it was first published' according to Dent's dust jacket. More than one hundred of Everyman's reprint titles were out of print by 1942, despite booksellers having trebled their orders and the series' popularity with the forces and Prisoner-of-War organisations.[445] Presumably, *Dead Souls* was propped up by official government paper supplies in 1942 to give readers insight into Britain's new Soviet allies.

For the Book Society, 1942 was the first year in which the crisis in book production and supply really hit home. 'While the war lasts we must needs cut our book-cloth to suit the paper rationing,' the club cautioned in April, 'One month will be missed in 1942: that is, it will be an 11-book year as regards Book Society "choices".' Hoping to save on packing materials and wartime labour, they moved to a system of advance notice, asking readers to make their decisions and let them know ahead of distribution if they wanted to receive a recommended title instead of next month's chosen book. Further niceties of membership fell by the wayside. When the gummed paper used for the club's bookplates ran out, no more could be obtained. 'The book-plate for April and later months will perforce arrive ungummed,' the club explained, 'It can either be pasted in the monthly book, or else left loose in the end-papers, where it will still serve as a reminder to borrowers.' By November, the paper cartons that books were delivered in were restricted by Order of the Paper Control (except for copies going overseas), meaning the club could no longer undertake exchanges for accidental damage in the post. And while they could serve the existing membership, marketing and recruitment shifted gear. 'Because of paper rationing, The Book Society may soon have to institute a waiting list for membership,' they advised at the end of the year.[446]

II

The platform at Paddington station was packed as Cecil jostled onto the blacked-out train for Reading. Pushing past swarms of servicemen and personnel going back to RAF Harwell, he found a standing space tucked in by the heaving luggage racks at the end of the carriage and put down his wet umbrella. He was a little out of breath from the rush across town in the snow.

That day he'd sorted out several picture captions, squaring off the words to fit beneath the photographs; a fiddly job he liked doing, like the wordplay of sonnets. Since joining the Ministry of Information's Publications Division as chief copyeditor the previous year, Cecil had been part of a team which produced thrilling, visually attractive Official War Books that its Director, Australian-born journalist Robert 'Bob' Fraser, dubbed 'propaganda bestsellers'.[447] The phenomenal success of *The Battle of Britain* (first published March 1941, then in a cheap illustrated edition) followed by *Bomber Command* in October, meant more work pouring in. All through January, Cecil had been working nine-to-twelve-hour stints at his desk, juggling over twenty pamphlets and book projects on the go simultaneously, all needing to get through the MoI's tortuous admin before they could publish.

He was suffering after two nights half-sleep that week in a bunkbed in the icy basement of Senate House, and in theory had more work to do before leaving the office; but Cecil was desperate to get out of London, see Rosamond Lehmann, and share in her delight over Diamond Cottage. It had been torture not seeing her throughout that cold Christmas and hearing about her move second-hand, while he was with his own family in Devon. 'My own love…I wish we were going for a walk together and then having a huge tea and then going to bed and loving each other silly,' he'd written. 'I shall drown you with love when we meet, my beautiful girl.'[448]

Trying to ignore the bodies in the carriage around him, his mind travelled back to his Book Society reviews. It was irksome that the new Waugh book was still niggling him, interfering with his dreams about Rosamond. He'd get it out of the way early on this weekend, so he could focus on her.

> You were the magic answer, the sprite fire-fingered who came
> To lighten my heart, my house, my heirlooms; you are the wax
> That melts at my touch and still supports my prodigal flame
> ('The Lighted House' in *Word Over All*, 1943)

***

Cecil Day-Lewis lived for weekends with Rosamond Lehmann during the first half of 1942. He'd seen her less during the week – apart from the odd night together in Gordon Place, the small, rented house they'd shared since the previous September – after Rosamond had decided before Christmas that she needed a space in the country for her two children (Hugo and Sally, both boarders), asking her tenant to leave the cottage in Aldworth in Berkshire that she'd bought before the war. Their 'tremendous affair,' as Rosamond put it, which would last for the next nine years, was all-consuming and overwhelming. 'I felt completely married to him,' she later said, 'as he did to me.'[449] Cecil made only three weekends home to Mary and the children in Musbury in the first six months of 1942.

Cecil and Rosamond had circled each other for years. First meeting at their mutual friend Elizabeth Bowen's house five years earlier, Rosamond had visited Cheltenham afterwards to give a talk and stayed overnight at Box Cottage with the Day-Lewises; in 1938 they'd shared a platform at the crucial anti-fascist meeting at the Queen's Hall where Cecil had realised that he needed to relinquish party politics to preserve his poetry. Cecil's days in wartime London were awash with books and publishing schedules: knocking manuscripts into shape for the Ministry; dealing with authors, artists, and cartographers; reading new books in proof for the Book Society; squeezing poetry in here and there, plus making broadcasts for the BBC. But after inviting Rosamond to dinner sometime during May 1941, pleased by her review of his work in the *New Statesman* as 'a writer with a profound and happy experience of love,' his life in wartime London was radically transformed.[450] For Cecil, the beautiful, talented Rosamond Lehmann was a writing equal and her well-placed connections took him to life at the literary centre, helping him become part of the establishment. She was also a spirit to revive:

> But you were also the dead-beat traveller out of the storm
> Returned to yourself by almost obliterated tracks,
> Peeling off fear after fear, revealing love's true form.
> ('The Lighted House')

After she moved in with Cecil in 1941, Rosamond's second husband, Wogan Phillips, had threatened to divorce her (citing Cecil as co-respondent) and request custody of their children, pushing her into court proceedings to sue Wogan for divorce on grounds of his own adultery. She and Wogan had been married since 1928, at the peak of Rosamond's fame and run with the book clubs (all of her first six novels, published between 1927 and 1953, were American Book-of-the-Months or Book Society choices).[451] But they had been estranged since the war, both involved with other people. Cecil came after two marriages and a painful break-up with the writer Goronwy Rees (this ended dramatically in 1940 when Rosamond found out about his engagement to another woman through an announcement in *The Times*). Cecil's love and genuine interest in her writing was a tonic. 'I think I feel confidence in myself for the first time in my life' she wrote to a friend. 'I never thought it could happen, but he has given me this by the incredible goodness & patience of his love. You've no idea what a true, reliable, grown-up character he is.'[452]

***

Had it been up to him alone, Cecil would have returned the proofs of Evelyn Waugh's *Put Out More Flags* to the publisher with a firm rejection. Waugh was a snob and, it seemed to him, a budding apologist for right-wing Catholicism. Since the publication of Waugh's third travel book, *Waugh in Abyssinia* (1936) – a journalistic account of the Italian invasion of Ethiopia – he'd also shown himself to be a pro-fascist sympathiser. Cecil hated promoting Waugh's work and this new book that was equally offensive to both inner city evacuees and left-wing 'travellers' like himself. But the Book Society and its readers couldn't afford to ignore it. Waugh was a star and a comic bestseller, one of the best-paid authors of his generation, and this would make his third Book Society choice after *Black Mischief* and *Scoop*.

His new book was a product of active service. As an intelligence officer with the Royal Marines, Waugh had seen Allied failures and disorganisation first-hand, especially in Dakar (now Senegal, then French West Africa), where the Allies had tried to land General de Gaulle for the Free French in September 1940, and in Libya when the Axis powers retook Bardia in April 1941. Waugh began *Put Out More Flags* on the journey home by troop ship in July 1941, after his unit had assisted in the chaotic evacuation of Crete. The breakdown in discipline among the fleeing troops would stay with him. 'I have been in a serious battle,' he wrote to his wife Laura in June, 'and have decided I abominate military life.'[453] *Put Out More Flags* was set 'in that odd, dead period before the Churchillian renaissance, which people called at the time the Great Bore War'. Like *Scoop*, it satirised high society, exposing the pretensions of people 'who did well out of the war' and the foolishness of some early war talk:

> 'There will be no air attack on London. The Germans will never attempt the Maginot line. The French will hold on for ever, if needs be, and the German air-bases are too far away for them to be able to attack us.'[454]

Following a set of upper-class characters doing their best to avoid the Front and privations on the Homefront, the book rankled with Cecil in just about every way possible. There were comic scenes of confusion in the Ministry of Information, 'that gross mass of masonry,' as Waugh put it, contributing to the popular stereotype of the Ministry and the writers who sheltered there as shirkers, just as Graham Greene's short story, 'Men at Work', had done the previous year. In an early scene, left-wing poet Ambrose visits his publisher at the MoI to try and get taken on:

> 'What is your work, Geoffrey?'
>
> 'Well mostly it consists of sending people who want to see me on to someone they don't want to see. I've never liked authors - except of course,' he added, 'my personal friends. I'd no idea there were so many of them.'

Ambrose could have been based on Cecil, while the characters 'Parsnip' and 'Pimpernell' were clearly Auden and Isherwood, 'two great poets [...] who had recently fled to New York'. The mockery and supposed sell-out of the Auden gang was hard to stomach:

> 'What I don't see is how these two can claim to be *Contemporary* if they run away from the biggest event in contemporary history. They were contemporary enough about Spain when no one threatened to come and bomb *them.*'[455]

Jack Priestley had goaded Cecil at the last Book Society meeting, persuading him to take this on. At least Waugh's satire was so blunt that Cecil could mock the futility of his cartoon-like villains: those 'sinister off-stage figures, the poets Parsnip and Pimpernell, who represent all that Mr. Waugh finds most undesirable in contemporary poetry'. Smiling to himself, Cecil thought more lines through. Waugh's characters were 'a bit fusty and self-conscious at first,' he tried out. The style was typical of Waugh in the 1920s – 'an idiom compounded of effrontery, mateyness and bright young anarchism' but now a bit out-dated, Cecil thought:

> So everyone can be happy – everyone except the critic who remembers how *A Handful of Dust* revealed in Mr Waugh a satirical power which few could have suspected, a depth and imaginative acuteness of feeling which make his new book, for all its buoyancy and narrative charm, by contrast less estimable.[456]

No one would miss this as a barbed, unsubtle review. But in all fairness, Cecil felt, Waugh deserved it. The book was bitter and blind in its attacks, a world away from the gravitas of that month's choice, Austrian Hans Habe's account of the fall of France. *A Thousand Shall Fall* was 'certainly the most remarkable book yet produced by this war,' Cecil had told readers in that month's *Book Society News*. The Waugh was quite different. He had better things in him yet, Cecil would conclude.

III

March 1942 brought heavy snows to much of Britain, along with more food rationing and the reduction of coal, gas, and electricity supplies. In the press, there was concern about the Allies waning influence as the Axis powers advanced, along with horror stories seeping out from the Japanese prison camps.

As Cecil's leader on *Put Out More Flags* appeared in the club magazine, the selection committee were plunged into mourning with news of a second judge's death. But unlike the previous summer with the sudden death of Hugh Walpole, George Gordon's passing came as less of a surprise. George had been ill, largely bed-ridden, since before Christmas, and the judges had known that his cancer was seriously advanced. He hadn't made any Book Society meetings since the previous autumn, when he'd finished his three-year stint as Vice-Chancellor of Oxford, and they'd agreed to take his name off the selection committee for the February *Book Society News*. It was the first time he'd not been a part of it since the club began.

The late diagnosis robbed George of his retirement plans. 'These were the completion and publication of such writing as I have been able to do in the last 25 years, most of it still in MS,' as he wrote to a friend.[457] 'Time denied' George reflected, in his last note to Edmund.[458]

* * *

Edmund and Sylva were late to the funeral and had to squeeze into a space by the altar. Magdalen college chapel was packed, full to the brim on the last Saturday morning of term, before the students departed for Easter. The other judges couldn't attend due to travel restrictions and the university congregation looked 'only just alive,' Edmund wrote later that evening, 'the sad intellectual cast is oppressive'. Edmund was still struggling with his mother-in-law's company at home and her unconcealed antipathy for 'Oxford, literature etc.' 'I believe I am long suffering,' he wrote in his diary, '& am really bored beyond words at having this strange woman about the place.'[459] He was contemplating leaving for a Chair in Ankara, a position he'd been nominated for by the British Council. But there was Claire to think about, not to mention whether war would extend into Turkey, and he felt generally indecisive, wanting to pay heed to 'some of my brilliant sudden acceptances in the past'.

The afternoon of George's funeral was warm for early March. The aconites formed a golden carpet as the coffin was borne in stately procession through Fellows Garden and Addison's Walk, on past Holywell Mill to the graveyard. Edmund shuffled along with the mourners, graciously acknowledging the few muttered congratulations about his new book on *Thomas Hardy*. There was some chatter about George's literary remains, which the obituary notice in Friday's *Times* had suggested were substantial, prompting excitement over the 'books in his desk which only he regarded as unfinished'.[460] After his death, George's wife Mary would take these on, trusting friends with 'fit to print' lectures and typescripts, so that much of his writing was eventually published posthumously.[461] Mary edited a collection of George's letters herself, obscuring her contribution by publishing under her initials, 'M. C. G.', and worked on a biography for the rest of the war. 'Perhaps, after all, George Gordon would not have frowned upon a memoir written by his wife,' she wrote in the preface for the book published in 1945, 'supported by the vigilance and recollections of his friends, and founded on material provided, all unconsciously, by himself.'[462]

***

George Gordon's death left just four judges to carry on the selection committee. Jack Priestley was appointed chairman and managed the club with Cecil for the first half of 1942, alternating between them to review the chosen books of the month. Edmund and Sylvia were preoccupied, both struggling with personal problems. Edmund found himself giving way to depression in Oxford – 'not finding anything to set me to work, – I mean to take an interest' – appalled by the shift that spring to area bombing of German cities with the indiscriminate killing of civilians. 'I believe that those who are to carry out this task have been persuaded that they will only be destroying a kind of subhuman miscreants,' he reflected in his diary.[463] Turning down the Ankara position, he retreated into army lectures and examinations, obsessing about Claire being called up.

Sylvia meanwhile was overwhelmed with work and in keeping Robert afloat. Busy writing copy for her contribution on *English Children* to publisher William Collins's patriotic 'Britain in Pictures' series, she was also trying to protect Robert, whose alcoholism had worsened with the strain of war. Sylvia covered for him as best she could. 'Robert Lynd' she would mourn later after his death in 1949, 'for whom I had to do everything.'[464]

So, Cecil was forced to step up and take on more Book Society reading through 1942. In March, when his review of Waugh's *Put Out More Flags* appeared in the *Book Society News*, Cecil reviewed another three works of fiction including Warren Stuart's *The Sword and the Net*, a John Buchan-style action story about a 'good Nazi' ace pilot. For April, he recommended a further three novels: *Storm* by George R. Stewart was an unusual book about a meteorologist; then there was *The High Courts of Heaven*, an R.A.F. story about the Battle of Britain; along with a 950-page historical romp – *Miledi* – by Bradda Field, 'a lengthy course which neither she nor her heroine quite stays'. It was a lot on top of long hours at the MoI, but the Book Society helped him connect directly with readers, keep up with new authors, and promote trade books aiding the war effort. It was another type of war work for the writer, as he put it, 'still evading the draft'.[465]

Mid-May 1942, Mary, Cecil's wife, visited him in London for a weekend. He had barely been home to Devon since the start of that year and couldn't blame her for wanting to check up on him. He'd heard about the bombing of Exeter from her, which had shaken them all down in Musbury, and he was glad to see her to salve his conscience a little. Persuading Mary that his digs in Gordon Place were unsuitable – he couldn't have his wife staying in the house where he'd spent so much time with Rosamond Lehmann – he arranged for her to stay at Charles Fenby's flat nearby. Needing to prove how busy he was in the capital, he worked both days of the weekend, inviting Mary to an awful lunch in the Ministry canteen on Saturday – where there were poor rations as usual – before a revue and concert at the Albert Hall that evening. Sunday, he took her along to Broadcasting House, where she smiled with encouragement as he delivered his talk on British war artists. Mary's visit jolted Cecil into remorse, reminding him of his commitments to family life in Devon that Rosamond, the bombing, and the MoI had almost caused or allowed him to forget. 'Oh Rosamond, sweet, I do so want you to have a home of your own & to be there with you,' he wrote her, 'but we shouldn't make a success of it if we knew I had done it at the expense of my own family; either it would haunt me forever, or I should succeed in convincing myself that I had really done them no important harm - & lose what integrity I have left in the process.'[466]

***

That summer the club promoted more topical war-books. 1942 was the year of Japan's great advance, as the imperial army conquered enormous areas of Southeast Asia and went further into mainland China, with Australia also coming under attack. A series of Allied defeats through the first half of the year saw tens of thousands of Allied soldiers captured as European colonies fell in rapid succession: Hong Kong, Borneo, Malaya. The shocking defeat of Singapore to General Yamashita in just a week, with tens of thousands of British, Australian, and Indian soldiers taken prisoner, was especially devastating. 'Sometimes now the name of Hitler reappears!' Edmund noted, surveying the morning papers. 'But he is not the fashion. Something bigger than even his queer genius is occupying our central mind. The East is on the move and a whole period of race history is in process of collapse or revival.'[467]

As a former communist, Cecil had long been interested in books about China. Before the outbreak of war, he'd praised Nobel laureate Pearl Buck's *The Patriot* for its sensitive handling of 'the psychological and physical clash between Chinese and Japanese,' remarking on how the book refused to be 'blurred, over-complicated, or in any way stampeded by the violence which is latent in its subject'. Cecil had noticed a glut of novels about China by western writers during the war years and he was sensitive to their tendency to 'occidentalise' their characters, as he put it, 'in moments of excitement'.[468] In March 1942, for instance, as readers processed the military disaster of surrender to the Japanese in Singapore, Cecil recommended Robert Payne's historical novel *Singapore River* specifically because it didn't orientalise the Chinese; he'd been pleased to see Lin Yutang's new novel, *A Leaf in the Storm*, fall onto his desk that spring.

Lin Yutang was one of the best-known Chinese writers in the West. Trained as a linguist, he'd studied in Shanghai, Beijing, Harvard, and Leipzig, renowned internationally as a translator and populariser of Chinese philosophy, culture, and myth. Yutang started publishing in English in 1935 with the bestselling *My Country and My People*, after meeting Pearl Buck in Shanghai who introduced him to her second husband, publisher Richard Walsh, head of the American firm of John Day. Yutang's new book, already published to acclaim in the US, where he now lived, was an epic 'Novel of War-Swept China.' His earlier works were widely regarded as shortcuts to understanding Chinese culture and temperament. For members of the Book Society, this novel brought the Pacific war home.

In his lead review for the club that May, Cecil empathised with western readers' sense of the complexity of the Pacific theatre: 'so vast, so distant are the battle-lines of the East, with their myriads of fighters, that no account of them can give us more than a bird's-eye view of the struggle as a whole'. But Lin Yutang did, it seemed to Cecil, what only great fiction writers could do: animated the epic through the specific, allowing readers to feel the effects of a country at war through imaginative sympathy and identification with a specific group of characters. The book showed readers 'unforgettable scenes of China at war':

> We see the bombing of cities, the migration of millions; young students, used to motor-cars, trudging thousands of miles across mountains and valleys; the avenging ferocity of the Chinese guerrillas; [...] the work of relief amongst the orphans left by the Japanese along their withering path.

A Leaf in the Storm was recommended as a timely insight into 'the voice of a great ally'. Cecil identified an 'under-emphasis' of tone in the book that would appeal broadly, picking out a scene where an elderly Chinese leader describes the brutality of the 'damned Japs' as so 'ungentlemanly' that 'you lose all fear of them'. Cecil's review chimed with Churchill's public emphasis on dignity and resilience after the heavy losses and surrenders in the Pacific. 'Here is the moment to display the calm and poise combined with grim determination which not so long ago brought us out of the very jaws of death,' Churchill had said after the fall of Singapore in February 1942. 'Here is another occasion to show—as so often in our long history—that we can meet reverses with dignity and renewed accessions of strength.'[469] Cecil saw plenty of memos on the necessity of keeping up civilian morale in the MoI. *A Leaf in the Storm* was an opportunity to remind readers that they were not alone: their Chinese allies shared a down-to-earth stoicism that would have gone down well with his old drinking buddies in the Red Lion.

***

June 1942, readers received a dual choice from the Book Society. The two books were shorter than normal and issued at less than the usual wartime price for novels of eight shillings and threepence, thanks in one case to the larger print run enabled by the club's bulk order, and in the other to the paper reserves of the MoI. The first book, *The Last Enemy*, was Richard Hillary's autobiographical account of serving as a fighter pilot; the second was John Steinbeck's *The Moon is Down*.

The Last Enemy began in Oxford before the war and moved through RAF training to the Battle of Britain, where Hillary was shot down over the North Sea three weeks into combat, and badly injured. Hillary paints a candid view of the laziness of middle-class undergraduates at Oxford before the war (himself included), bedazzled by 'their literary idols' and 'unquestioning allegiance to Auden, Isherwood, Spender and Day Lewis,' with whom 'they affected a dilettante political leaning to the left'.[470] The second half of the book focussed on the author's convalescence, describing the radical plastic surgery he received on his nose, lips and eyelids. Conscious of the many wartime adventure stories now being published, Jack Priestley emphasised the book as the work of 'a real writer,' 'something more than an account of a fighter pilot's life, something more than a piece of wartime documentary writing'.[471] His words were to be prophetic. *The Last Enemy* would go on to be one of the most popular titles of the war, 'grimly realistic' in its treatment of the war theme, as Cecil later commented.[472]

Steinbeck's *The Moon is Down* was a short propaganda novel, designed to encourage hope and resistance in the occupied countries of Europe. Backed by the MoI, Cecil felt a conflict of interest with this one, so Edmund provided a sympathetic review for the club. While some critics felt Steinbeck was too soft on the Nazis, Edmund underscored the humanity and complexity of Steinbeck's portrayal of nations at war, acknowledging the writer's unwillingness to demonise Germany. 'He does not make his invaders one and all a series of savage brutes; nor does he invest all the invaded with showy heroism,' Edmund counselled the Book Society.[473]

But with no resolution in sight, some readers were wearying of contemporary war books, and the glut on the club's lists that summer threatened to overwhelm even the most news-conscious reader. Part of the club's Recommended section had been given over to 'The World at War' (books of Hitler's and Churchill's speeches were included), while images of Hurricanes and Spitfires now regularly filled the pages of the *Book Society News*, with ads for signed prints of the 'RAF in action' carried for the Print Society. Back in May, Cecil had recommended Crichton Porteous's *The Farm by the Lake* as a 'simple and refreshing' country story about Derbyshire life for 'those who are looking for an antidote to war-preoccupation'. He'd perceived 'a decline in the general standard of novel-writing' since the war began; three years in, the war had 'nipped much young talent in the bud.'

'Many of our best novelists have been silent since the war,' Cecil argued in an article in 1944: 'E. M. Forster, Aldous Huxley, R. C. Hutchinson.'[474] Including Rosamond Lehmann in this list, Cecil teased her to write 'a happy book': 'a book like your eyes and your smile and your voice when you are with me'.[475] 'But this probably can't be done,' he acknowledged.

July's choice was Canadian writer Hugh MacLennan's *Barometer Rising*. This was a historical romance, thus different to what they'd sent out in June – but again a story of war and real-life disaster. It was set in the days leading up to and following the notorious Halifax Explosion in Nova Scotia in 1917, when a ship crammed with high explosives had blown up in the harbour, causing what was at that point 'the most devastating explosion of all time'. The book's Canadian setting made it relatively unusual for Book Society readers, something MacLennan pointed out in his foreword, declaring that there was 'as yet no tradition of Canadian literature,' and Cecil stressed the unusual geography to spike readers' interest in the *Book Society News*.[476] Nova Scotia was 'a locale so little exploited in fiction that we get no sense of reading just another novel in the period of the Great War,' he tried to assure them. The judges had plumped for another war-themed historical novel for their next choice: Norman Collins's *Anna*, set in the Franco-Prussian war and Siege of Paris. After that came James Lansdale Hodson's *War in the Sun*, essentially a notebook of war observations and impressions from the Middle East, India, Burma, and West Africa. This was 'one more of the kind of war books which truly belong to this actual date,' Edmund explained. It was becoming hard for the selection committee to balance the lists, with genuinely escapist reading in such short supply.

IV

After fire-practice, Edmund caught the train down to London to see Aki before the judges' meeting. 'Proofs for Book Society selection come along in fair number' he noted on the back of some club paperwork that November (his late 1942 diary is preserved as various unbound leaves, reused memos, and scraps of paper). 'But types of new book are, on this evidence, very few and transitory.' The fourth winter of war was approaching, and Edmund felt himself 'ill prepared for it. But the general acquiescence in a long war has its effect.'[477] He suggested to Aki they meet on the Heath that day rather than Farringdon Road. 'Book-hunting is not so good as in the old days,' he wrote her, what with forgeries starting to work their way into the depleted rare books market.[478] He'd just met a man who'd been offered one or two duds in London. 'Queer,' he acknowledged, 'with a world war all round.'[479]

Edmund had recently been part of a broadcast on war poetry to India ('George Orwell as chairman, & Herbert Read and William Empson among the speakers'), and had news for Aki that Orwell might have some work for her with the BBC's foreign broadcasting service. 'Don't be afraid of it', he counselled, 'you will find him and others very friendly.'[480] His son John, meanwhile, had his commission in the Navy but was 'yet undecided what to try for with it,' while Claire had finally been 'swallowed up' by the Army, stationed in Derby despite holding a teaching job in a recognised school.[481] 'The policy is to keep education going,' he grumbled as he and Aki stomped across the Heath, circumventing the trenches. 'And here she is on some technical point driven off to wash dishes or sweep huts.' Worried that the 'wild and rapid freedom' of army life would be too much for her, Edmund was sinking into depression, mourning Claire's 'Black Absence.'[482] He couldn't reveal to Aki his plans to divorce Sylva so he could remarry.

When he finally got to the meeting, Edmund found the selection committee delighted by plans for a special club edition of *War and Peace*, going out to members that Christmas. Unobtainable in Britain for many months, with two of the three English translations out of print, the BBC's dramatized radio version of *War and Peace* broadcast during the Battle of Stalingrad had stimulated public demand. The club's special would be attractively produced, 'bound in cream vellum bookcloth over flexible board,' they advised, 'with lettering and symbolic design in gold-leaf, and with burnished tops for the pages'. As the Battle of Stalingrad wore on and the Soviet counter-offensive began that November, the book's renewed topicality, grandeur, and humanity was obvious. It was 'Russia's – and perhaps the world's – greatest novel,' Jack Priestley would affirm to the club. The huge quantity of paper required for *War and Peace* meant one combined monthly choice for January and February in the new year. This was to be *Assignment in Brittany* by Helen MacInnes, a 'first-class adventure-story,'

Cecil said, even if it was a little far-fetched with the central character, a British officer, impersonating a French soldier planted in Vichy France to report on enemy movements after Dunkirk. The book had value in its portrayal of the French resistance, Cecil would advise readers, telling us 'more about that spirit than many of the journalistic or semi-historical books that have been published since June, 1940'.

***

The canteen in the Ministry of Information was emptying out, the afternoon shadows starting to lengthen, as Rosamond Lehmann waited for Cecil to appear. She'd come up to town to try and see him before the Christmas holidays and to steal some time alone together; the children had already broken up from school so she couldn't stay overnight at the flat. Travelling to see Cecil meant shirking one of her neighbour's fundraising luncheons for the armed forces and a host of domestic duties – wood-chopping, scrubbing, hens – that kept her in Aldworth 'tied here, an exhausted prisoner'.[483] But she needed to apologise for last weekend. Her divorce was going through, and she wanted to marry Cecil, just 'to live with him & look after him, and build mutual responsibilities, etc etc. In fact what women do want with the person they completely love & trust.'[484]

Cecil had told her that he believed they 'could make a success of living together,' 'and, oh Rosamond, sweet,' he wrote, 'I do so want you to have a home of your own & to be there with you.' But he hadn't told his wife about them yet, and Rosamond was mindful of not pushing too hard. The intensity and strain of their relationship was starting to test them. 'Darling, please don't think by "obsessed" I meant anything like that,' Cecil had written to apologise last Sunday, '<u>I</u> felt myself too much involved with <u>you</u>,' he went on, 'I'm so terribly afraid of hurting you, giving you more pain and regret than happiness.' 'And I certainly don't want you to feel that I'm fussing about your writing.'[485]

'I am very good three quarters of the time, & then I am very bad,' Rosamond had explained to their mutual friend, Laurie Lee, a new colleague in Cecil's editorial section at the MoI, 'and I am terrified of these crises coming quicker & quicker like capitalist wars, till disintegration is complete'.[486]

Stirring the coffee absentmindedly, Rosamond went back to her notebook, pulling her long trench coat around her for warmth. Her pen scurried across the page as the long passages of dialogue flowed freely and she paused only briefly, rarely going back to re-read what she'd written. A couple of wartime stories for her brother John's *New Writing* periodical had kept her busy over the last few months and she'd just started a new story, told like the last two by an inquisitive child called Rebecca. But a new, older character, Sibyl Jardine, was taking over the plot, and she thought she might have enough to develop this into her next novel. Mrs Jardine was a woman with a past, based loosely on Ménie Muriel Dowie, a New Woman writer and mother of Rosamond's first suitor, outcast from society after being divorced by her first husband and then marrying his best friend. Cecil had suggested *The Ballad and the Source* as a title, and she'd dedicate the book to him when it came out. In her mind's eye, Rosamond could hear the glamorous Sibyl defending her decision to run away from her husband, provoking the wrath of society by abandoning her first child as she did so:

> 'Sometimes', she said, 'the source is vitiated, choked. Then people live frail, wavering lives, their roots cut off from what should nourish them. That is what happens to people when love is betrayed – murdered.'[487]

Rosamond was enjoying this character and her melodramatic narrative but wondered vaguely if she'd 'produced a monster'.[488] No doubt they'd say Mrs Jardine was herself. 'Convention is another name for the habits of society,' she wrote carefully. 'When a habit is bad it should be broken. A bad marriage is the most detrimental, most vicious of habits – and one of the most difficult for a man or a woman to break.'[489]

***

In his study off the porch, Cecil sat down at his desk to contemplate the letter he'd written Rosamond before he and Laurie left London for the weekend in Musbury. 'What worries me more than my own situation and the future of my family even,' he'd written, 'is that – if I try to keep you, as I want to, by loving you more tenderly, more understandingly – I may destroy your chance of marrying again, of the security and companionship you could have, and yet still not succeed in giving you what you want and expect from me.'[490] The letter went on: 'I'm often so deathly tired now [...] – no stamina, no emotional reserves to face those bad hours at night when a demon seems to enter you and makes you say cruel, stabbing things to me in a voice I can't recognise, & a demon comes in to me and makes me just as bad.' Cecil folded it back in half and stuffed it into an envelope. He'd post it tomorrow.

Turning back to his draft introduction to *Anna Karenina* for J. M. Dent, he read back over his words. The Book Society was to receive another Tolstoy special edition that summer, published by the club by arrangement with Dent: a one-volume edition of Rochelle S. Townsend's popular 1912 translation, accompanied by a new introduction from C. Day Lewis. This was clearly written through the prism of his own love affair. 'In Anna Karenina, we have a character with great potentialities either for good or evil,' Cecil wrote, 'a woman of extraordinary beauty, vivacity, and charm; a personality so strong that, though for chapter after chapter she does not appear upon the scene at all, she still seems to be holding the centre of the stage.' But she was a 'phantasy-builder,' Cecil judged, 'the type of person who creates around himself a fictious world, more pleasant, more flattering, more amenable than the real one,' suffused by a 'warped love' that transformed her passion 'into a jealous demon.' So Anna is doomed to be 'for ever dissatisfied,' he summed up. 'She cannot accept real life on its own terms,' 'doomed now to destroy herself, and Vronsky with her.'[491] The classic book was 'a tragi-comedy, like life itself,' he'd tell Book Society readers when the choice was announced.[492] 'Romantic love [...] should be bracketed with gunpowder as man's most disastrous invention,' he'd written Rosamond.[493]

***

Following *Assignment in Brittany* and Kate O'Brien's *The Last of Summer* at the start of 1943, the judges selected *The Two Marshals* for April, historian Philip Guedalla's biography of Francois Bazaine and Henri Petain, a study of France's defeats in 1870 and 1940 respectively. The next choice (covering May to June, because of the paper shortages) was C. S. Forester's *The Ship*. Forester was well-known and loved by club readers, and *The Ship* was an exciting account of naval warfare, focussed on a British warship trying to break Mussolini's battle fleet and stranglehold on Malta. '[T]his time it is not the history of Napoleon's day that he makes live for us,' Sylvia Lynd admired in her review, 'but the history of our own.' The book was dedicated 'with the deepest respect to the officers and ship's company of H. M. S. Penelope,' whom Forester had stayed with for three weeks in 1942 to gather up-to-date material. Like *The Last Enemy*, *The Ship* would become one of the most popular novels of the war.

The club's special edition of *Anna Karenina* was sent out to readers in July 1943, kept on hold as a 'floating volume,' the judges explained, 'held ready for any month when a substitute for a normal Choice might be needed in these abnormal times'. The disruption they had feared over the last year or so to their services had finally caught up with them, as the *Book Society News* explained:

> In a period when many fewer new titles are published, and the vagaries of wartime production sometimes cause a future month to be particularly thin in outstanding new books, it is also possible that once in a while, our Committee may find no potential Choice which can be ready for a given month. That is now the case in regard to early July, 1943, when we shall already have waited 6 weeks between distributions.[494]

The fine edition of *Anna Karenina*, produced as a companion volume to 1942's *War and Peace*, was marketed 'as a Book Society Special to fill a wartime gap'. Cecil's 'new and penetrating Introduction' was advertised as a selling point, along with attractive endpapers in two-colour designed by artist Eric Fraser, purple vellum bookcloth and gold-leaf lettering, plus a bookmark for the readers' ease listing principal characters and family groups. 'As with *War and Peace*,' the club noted, 'the Book Society does not presume to "chose" *Anna Karenina*.' But like *War and Peace*, this was another classic now virtually unobtainable, a superb novel 'impregnated with Tolstoy's remarkable vitality and acute understanding of human nature'.

By now, Cecil and Rosamond were two years in, and Cecil moved away from the bitterness of his Introduction in this second appreciation for the club, leading instead with a nostalgic reference to the pre-war Greta Garbo film version. 'Garbo's Anna,' Cecil remembered, was 'smiling, vivacious, full of charm and caprice, perfectly yet dangerously poised on the glittering crest of love, admired, ardent and vulnerable as a spray of blossom against a darkening sky – and then the storm beating down and the blossom ruined.' He and Rosamond had passed beyond the 'jealous demon' of his Introduction. And he would dedicate his new book of poems to her to make amends.

***

Early September 1943, with the Allies landing in mainland Italy and the Germans still falling back on the Russian front, Cecil Day-Lewis's *Word Over All* was published by Jonathan Cape. Dedicated to Rosamond Lehmann, the slim volume was a public affirmation of their relationship, beginning with new love poems she'd inspired (there were also some older ones he'd written for former lover Billie Currell), followed by more poetry on the continuing war (some reprinted from Cape's 1940 limited edition of *Poems in Wartime*). Reviews were good, confirming Day-Lewis's rising establishment status and broadening popularity. 'Mr Day-Lewis has emerged from his entanglement of ideas and political preoccupations,' Richard Church wrote in *The Listener*. 'He is now fully himself. It is an impressive self, and likely to make a permanent mark on the history of English poetry.' 'It is because Mr Day-Lewis has matured, while his compeers, Auden and Spender, have not', G. W. Stonier opined in the *New Statesman*, 'that his new volume makes a more substantial appeal.'[495] Poetry was still selling surprisingly well, in numbers that would have staggered any publisher in peacetime, and Cecil had a theory for this:

> Good poetry, even more than fiction, has that quality of detachment (not the same thing as escapism), of being concerned with deeper truths and more permanent realities, which fortifies us against the unnatural stress we are undergoing by helping us to see it in perspective.[496]

Mary Day-Lewis received a copy of *Word Over All* through the post on 10 September with a personal inscription written inside the cover (before the printed dedication to Rosamond): 'Mary, with my love, Cecil, September 1943.' The autumn schedule was busy for the MoI's publishing division, and what with sharing a platform at the Wigmore Hall with Edmund and Louis MacNeice for the United Aid to China Fund, Cecil didn't make time to go home to Brimclose and see Mary until the end of October. He wrote two letters in advance, finally telling her about his relationship with Rosamond, offering to divide himself and his time and maintain their marriage until the boys had left home. Rosamond's divorce was coming through, and perhaps she was right that in being open with Mary he would feel less compromised, preventing, as he'd acknowledged to Rosamond, 'the rot you felt setting in on you'.[497]

It is out at last –

The truth that fevered my cheek and frostily glassed
My eyes against you: a creeping
Incurable disease, it passed
Into your heart from mine while we were sleeping.
('Married Dialogue' in *Poems 1943-1947*, 1948)

Mary enjoyed a close friendship with Barbara Cameron, a neighbour who had supported her through Cecil's earlier affair with Billie Currall. During the war, with both of their husbands away, this friendship had developed into something more (Cecil worried privately to Rosamond about his own part in this relationship, 'thinking there must have been some grave defect in myself which turned her that way'.)[498] Cecil's public betrayal was painful for Mary, but she had the boys, her relationship with Barbara, and life in Musbury to focus on, and she preferred Cecil's double life to divorce. 'Peace', she wrote in her diary after his visit that October 1943.[499] She would redirect his mail care of 'The Honourable Mrs R. N. Philipps' through the rest of the war, while his visits to Brimclose remained infrequent.[500]

***

Autumn 1943, Jack Priestley and Sylvia Lynd led on club choices, pleased, four years in, that quality works were finally coming out from writers well-known before the war. André Maurois's *Call No Man Happy* was an entertaining autobiography by an 'international celebrity and pillar of Anglo-French entente,' Priestley guided. Storm Jameson's *Cloudless May*, a powerful novel of France in 1940, was 'illuminated by pity and understanding'. It was 'certainly the author's best book' according to Sylvia.

They Were Sisters, Dorothy Whipple's first book since the outbreak of war, was selected for November 1943, another quiet triumph making Whipple's third Book Society choice to date. 'Sound, sensitive but unpretentious,' as Priestley told readers in the *Book Society News*. Set in an idyllic pre-war countryside where the ramifications of 'world unrest' and antisemitism are simmering but not fully understood, *They Were Sisters* showed how private lives could be disrupted by far-off political events. But unlike Elizabeth Bowen's *The Death of the Heart*, with which it shared a similar sense of foreboding, *They Were Sisters* was more bittersweet for knowing the full extent of what had been lost:

> She stood in the orchard. The sun had sunk out of sight, but the sky was banded with yellow behind the great elms on her right. On her left the moon was a pale china globe waiting to have its light turned on. This lovely world, she thought, and alas! So threatened. This time next year, William said, they'd be at war.[501]

Focussed on three charismatic sisters, the novel addressed domestic violence and made a case for reforming divorce law, pointing out the inequities and binds that married women could still find themselves in, as opposed to men. 'Why should he be able to divorce me because I won't go out to him when I can't divorce him because he won't come home to me?', asks Vera, one of the sisters. It was an absorbing, vaguely escapist and ultimately comforting plot from a Book Society favourite; perfect for long evenings in the fifth drawn-out winter of war.

Cecil was keen on December Choice, Nigel Balchin's semi-autobiographical thriller *The Small Back Room*. Like Balchin's first novel, *Darkness Falls from the Air*, which was set during the Blitz, *The Small Back Room* was 'developed with power and persuasive skill', bound to be popular with readers. Balchin was a fellow civil servant, based at the Ministry of Food, and this was an 'unusual novel', Cecil confirmed, about a secret war-research department, focussed upon the dilemmas of weapons researcher, Sam Rice, tasked with investigating a new type of bomb that German aircraft were dropping over Britain. Balchin wrote with particular insight, according to Cecil, from 'the bitter taste of experience in his description of the back-stairs work behind the back-room boys'. But more than that, the book was about compromise and ambiguity as much as heroics: the inevitability of mediocrity. '"The good chaps went and were killed and the crooks got away with it. I just stayed put" is his summing up,' Cecil took away from the novel. As he elaborated in his Book Society review:

> A few go all out for the side on which the bread is buttered: complete egoist, natural opportunists – whether they become, in the legal sense of the term, crooks, depends upon their luck too. The rest of us, the great majority, oscillate uneasily between principle and advantage, between alternatives which never seem clear-cut, between courses whose totals of good and evil cancel each other out.

1942

154	January	*A Thousand Shall Fall*, Hans Habe, trans. by Norbert Guterman
155	February	*H. M. Pulham, Esquire*, John P. Marquand
156	March	*Put Out More Flags*, Evelyn Waugh
157	April	*Musk and Amber*, A. E. W. Mason
158	May	*A Leaf in the Storm: A Novel of War-Swept China*, Lin Yutang
159	June	*The Last Enemy*, Richard Hillary
160		+ *The Moon is Down*, John Steinbeck
161	July	*Barometer Rising*, Hugh MacLennan
	August	[No selection]
162	September	*Anna*, Norman Collins
163	October	*War in the Sun*, James Lansdale Hodson
164	November	*The Song of Bernadette*, Franz Werfel, trans. by Ludwig Lewisohn
165	December	*War and Peace*, Leo Tolstoy, trans. by Louise and Aylmer Maude

1943

166	January + February	*Assignment in Brittany*, Helen McInnes
167	March	*The Last of Summer*, Kate O'Brien
168	April	*The Two Marshalls*, Philip Guedalla
169	May + June	*The Ship*, C. S. Forester
170	July	*Anna Karenina*, Leo Tolstoy, trans. by Rochelle S. Townsend
171	August	*Call No Man Happy*, André Maurois, trans. by Denver and Jane Hastings Lindley
172	September + October	*Cloudless May*, Storm Jameson
173	November	*They Were Sisters*, Dorothy Whipple
174	December	*The Small Back Room*, Nigel Balchin

Chapter 10. Edmund, 1944-5

Persuasion at the Dorchester hotel

I

Book Society special edition of *Persuasion*. Choice 183, December 1944, with an introduction by Edmund Blunden.

During Valentine's weekend February 1944, Edmund and Claire, following legal advice, stayed overnight at the Dorchester hotel. The 'Little Blitz' was terrorising London and the Southeast as the Luftwaffe retaliated to American bombing and the RAF's continued pounding of Berlin (stories were getting out of havoc in the streets as thousands of Berliners fled to the countryside on foot). The Dorchester, with its reinforced concrete, was known as one of the safest places in London, and several members of the government had taken rooms there, as well as General Eisenhower and his staff, planning the Normandy landings. For Claire and Edmund, their fourth anniversary coincided with her leave, and Edmund could no longer keep up a double life. 'I have resolved on taking a step which should enable you to bring these difficulties and the unhappy situation as a whole to an end,' he wrote Sylva afterwards, enclosing the hotel bill as official evidence. 'If you could cause enquiries to be made at that hotel, I believe you could obtain further evidence which would lead to your being able to take action and allow us both to begin things again in our own paths...'[502]

Since the previous autumn, Sylva had been training as a bookseller's apprentice at Sanders in Oxford and was taking in work for MGM. Conscious of Edmund's long-term absence she received his news graciously, declaring she would not stand in the way of his happiness, and would begin divorce proceedings. She wrote to Claire separately, wishing 'that all may go smoothly', advising that 'if you can get out of that Derby circus and live a Christian life, and become a devoted mother, then I think the sun may shine on you both'.[503] How to get Claire out of the army was indeed their next challenge, Edmund admitted to Siegfried Sassoon, revealing they'd considered the obvious and were 'prepared to try it and risk all the "disgrace".' Siegfried however cautioned that would be a mistake, involving them 'both in worries and conflicts which I dread. You must both cling to the happiness which you have,' he counselled, 'beset though it be by the damnable circumstances of the war. I *can't* believe that Germany will hold out beyond the autumn.'[504]

Not quite fifty, Edmund was throwing caution to the wind that new year, having also resigned from his Merton fellowship in Oxford with effect from January 1944 to return to a literary career. The routines of academic life had disconnected him from his roots as a rural, nature poet. Moving back into his sister-in-law's home in Tonbridge while waiting for the divorce to come through (recalling a decade earlier when Annie had supported him during his divorce from Mary), Edmund pursued work on a biography of Shelley. 'It's good – very good – to know you've returned to your native country, where undergraduates cannot plague you,' Rupert Hart-Davis wrote him that spring.[505] Edmund's *Cricket Country* was due out with Collins in April and destined to be a classic, Rupert reassured him, 'The book is real balm for a war-bruised mind.' 'People are glad I suspect to receive something which is not written allegedly in a jeep about jeeps,' Edmund agreed.[506] A new collection of poems, *Shells by a Stream* – dedicated 'To Claire with devotion' – would appear in October. This would include a heartfelt tribute to Claire's ability to restore Edmund to life:

And make the colourless words look fair
With your resource of love, and love's all-seeing skill
('The Gift: For C.M.P')

***

As preparations for the liberation of Europe proceeded behind closed doors through the first half of 1944, anticipation for the Second Front built on the street. Allied traffic streamed down to the south coast, amassing in the port of Southampton, while tens of thousands of workers were redeployed on top-secret construction projects creating floating harbours to be towed across the Channel, along with an undersea pipeline between the Isle of Wight and Cherbourg to supply fuel to the invading armies in northwest France. After the successes in North Africa and southern Europe in 1943, the possibility of peace and a world beyond the war was starting to seem credible. As Edmund advised in the *Book Society News*, recommending E. Amy Buller's *Darkness Over Germany* – a well-researched book about pre-war German attitudes in the liberal minority – the author's 'knowledge is now usefully at the service of all who are able to contemplate the post-war period'.

The Book Society began the fifth winter of war with a flurry of Allied choices. The January-February choice was a long American novel by Pulitzer-prize winning John P. Marquand. Written 'For The Reader Who Takes His Fiction Seriously,' as Marquand wrote in the Preface, *So Little Time* was 'an attempt to depict certain phases of contemporary life'. Already successful in the States thanks to the Book-of-the-Month club, *So Little Time* offered a melancholy portrait of America in 1940-41, taking readers back to the early years of the war and the run-up to Pearl Harbour. It was 'immensely readable and likeable,' Jack Priestley pointed out in his review, drawing readers' attention to powerful scenes such as when the hero, Jeffrey, first hears about the London Blitz at a party when someone puts on the radio:

> 'This-is London.' It had been London for just a moment. Jeffrey had been conscious of the planes and the antiaircraft, although there had not been a sound. He could feel his own utter insignificance and the imminence of danger all around him, although the night was clear October moonlight, beautiful, and very still.[507]

'There are times when we are made to feel that America itself is the central character in the chronicle', Jack perceived. The book made poignant reading for British and commonwealth readers contemplating America's role in the war, now looking to General Eisenhower as Supreme Allied Commander for the invasion of Nazi-occupied Europe. 'The battles in France will surely be appalling – And is the outcome certain – for adequate success?' Siegfried Sassoon asked Edmund that May. Sassoon's home and village of Heytesbury in Wiltshire had been given over to 'blooming Americans' (they had nearly sixty using the house) preparing for the Normandy landings. 'I watch the young Americans of the Armoured Group practising baseball among their huts outside the garden hedge, and wonder where they will be in a few weeks time,' Sassoon confided in Edmund, 'while I, an elderly civilian shall be pacing up and down among my peonies.'[508]

For March the club chose *Other Men's Flowers*, an anthology of poetry quoting nearly two hundred and fifty poems whole or in part. The book's two-tone typography on the dust jacket called attention to the word 'Flowers': 'anthology' comes from the Greek 'anthologia,' translated literally as 'flower-gathering'. The poems themselves were not difficult according to the judges: 'Nearly everything is here that the occasional reader of English poetry remembers or misremembers,' the club magazine pointed out. But the 'flowers' had been picked by Field-Marshall Lord Wavell, an early war hero who, as Commander in Chief of the Middle East, had with his troops defeated the Italians in North Africa in 1941. Wavell was then appointed Commander-in-Chief in India, responsible for the defence of Burma, and since September 1943 had been Governor General and Viceroy of India, tasked with organising the plan for Indian self-governance after the war. The compiler himself was the chief interest, Sylvia admitted in her review, for 'This, above everything else, is the anthology of a man of action.' Poetry should be memorable and written to be recited out loud, Wavell admonished, 'and the chief fault he finds with much contemporary poetry is that it cannot be remembered,' Sylvia explained. The anthology was a personal celebration of Anglophone poets and a call for poetry as action. 'To speak verse aloud because the exhilaration of the moment calls for it, that is clear proof that he loves it,' Sylvia wrote:

> He has frequently declaimed verse while on manoeuvres, while waiting in battle for planned events to unroll into action, while driving a car or riding a horse or travelling by train.

It was 'altogether a delightful book,' Sylvia concluded, 'and I hope every child who can read will be given the pleasure and excitement of it'.

The April and May-June club selections focussed readers' minds on the wider world at war. April's choice, *Indigo* by Christine Weston, was 'a balanced novel about India,' according to Cecil, which 'should be one of the outstanding novels of 1944'. Weston was born of French and English parents in the United Provinces of British India, and had lived in India until marrying an American in her twenties. *Indigo*, her first book, already published to critical acclaim in the States, was set between the Boer War and 1914, exploring the complexity of male friendship in the British Raj through the characters of Jacques, a French boy, Macbeth, an Anglo-Indian (who grows up to be 'a just, liberal minded administrator', Cecil noted); and Hardyal, an upper-caste Indian, 'torn between affection for his white friends and love of his country'.

To Cecil, Hardyal was 'a brilliant creation: I cannot remember any Indian character in fiction more imaginatively authentic,' he affirmed. The book answered a widely felt need to better understand the current political situation. For while the impact of the Bengal famine – compounded by the British military's scorched-earth policy in anticipation of a Japanese invasion of British India – was still being debated in the Commons early 1944, British, Indian, and Chinese troops were beginning a second Allied offensive in Burma. In February 1944, the success of British and Indian soldiers in holding back and defeating a Japanese attack for the first time at the Battle of the Admin Box on the southern front of the Burma campaign was widely celebrated. Close-quarter fighting in Imphal and Kohima in India during the following months was seen as a turning-point against the Japanese. Meanwhile, questions of the future governance of India that would be acceptable to both the Indian National Congress and the All-India Muslim League were being debated. Weston's book did a good job, Cecil felt, in achieving 'a very fair balance' between Indian and Anglo-Indian perspectives, even if the historical setting gave contemporary readers a get-out from the racism the book explored, enabling 'the queasy reader to comfort himself, in respect of one of two minor episodes, that "anyway such things couldn't happen to-day"'. Like the very best fiction, *Indigo* was an important book, in Cecil's eyes, that had the grace not to be weighed down by the topical issues it dealt with.

May-June choice was *Ma Wei Slope* by Keith West, a historical novel of the T'ang Dynasty. West was a British authority on Chinese history and culture, friends with the late Stella Benson of the bestselling *Tobit Transplanted*, and this was his fourth book with a Chinese background. The novel was such an achievement 'that [it] might almost be a translation from some classical Chinese story-teller of the period,' Cecil believed. With the dramatic action focused on the emperor, heroine Winter Cherry, and a chequered love story, the book reminded Cecil of some of the earlier stories he'd recommended on China, especially *A Leaf in the Storm*. 'We share with the Chinese, it seems,' he wrote in the *Book Society News*, 'a love of understatement, a certain phlegm under emotional stress.' He and Edmund had been at the Wigmore Hall in London a few months previously, raising funds at a charity event for the Chinese who had suffered so much during seven years of Japanese occupation. *Ma Wei Slope* was a welcome opportunity for the club to remind readers of the hopes and fortunes of their wider Allies.

II

On Friday 9 June 1944, Edmund took the train up from Tonbridge. The continued ban on leave affecting Claire plus the general uncertainty of own his circumstances – significantly the question of how long he would stay at Annie's and where he and Claire would live when they were married – were beginning to grate. To Edmund, Annie's home had always been a sanctuary, but he felt she was possessive about their relationship. Now she had lodgers in too, he was feeling oppressed. Waiting on the platform, he noticed that the high winds and unseasonable weather that had delayed Operation Overlord by a day at the beginning of the week were still with them. 'Don't you think we must have made a remarkably good start?' he'd asked Siegfried on D-Day, 'but I suppose the other side will be dangerous a while we are trying to dig in a bit.'[509] There were reports of fierce fighting in Normandy, along with heavy German losses as the Allies pushed on, breaking the formidable Atlantic Wall. Rome had fallen to the Allies a few days before the D-Day landings began, with the army continuing to move north into Fascist-controlled areas. 'I can't keep my thoughts from the experiences of the individual men in such a terrible attack,' Edmund wrote Siegfried, 'and imagine you are living them all.' The poet Keith Douglas, one of Edmund's former pupils at Merton, would be killed on high ground above Tilly-sur-Suells, west of Caen, that day. Edmund had offered him advice on his manuscript of *Alamein to Zem Zem*, a wry memoir of the desert war in North Africa, published posthumously after the war. Douglas had produced some of the finest poems of WWII, Edmund felt, leaving a legacy on a par with Wilfred Owen.

Remember me when I am dead
And simplify me when I'm dead.
('Simplify Me When I'm Dead', Keith Douglas)

***

On the train, Edmund gathered his thoughts for the Book Society. He had the usual mixture of non-fiction to review, including a new edition of a book about Milton and a lively account of the civil engineering projects needed by the Eighth Army fighting in North Africa, along with the building of a desert pipeline. Edmund was happy with next month's main selection, *Memories of Happy Days*, an autobiography by the American writer, Julian Green, born and resident in France. Green had driven ambulances near Verdun before enlisting in the French Artillery at eighteen and was a star of the French Academy after writing his first novel in his early twenties. *Memories* was his first book written in English and showed French life and culture from an insider's and observer's perspective, making 'a valuable tribute to France at a time when such tributes are as valuable as they are rare,' Jack argued.[510]

There was much anticipation for Squadron leader H. E. Bates's new novel, *Fair Stood the Wind for France*, due out in autumn and already chosen by the American Book-of-the-Month Club. Meanwhile on the domestic front, Jack had been canvassing everyone about Helen Ashton's *Yeoman's Hospital*. Written by a qualified Doctor, *Yeoman's Hospital* offered some insight into the voluntary institutions likely to go, or be nationalised, under Beveridge's proposed National Health Service reforms. The book didn't take sides but acknowledged in 'an all-round picture [...] the good they have done', Jack pointed out.

There was also Rosamond Lehmann's new novel to consider. *The Ballad and the Source*, dedicated 'To C. D. L.', was her first book since the start of the war. Personally, Edmund admired the fine parts on WWI – 'they talked about the war, the war, the war' – which shifted between tragic and banal to capture war's impact on those left at home:

> Here, there, on every hand, inchmeal, the view beyond the windows of our home contracted, clouded. Our friend's brothers, the big boys who had partnered us in the polka, were being killed in Flanders, at Gallipoli; were being torpedoed and drowned at sea. An unrelenting diet of maize and lentils brought us out in spots, chilblains caused us to limp, the bath water stopped being hot at night.[511]

Cecil had plunged even further into his double life that year, moving with Rosamond into a small, terraced house in South Kensington (Lauric Lee was living in the basement flat with them, trying to ward off the rumour mill). Sylvia would take the lead review on this book. The following year, *The Ballad and the Source* would be chosen by the American Book-of-the-Month club, ensuring a transatlantic bestseller with Lehmann's first double whammy.

***

On the way up to town that day, Edmund also had to check the proofs of his Introduction to the club's new edition of Jane Austen's *Persuasion*. This was the Book Society's floating volume, a special edition like the two recent Tolstoy's, for when they were next hit by war delays. The critical and textual history was interesting to Edmund and the book was topical enough, with the role of the Navy written out of experience, as Austen's two brothers were sailors who became Admirals. The story captured powerfully civilian anxieties and those waiting-at-home in wartime:

> Anne was tenderness itself, and she had the full worth of it in

> Captain Wentworth's affection. His profession was all that could ever make her friends wish that tenderness less; the dread of a future war all that could dim her sunshine. She gloried in being a sailor's wife, but she must pay the tax of quick alarm for belonging to that profession.[512]

But Edmund had focussed his Introduction on Austen's main business, 'the search for husbands and the questions of caste and of property relating to it'. Austen was serious about marriage as a writer, Edmund felt, because 'the search was then, as it is now, among the biggest things in the world'. Claire was a lot like Anne, Austen's heroine, Edmund thought. 'Her women are not out for fun', he'd explain, 'they are individuals, none the less passionate because they are trained in a certain reserve; the "nervous thrill" of Anne is the true hint of what they are.' Still in awe of Claire, she was his last chance at this most important business in life.

Such is your well-tuned, wild-flowered, world-bright grace,
Giving me sense of wide free ways, so free
And wide that I count nothing of time and space
But think these present gifts will ever be
('Time Together' in *Shells by a Stream*, 1944)

***

Book Society members received their special edition of *Persuasion* for Christmas 1944 along with seasonal wishes that it may be 'the last Christmas before the war ends everywhere outside Asia'. In August, Paris had been liberated through the Normandy campaign, and though the Germans had stabilised their eastern and western fronts, confidence that the Allies would break through was widespread. The unmanned buzz bombs and rockets – 'infernal machines', Siegfried Sassoon wrote Edmund, recalling the bomb intended for Napoleon – that had been terrorising civilians since June, were still causing deaths and casualties.[513] But the Home Guard had been stood down, and war industry was slowly releasing workers. Winning the war against Japan might take another eighteen months after the victory over Germany, Churchill had warned, but there was cautious room for optimism.

For the club, the difficulties in procuring stock – 'the lack of paper, and lack of labour among printers, engravers, binders' – was more apparent than ever that winter, palpably affecting the Christmas season. 'There is no need, in the sixth Christmas of the war,' they told members, 'to stress the fact that books are in great demand and short supply.' The market for illustrated Gift Books was one of the worse hit parts of the book trade: 'The trouble in 1944 has been to collect, from anywhere and everywhere, enough that demand inclusion and are still obtainable for members.' There were some spare copies of the fine edition of *Persuasion* which could be ordered as gifts on a first-come first-served basis, after some had been reserved for members overseas. But the amount of stock the club could guarantee to have in now was unreliable, and readers were encouraged to order early if they wanted any of the alternative titles from the recommended list, in case their first preference had gone out of print. 'Every book mentioned in our editorial pages is obtainable at the time of writing,' the *Book Society News* assured members, but stock ranged from ample to small, and readers needed to get in quick.

The judges' own books, out in time for Christmas, were selling well. Edmund's *Shells by a Stream* was scheduled to be reprinted in the new year, while Cecil's *Poetry for You: A Book for Boys and Girls on the Enjoyment of Poetry* looked set to be a bestseller, striking a chord with teachers and young readers. Cecil had dedicated this to his sons, 'Sean and Nico', pleasing Mary. Sylvia meanwhile, now a grandmother, was finalising her *Collected Poems* for Macmillan and shared two new ones in the *Book Society* annual. She and Robert were contemplating selling up at Forest Green and moving back to Hampstead when the war ended. She 'does not profess anything of dazzling brilliance or fierce energy,' Edmund wrote Siegfried after reviewing the volume for the *Sunday Times* the following March, 'but designs her pieces properly and remembers what she was to write about'.[514] Jack was back on the airwaves with a new series called *Questions for Tomorrow*, beavering away on a play – *An Inspector Calls* – and drafting a *Letter to a Returning Serviceman*, plus rallying fellow writers to support better relations between London and Moscow (*An Inspector Calls* would first be staged in the USSR in 1945, before a London theatre became vacant the following year). His new novel, *Three Men in New Suits*, addressed some of the challenges of demobilisation. Memories of his own struggles as a returning serviceman were still fresh. 'I think you celebrated your twenty-first birthday in the desert,' he wrote in *A Letter to a Returning Serviceman* (published 1945), 'I know I celebrated mine in the water-logged trenches of 1915.'

The book which the committee had wanted for December 1944 that couldn't be prepared in time because of the illustrations – meaning they had to send out Austen's *Persuasion* instead – was advertised in the Christmas annual as choice for January/February 1945. This was William Gaunt's *The Aesthetic Adventure*, an entertaining book about nineteenth-century painters and artists. Baudelaire, Degas, Beardsley and Wilde were included in what was 'a distinct achievement in collective biography,' according to Jack, making 'very easy and lively reading.'

The next choice, *To All The Living*, advertised in the January/February *Book Society News* and selected for March, was a realistic novel concerning women factory workers. The author, Dr Monica Felton, had worked in several government departments and was one of only two women to have served as clerk to the House of Commons. The book wove together individual histories into a mass-pattern of factory life, giving readers some insight, as Cecil explained in his review, into 'the life which thousands of girls have been living for the last four years, uprooted from their homes and thrown into a hard, unfamiliar, sometimes dangerous routine.' Cecil believed in this book, admiring how Felton had gone beyond reportage and documentary – like the 'flat recording detail and dialogue in the Mass Observation manner' – by moulding authentic experience 'in a truly imaginative form'. *To All The Living* showed how industrial production and social welfare were connected, teaching readers about 'a great industrial community going through all the growing pains of a human organism, a structure of such complexity that good intentions and technical skill are not enough in themselves to assure its development. You felt, when you have finished it,' Cecil summed up, 'that you really know something.' *To All The Living* was the kind of book Cecil had hoped to promote when he joined the club. It was a good one to sign off on.

III

January 1945 was the coldest winter for fifty years according to the papers, with endless snow and polar temperatures. As the Allies in the Ardennes defeated the last major German offensive, with huge losses on both sides, the army was brought in to address national fuel shortages in Britain and help move dwindling supplies of coal around the country. On 19 January, with news surfacing that

Soviet troops had liberated Kraków and the German forces were in headlong retreat, Cecil was signed off from the Ministry and sent home on sick leave. He was suffering 'a complete emotional exhaustion', as he wrote Rosamond, manifesting among other things in an irrational jealousy of her friendship with Laurie Lee, when 'I want to be everything to you, as you want to be everything to me.'[515] He spent the next two weeks in a snow-covered Musbury convalescing, taking long walks and dreaming up the plot for his next Nicholas Blake. There was so much material to be mined from wartime London. *Minute for Murder* (published 1946) would include a character like Laurie, bomb-spotting on the window ledge of Senate House, seeing what the doodlebugs were doing to prevent 'the whole Division piling themselves down the stairway once or twice every hour'. Nigel Strangeways would be brought in to the Ministry to solve a case where the murderer was divided, caught between a lover and his wife, with the prospect of peace bringing it all to a head:

> It must be common enough just now in such liaisons, Nigel reflected – war had prevented people looking far ahead or envisaging the consequences of their private actions: there must be many lovers now wondering if their affairs could last beyond the cessation of hostilities, almost dreading the return of peace.[516]

Killing off 'Our Blonde' would be one way out of Cecil's dilemma.

Cecil had begun another literary enterprise recently, starting a new journal in association with Rosamond, poet Edwin Muir, and Denys Kilham Roberts from the Society of Authors. The first issue of *Orion: A Miscellany* was published that January – Rosamond very unhappy with the 'filthy shiny paper with revolting paper cover' the publishers had decided on – with a second due out in autumn (two more issues would appear, one in 1946 and the last, Cecil and Rosamond no longer involved, in 1947).[517] Readers were hungry for good writing and other literary magazines set up in wartime, like Cyril Connolly's *Horizon*, were still doing well. Rosamond had editorial experience from working on her brother John's *New Writing* and she and Cecil could easily persuade friends to contribute: Edmund, Laurie Lee, Stephen Spender, Leonard Woolf, Elizabeth Bowen all offered something. The first issue included Cecil's new translation of Paul Valéry's poem 'Le Cimetière Marin' ['The Graveyard by the Sea], developed from Rosamond's literal translation from the French.

> The wind is rising!....We must try to live!
> The huge air opens and shuts my book
> ('The Graveyard by the Sea' from Paul Valery's '*Le Cimetière Marin*')

Away from London that January on Doctor's orders, Cecil also came to a decision on the Book Society. His commitments to the club had overextended him for some time, and he needed to move on. Jack wanted an industry insider on the selection committee to help them find new writers after the war and had begun discussions with Daniel George Bunting, chief reader at Jonathan Cape (Daniel George had recommended they publish George Orwell's *Animal Farm* when it landed on his desk in 1944 but Cape, like many others, declined). As a reader, Daniel was known for candid criticism and the time he spent, despite his own writing, on author development. Self-taught from a second-hand shilling library himself, with a design and managerial background in motor cars and engineering, Daniel was an essayist and poet, known for witty collections like *A Peck of Troubles. Or an Anatomy of Woe* in which anecdotes from the world of letters on subjects ranging from in-growing toenails to fancy dress were 'conveniently displayed in an alphabetical arrangement for the purpose of Comparison, Consolation and Diversion'. Prior to the Munich Crisis, he'd collaborated with Rose Macaulay on an anti-war anthology, *All in a Maze.* 'Fools rush on war, said Euripides' Rose Macaulay wrote in the Introduction, 'and mankind are fools.'

By March 1945, the same month the Allies crossed over the Rhine and in Britain the air raid sirens finally stopped, Daniel George had joined the judges. Cecil had a smattering of reviews, overdue, published in the recommended pages of that month's *Book Society News*, but there were no farewells or special features to explain his unceremonious departure. Sylvia took the lead on the selected book for April, a murder mystery set in India by Philip Woodruff: 'a writer about India in the Kipling tradition,' she conceded, anticipating Cecil's displeasure. The book made a good talking point, Sylvia advised, because 'India is going to be increasingly in the political news, and we must all be prepared to hold opinions of one kind or another on the "India" question. The fact that in this country the problem can be so dispassionately posed,' Sylvia went on, 'indicates how far we have travelled from the old sort of Imperialism.'

IV

> Oh, is it Peace? The young child said,
> Seeing the light across the Green.
> Oh, is it Peace, that square of light,
> Where always night has been?
> A lighted window in the gloom
> Like honey in a honeycomb?
> (Sylvia Lynd, 'Sweeter Than Honey' in *Collected Poems*, 1945)

Daniel George's first lead review for the club announced Evelyn Waugh's *Brideshead Revisited* as the selected title for May 1945, the month war in Europe finally ended after the Germans signed a document of military surrender on 7 May. Crowds celebrated and danced for Victory in Europe on Tuesday 8, but it was 'a victory only half won' as President Truman reminded, while Japan fought on. The horrific reports coming out from the liberated concentration camps in Europe and the trauma of what the world had been through remained. 'I contemplate the world with a shudder,' Siegfried Sassoon wrote Edmund late April, speculating on rumours of German surrender:

> Violence, destruction, and brutalisation everywhere – All sensitive values destroyed, it seems. "Vision be love, be light" etc. – The words cry out; but a tank comes along and crashes through...saying "Take that!" I feel like a glow-worm with a V.2 descending on it, when I measure my simple humanity against life as it is now.[518]

For the Book Society, Daniel framed *Brideshead Revisited* as light reading for the war weary but a dangerous tonic postwar. 'To be young in 1923 was bliss – in Oxford,' he mocked pointedly. Finding the novel's conservative, nostalgic elitism jarring, Daniel questioned: 'At least we must suppose [Waugh] had a purpose in committing his story to the charge of a narrator so provocative, so determined to wring our hearts with lamentations for a past shared by a precious few.' The public, along with returning soldiers, were facing mass housing problems, clothing and food shortages, and continued austerity, with widespread demands for a more equitable social policy. *Brideshead Revisited* would go on to be a transatlantic bestseller, but in a revised edition fifteen years later where he 'modified the grosser passages', Waugh would concede how wartime deprivation had influenced the novel's excesses:

> It was a bleak period of present privation and threatening disaster – the period of soya beans and Basic English – and in consequence the book is infused with a kind of gluttony, for food and wine, for the splendours of the recent past, and for rhetorical and ornamental language, which now with a full stomach I find distasteful.[519]

In the context of an impending General Election after Churchill stood down mid-May and a caretaker government of old guard Conservatives was put in play, Waugh's satire of meritocracy as the dreadful age of the harmless Hooper, with his 'flat, Midland accent' was potentially exasperating.[520] 'There are social problems more urgent than the maintenance of facilities for aesthetic, amorous and spiritual dilettantism,' Daniel concluded for the Book Society. His criticism of *Brideshead Revisited* was a sign that the club would be on the right side of history when July's General Election took place, part of a groundswell of opinion that was to sweep Clement Attlee and the Labour Party to victory in a spectacular landslide (Jack Priestley stood unsuccessfully as an independent candidate for the still existing seat of Cambridge University, campaigning also on behalf of Labour candidates). The tolerance for Lord Sebastians, Anthony Blanche, and the Man with the Big Cigar was over. 'Better fifty years – or more – of Hooper than a cycle of decay,' as Daniel declared for the Book Society. 'The more ideas for the future we have, the richer we will later be,' Hugh Walpole had said in one of his last radio broadcasts.[521] With Attlee's election marking a programme of nationalization, a new National Insurance scheme and the formation of a National Health Service, Hugh's dreams of a new social order after the war would be given a shot.

***

On Monday 28 May 1945, three weeks after VE Day, the first portion of the sale of 'The Famous Library of the late Sir Hugh Walpole CBE' was sold at auction by Christie, Manson & Woods at Derby House in Stratford Place, off Oxford Street. The building's fine Georgian stonework was blackened and grimy, but it was still intact, unlike Christie's former home on King Street, not far from Book Society House, which needed rebuilding after being bombed-out during the Blitz. The sale was the first over nine days (there were two more early July and one in autumn, then in February, May, and July the following year), totalling more than two thousand lots. Built with enthusiasm and eclectic taste over many years, Hugh's enormous library boasted first editions, finely printed private press books, and association copies signed by contemporary authors – many of them part of the Book Society.[522] The sale attracted the big London rare book dealers and out-of-town buyers from Bath and Hugh's native Cumberland, frustrating later bibliophiles with the library scattered and broken up.[523] Hugh's impressive art collection was sold and exhibited separately at the Leicester Art Galleries in London in three parts between April and July. 'He was, to my mind, the best kind of collector,' Jack wrote in the exhibition catalogue, 'if only because he pleased himself and did not follow fashion.' 'And let us hope, in this grim time,' Jack went on, 'that a lot of other people, visiting this show, may be able to recapture some of his happy excitement.'[524]

The following day at noon, Tuesday 29 May, Edmund and Claire married 'without fuss' in a quiet registry office in Tonbridge; Edmund invited Rupert Hart-Davis and Siegfried Sassoon. 'There will be a cake, a bottle of whisky and some scrap at 1 afterwards.' His divorce from Sylva had been finalised earlier that month. 'She is still as reasonable and as generous about all as I have described her,' he confirmed.[525] Edmund had been offered regular literary work as assistant editor of the *Times Literary Supplement* from 1 July, an office job at £650 a year, meaning taking a flat in London with Claire once she was demobilised from the army that summer. His working and domestic life post-Oxford was falling into place and when, shortly after VE Day, international cricket resumed with the Victory Tests – England playing an Australian Services team of military personnel – Edmund and Claire 'encamped at Lord's' to marvel at 'the batting displays' of English captain Wally Hammond.[526]

That August, 'In the midst of VJ and atom bombs,' Edmund received a Leigh Hunt item through the post courtesy of Hugh's library. Rupert Hart-Davis was up in Cumberland still sorting through 'more of dear old Hugh's books'. It was 'not I fancy of any great negotiable value,' Rupert admitted, but 'I thought might amuse you. I'm sure old Hugh would want you to have it.'[527] For Edmund, the atomic bombs at Hiroshima and Nagasaki which ended the war on 14 August defied comprehension. 'I am more convinced that the overwhelming of Japan in this manner (for it is now generally admitted that they were hardly able to hold out three months, *without* Atom bombs) will have strengthened the feelings of all the Orient from Persia onward that the Western Civilisation is *the* barbarism,' he wrote his brother in confidence at the end of that month.[528] 'You will have shared my hopes that the events in the East at least mean the restoration of freedom and quiet interests to such completely beautiful characters as T. Saito' he confessed more sanguinely to Sassoon.[529] Claire was pregnant, he revealed in the same letter, meaning they were looking into maternity hospitals 'which it seems she will be needing about March or April 1946.'

***

On the Book Society that autumn, novelist and critic Compton Mackenzie (now in his sixties a literary statesman) joined the selection committee to take them back up to five, while Edmund secured Sassoon's memoir, *Siegfried's Journey 1916-1920*, as December choice. Edmund had shared intimately in the development of this book, receiving regular updates from his friend during the years of writing, and arranged to review it for Christmas; a season of peace but not of plenty, as readers were consoled in the magazine, 'the dearth of things to buy and give is more evident than at any Christmas in the war'. Paper mills, printers and bookbinders were months behind, with most new planned books delayed at some point in the production process. Though Sassoon disliked the continuing 'prospect of "war economy" format', as he told Edmund, his publishers had rushed the book out before the anticipated 'spate of "post-war literature"' began.[530] Looking back to the years after the end of WWI, *Siegfried's Journey* took 'the story of a young man who had devoted himself to the soldiering business of a world war and had become almost diseducated in the world's normal affairs, returning to these last and discovering the deeps and the shallows' Edmund advised readers. It was 'an oasis in the dreary drifts of world-chaos scrabblings,' he praised Sassoon.[531] 'Those who now come from the second world war into the problems of peace may find great virtue in his words by the way.'

1944

175 January + February *So Little Time,* John P. Marquand
176 March *Other Men's Flowers*, ed. by A. P. Wavell
177 April *Indigo*, Christine Weston
178 May + June *Ma Wei Slope*, Keith Weston
179 July *Memories of Happy Days*, Julian Green
180 August *Yeoman's Hospital*, Helen Ashton
181 September + October *The Ballad and the Source*, Rosamond Lehmann
182 November *Fair Stood the Wind for France*, H. E. Bates
183 December *Persuasion*, Jane Austen

1945

184 January + February *The Aesthetic Adventure*, William Gaunt
185 March *To All The Living*, Monica Felton
186 April *Call The Next Witness*, Philip Woodruff
187 May + June *Brideshead Revisited*, Evelyn Waugh
188 July *Folly Bridge. A Romantic Tale*, D. L. Murray
189 August *Singing Waters*, Ann Bridge
190 September + October *Mine Own Executioner*, Nigel Balchin
191 November *London Belongs to Me*, Norman Collins
192 December *Siegfried's Journey*, Siegfried Sassoon

Postscript

I

The club magazine after WWII. *The Bookman*, incorporating the *Book Society News*

March 1946, the *Book Society News* relaunched as *The Bookman*. 'The title is that of the famous magazine founded by Sir William Robertson Nicoll in 1891,' they explained of its circuitous history, 'which in 1935 was incorporated with *The London Mercury*. When the latter was itself incorporated with *Life and Letters*, the title of *The Bookman* passed with it; and the Book Society has now obtained the rights for a title which for over fifty years has been associated with some of the best traditions of English literature.' A strike for tradition, the rebrand signalled a desire for gravitas postwar and met with critical approval. As the foremost journal for book buyers, book readers and booksellers, 'It seems very right and proper that the Book Society should revive the title of *The Bookman*,' wrote Lady Rhondda, once a club adversary, and still editor of *Time and Tide*.[532]

Later that year, journalist and short story writer V. S. Pritchett was brought onto the selection committee. As assistant literary editor at the *New Statesman and Nation*, Pritchett was an up-and-coming star. 'Pritchett is a writer whom other writers should read,' Sylvia had said in an admiring review of his recent essay collection on *The Living Novel*. Edmund was uncertain of his own continued involvement after accepting an invitation to join a cultural delegation to Japan. He and Claire set sail for Tokyo, along with their first daughter, Margaret, in November 1947 for what became a three-year trip. Nevertheless, Edmund remained on the selection committee, reading for the club until the end of 1952.

Sylvia stayed with the judges until the summer of 1951, not long before her death, aged sixty-four, the following year. Jack retired earlier, at the end of 1948. So, it was the younger men Daniel George and V. S Pritchett who steered the club through the late 1940s and into the 1950s, weathering continued paper shortages (paper rationing in Britain did not end until 1949) while at the same time benefiting from efficiencies in air mail that improved services to readers overseas. By 1960 a new roster of celebrity judges was involved. The 1960 selection committee comprised poets Richard Church and Kathleen Nott, naturalist James Fisher, novelists William Golding and Penelope Mortimer, classicist Peter Green, and historian Dr J. H. Plumb. Later, other writers came in. 'Angry Young Man' Alan Sillitoe, authors Beverley Nichols and Lettice Cooper, critics and translators Stella Rodway and Isobel Quigly, science fiction writer Brian W. Aldiss. The calibre indicates that the club was still a well-respected institution for writers and critics who continued to do the work, spotting and promoting writers who would become famous including Laurens van der Post, Mary Renault, Iris Murdoch, Samuel Beckett, John Fowles, Maurice Edelman, Dudley Pope. Popular Book Society choices in the late 1940s, '50s, and '60s include *The Heat of the Day* by Elizabeth Bowen and *I Capture the Castle* by Dodie Smith, *The Kon-Tiki Expedition* by Thor Heyerdahl, Nevile Shute's *A Town like Alice*, *Seven Years in Tibet* by Heinrich Harrer, L. P. Hartley's *The Go-Between*, *To Cider with Rosie* by Laurie Lee, Harper Lee's *To Kill a Mockingbird*, Lynne Reid Bank's *The L-Shaped Room*... With nearly five hundred Book Society choices between 1929 and 1968, the lists of well-known titles go on and on.

But times were changing, and in a more democratic era of book-buying and publishing after the war, a collision of factors contributed to the club's demise. First up, the paperback revolution of the 1960s, when new imprints joined Penguin to cultivate a mass-market of book-buyers, dramatically upended the club's finances. In October 1960, readers in Britain could buy Pan's paperback version of Alan Sillitoe's *Saturday Night and Sunday Morning* for two shillings and sixpence (approximately £2.60 in today's money) while Book Society members that same month received *To Kill a Mockingbird* at sixteen shillings in hardback (today's £16.80).[533] The introduction of compulsory secondary education after 1944 widened the potential reading public as paperback titles began to sell in the millions (Pan's first million-selling paperback was *The Dam Busters* of 1956, published in hardback in 1951). By the end of the '60s, four paperback publishers – Penguin, Fontana, Corgi, and Panther – accounted for eighty per cent of the UK's book market sales.[534]

Yet the Book Society (like the broadsheets, who didn't review paperbacks) continued to ignore how the new paperback publishers were disrupting the market, expecting their members to keep buying new hardbacks for their bookshelves. By the late 1960s, these averaged around thirty shillings (over £21) on publication: the club's whopper was *Chips: The Diaries of Sir Henry Channon*, November 1967 choice, which was three guineas and three shillings when it came out (about £44 today), offered to club members at fifty-five shillings (nearly £39). Hardback publishers powered on, acquiring the paperback rights that they would then sublicense, but when so much of an author's profits came from the paperback edition, it was only a matter of time before agents would start selling the rights separately, challenging the legacy power of hardback publishers and institutions like the Book Society who clung to them.

Arguably, there was also less need to subscribe to a members' book club for literary advice after the war when the welfare state modelled access to culture – alongside education, the NHS, employment, and pensions – as a public good. In 1946, the Arts Council received a royal charter to make what had once been the privilege of a few the 'democratic right of the entire community', subsidising writers and institutions to support public accessibility (in the 1960s, Cecil Day-Lewis would channel his earlier support for new writers on the Book Society into chairing the Art Council's Poetry and Literature panels).[535] The Public Libraries Act of 1964 made it a statutory duty for local authorities in England and Wales to provide a comprehensive and efficient library service for all, stipulating minimum staffing levels and annual acquisition targets. And, if many readers still preferred to receive books through the post in the '60s, there were other book clubs to choose from. Alan Bott's Reprint Society (or World Books), selling cheap reprint hardbacks at two shillings and sixpence, had over two hundred thousand members by the mid-1950s; the Folio Society, selling at the premium end, brought expensive hardbacks with fine bindings and design to the collector's market. The loss of Book Society members overseas in a postcolonial world, as civil servants and other workers once based abroad returned home, further affected their membership.

But the Book Society limped on. Postwar, the judges saw African American, working-class, and more gay writers break into the mainstream, recommending Ann Petry's debut *The Street* in 1946 (the first novel by an African American woman to sell over a million copies) and writing by David Storey and Stan Barstow in the 1960s 'when most novelists seem to hail from working-class homes in gloomy industrial towns in the provinces'.[536] As a club, they continued to educate readers, opening their eyes to the world through history, travel, and literature in translation. Though the vast majority of Anglophone fiction the selection committee chose postwar was still largely western in perspective, they did seek to promote original voices from newly independent nations ('I have always hoped and believed that one day a big novel, written by an Indian, would come out of India' wrote judge Rumer Gooden in 1959 in reference to the club's choice of Balachandra Rajan's debut novel, *The Dark Dancer*).

Yet while the bestseller charts became dominated by sex, erotic books, and those 'whose notoriety springs from their ability to type those four and six-letter words that at one time were written only by creators of graffiti', as Anthony Hern (literary editor at the *Daily Express*, cartoonist and serial writer for James Bond) put it in a review of *Lucy: A Novel of the Restoration Theatre* by Hester Chapman in summer 1965, the club continued to promote what 'used to be called A Good Long Read'. 'A best-seller, however, is not necessarily a Book Society Choice' the club endeavoured to remind readers in September 1966. The judges were still choosing from publishers' manuscripts (unlike reprint book clubs who operated with knowledge of a book's sales and reception) therefore selecting for 'a generalist of intelligent readers who actively share with us a sense of discovery and who in so doing acquire a collection of first editions of books'. But choosing titles based on their 'depth, pace and intrinsic interest' alongside what the club dubbed an 'elusive quality of re-readability' was no longer enough. In a disrupted and disruptive, more liberal, and democratic world for books after the war, it was an unsustainable formula.

In April 1959, thirty years after they began, the Book Society announced a cost-saving merger with Bumpus books, one of London's oldest and most prestigious booksellers.[537] The year previous, Bumpus had been saved from liquidation by a consortium of publishers who bought it out and engaged Tony Godwin as managing director. Future distribution for the Book Society would be handled through Bumpus, booksellers by Appointment to Her Majesty the Queen, with members directed to send future correspondence to the club's new address, 6 Baker Street, where Bumpus were converting their premises to house the club. Members visiting London were invited to take advantage of the new partnership by spending 'a leisurely half-hour' exploring Bumpus's liberal shelves, with back-page maps on the *Bookman* directing readers to 'Bumpus Book Society', just off Oxford Street. 'Comfortable seats and an unhurried atmosphere combine to make this spacious bookshop a bibliophile's sanctuary', the *Bookman* announced.[538] It was 'the most luxurious bookshop in Europe' subsequent ads declared.

The new association brought further changes. *The Bookman* was redesigned, edited and designed professionally to carry more gravitas, and began to include additional feature writers alongside the regular selection committee. The later (all new, bar Richard Church who stayed on) was expanded from five to seven judges to manage workloads ('with something in the region of 1400 new titles each year to sift, read, evaluate and discuss, it called for prodigious application'). Committee members' own books were to be considered for future selection, and new individual bindings would mark future club choices.

The Bookman of the 1960s reveals an increasingly diversified business seeking new markets, trying to stay relevant and add revenue streams. In November 1962, 'The Junior Book Society' was introduced: seven shillings and sixpence for a book a month, aimed at 'those parents whose children are away at boarding school'. In April 1964, Paul Gallico became the first author to make a club recording. Vinyl records, to be played at 33 r.p.m, would be issued from time to time. '*Now* – the authors of our Choices speak to you in your home!', the club related this 'milestone in literary history'. In 1965, the Book Society set up an antiquarian books department to source rare titles for members, while finally introducing a postal charge on their choices, blaming increases in overheads and postage. That same year, after Bumpus ceased trading following the death of its chairman, J. G. Wilson, the club changed premises twice, first moving to Ludgate Hill in the City of London, and then to Fitzroy Square, Euston. The *Bookman* still advertised a club that saved time and money. But the Book Society that had opened reading and book-buying to 'the Man in the Street,' as dreamt by Hugh Walpole in the late 1920s, had run its course.[539]

II

> and many days we came,
> And many books we chose;
> I fear I have forgotten some of those,
> But not the brilliant and delightful crew
> Who then assembled, led by 'piping' Hugh.
>
> Edmund Blunden, 'On Rupert Hart-Davis; a good friend' (nd, Hong Kong)[540]

Edmund Blunden was in Japan between December 1947 and May 1950, then in 1953 took up a tenured position as Professor of English Literature at the University of Hong Kong, where he stayed until 1964. In 1951 he stood aside after being nominated for Professor of Poetry at Oxford to allow his friend, Cecil Day-Lewis, to be voted in, and was instead elected Oxford Professor of Poetry after his return from Hong Kong in 1966, aged seventy. Edmund and Claire had four daughters and lived together happily until his death in 1974. He remained in contact with Sylva and Aki for the rest of his life.

After his death, Edmund's personal library of over 10,000 books was sold to the University of Ohio, where the Head of English agreed to keep it intact. In 1985, Edmund joined Siegfried Sassoon and fourteen others on a memorial dedicated to First World War poets in Poets' Corner in Westminster Abbey.

***

Sylvia and Robert Lynd returned to London after the war, selling their beloved cottage in Forest Green in 1947. Robert passed away in 1949 and Sylvia died at home in Hampstead three years later, aged sixty-four, outlived by her lover, Gordon Campbell, by another ten years.

In the last years of her life, Sylvia worked on an autobiography. This included chapters on her upbringing and her mother's radical anarchist and suffrage views, their support for Irish home rule, portraits of literary friends including Yeats, D. H. Lawrence and Katherine Mansfield, and sections on her married life in Hampstead as literary patron, socialite, and book club judge. This writing project, called *Slices of Autobiography*, was taken up by Máire Gaster, Sylvia's second daughter, after the archive came to her following her elder sister Sheila's death in 1976. Máire edited the material with a view to publication but didn't pursue this further after it was rejected by Livia Gollancz, who had taken over her father's publishing house in 1967. Along with excerpts from Sylvia's diaries, *Slices of Autobiography* exists in several different versions in the archives and remains unpublished. Sylvia's great-granddaughter, writer Lydia Syson, is now working with this material.

***

Cecil Day-Lewis broke from Rosamond Lehmann and divorced his wife Mary Day-Lewis in 1950, marrying the actress Jill Balcon the following year. They had two children and lived together until the end of his life, despite Cecil's continued affairs.

After the war Cecil went into publishing, working as a reader at Chatto & Windus from 1946, then as editor and publishing director (among authors he supported in the 1960s were Attia Hosain and A. S. Byatt). He was made a CBE in the Queen's 1950 Birthday Honours and elected Professor of Poetry at Oxford between 1951-6. In 1963, Cecil edited *The Collected Poems of Wilfred Owen* for Chatto's, almost doubling the number of poems available to the public since Edmund's 1931 edition of *The Poems of Wilfred Owen*.

Cecil worked for the Royal Society of Literature and the Arts Council in the 1960s, leading on the state's programme of intervention for struggling writers. In 1966 he recorded a selection of Edmund Blunden's poems for gramophone record with Jill Balcon to mark his friend's seventieth birthday. On New Year's Eve 1967, he was appointed Poet Laureate.

Cecil Day-Lewis died in 1972, aged sixty-eight, two years before Edmund passed away. Despite petitioning from the Royal Society of Literature in 2001, he has so far been denied a posthumous space in Poet's Corner.

***

Aki Hayaski was naturalised as a British citizen in 1949. After the war, she published some articles in her own name in *The Rising Generation*, a bilingual Japanese/English journal, and *Today's Japan*. She remained in London for the rest of her life, researching in the British Museum and contributing to Edmund's scores of books.

In 1962, Aki died alone in her rooms in Hampstead, aged seventy-three. She left all her property and savings to Edmund and his family, care of the University of Hong Kong. Her story and contributions to Edmund's oeuvre was resurrected in the late 1980s in Sumie Okada's *Edmund Blunden and Japan: The History of a Relationship*.

***

III

Book Society bookplates, from the Francis and Margaret Crichton collection.

In 1996, Oprah's Book Club began as a segment on *The Oprah Winfrey Show*, the highest-rated daytime talk show in television history. Aiming 'to get the whole country reading again,' the club was a cultural phenomenon, catapulting titles into the bestseller lists and proving – via a studio sofa, Oprah's non-threatening demeanour, and a democratic formula based on audience engagement and community – that there was a much wider audience willing to buy books than the world of mainstream publishing realised.[541] Eight years later, the first TV book club in Britain followed in Oprah's steps. Sharing her inclusive model, the Richard and Judy Book Club was initially a ten-minute segment on the couple's teatime chat show, the vision of producer Amanda Ross (in 2006, Ross was voted one of the most influential people in publishing by an industry panel). Both clubs are still powerful in different formats online since 2010, Richard and Judy working with W. H. Smith bookshops to promote paid-for titles. Since then, countless celebrities have jumped on the bookselling waggon, whether to promote their own brand, to boost literacy, or create a sense of community around books and the shared experience of reading.

The Covid 19 lockdowns of 2020-21 saw a dramatic rise in digital and physical subscription book clubs, not all of which survived the pandemic. According to market aggregator 'My Subscription Addiction', in 2024 over one hundred and fifty book-subscription services exist across Canada, the UK, New Zealand and the US (roughly consistent with figures dating back to 2018).[542] Many of these are niche and specialist, offering packages for instance of Young Adult literature, international writers, or literature in translation. Some independent publishers and booksellers have embraced subscription models as a way of defining their brand and building customer support in a concentrated marketplace. For in a world of excess, as Michael Bhaskar reminds us, 'value today lies in better curating information'.[543]

The Oprah phenomena of the late 1990s coincided with two important studies revealing the impact of the American Book-of-the-Month Club on readers decades earlier. Joan Shelley Rubin's *The Making of Middlebrow Culture* (1992) and Janice A. Radway's *A Feeling for Books: The Book-of-the-Month Club, Literary Taste, and Middle-Class Desire* (1997) indicated how the BOMC had transformed readers' access to literature across the US. The archives of the Book-of-the Month Club (including the first layer of initial readers reports) are housed in prestigious national institutions – Yale, the Library of Congress, Columbia – with the club a recognised part of American cultural history. In 2016, the BOMC (now owned by conglomerate Bookspan) was rebranded Book-of-the-Month. Currently marketed as 'a popular online subscription service for books that helps millennial women discover the best new reads,' the BOTM offers members 'a curated selection of between 5 - 7 new and early release hardcover books every month' to choose from, shipped out in a bright blue box.[544] You can watch BOTM members unboxing online.

In contrast, Hugh Walpole and the Book Society's place in the longer history of reading and subscription book clubs in Britain and the commonwealth is largely unknown. The loss of archives and records when the company was dissolved in the late 1960s has thwarted understandings of the club's social and cultural impact and worked against the kind of interest the American BOMC has received. But the Book Society is part of shared memory and a living history that still marks many readers' bookshelves. While writing this book, I've heard from families who've inherited Book Society collections from Canada to Tanzania. And if you're buying older books second-hand it won't be long before a bookplate from the Book

Society turns up pasted inside the cover, a member's name handwritten in, providing a living connection to a former reader and a tantalising connection to recent history, just out of reach.

In the summer of 2024, deep in the final stages of writing, I was contacted by Kate McKinnon from Perth in Scotland. Kate had seen my Book Society website and wanted to know if I would be interested in seeing the collection of books she'd inherited from her maternal grandparents when they lived in India? Kate's grandfather, Francis Crichton (known as Frank), had worked in the Calcutta jute trade from the early 1920s until 1950, when the family returned home to northeast Scotland (the Scottish connections to the Indian jute trade run deep; in the late nineteenth century Dundee and its surrounding area was known as 'Juteopolis', the centre of a process of imperial globalisation that benefited from low-wages in Bengal and imports of raw material while sending out capital, machinery, and migrants).[545] Kate's grandmother, Margaret, joined Frank in India in 1937 when they married and had numbered the books they received from the Book Society each month, carefully labelling their growing collection. Frank and Margaret were now deceased, and the books were living in Kate's house in boxes. Kate and I shared research and book lists (I still had some gaps as the *Book Society News* hasn't survived in a complete run pre-1936), and Kate and her son went through the collection systematically, initially thinking they had about eighty Book Society choices mixed up with other titles, later realising they had several hundred choices from between 1929 and 1965.

We chatted on the phone, Kate wanting to rehome the collection, and when my husband made plans to go bike-packing in Scotland that autumn, he offered to pick them up. A car boot full, eight boxes, and much happy unpacking later, these are some of the books, complete with dust jackets, reproduced in colour in this book. For me, having worked on this project for the best part of a decade and after a fair amount of book-hunting myself, the opportunity to see an entire, near complete collection, carefully numbered, was overwhelming. Some of my gaps could now be filled in. Perhaps unsurprisingly, these initially seemed to be more obscure, forgotten, titles: Mary Mitchell's 1934 'fantastic romance' *A Warning to Wantons* (which of course turns out to have been less obscure once – there was a 1949 film directed by Donald Wilson), or *The Life & Adventures of Aloysius O'Callaghan* by Thomas Washington-Metcalfe.

Seeing the choices altogether made me appreciate better the early *Time and Tide* critique. Gollancz's bright yellow dust jackets, distinctive at the time for their lack of illustrations and bold use of type, are well represented in Kate's grandparents' collection. The Gollancz wrappers are more fragile than other publishers' covers, a sign of poorer paper quality perhaps, or of being more eagerly read. And thinking of the Crichtons in Calcutta receiving these books by parcel every month, the preponderance of titles exploring expat, or early 'frontier' life was striking (the early Australian titles *The Adventures of Ralph Rashleigh. A Penal Exile in Australia 1825-1844*, *The Fortunes of Richard Mahoney*; Frederick Niven's *Mine Inheritance*; Kenneth Roberts's *Northwest Passage* – this later chosen by the Book Society and the American Book-of-the-Month Club). Perhaps because of where I'd first discovered the Book Society, in the archives of Leonard and Virginia Woolf's Hogarth Press, and no doubt due to my own interests, I'd looked past some of these titles in my club reading. But there are many ways to parse the hundreds of choices in a Book Society collection, and many more stories to be told.

The three hundred and twenty-two books in these eight boxes represent a lifetime of reading and collecting far away from home. Hopefully they'll have found a good resting place by the time you read this. So, the legacy of the Book Society and its connection to a shared history of reading, opening us up to other lives lived in other times and places, goes on. You'll recognise many club choices and recommendations from your own reading and bookshelves. And that is surely more than the judges, caught up in the daily grind, overwhelmed by manuscripts and meetings and review deadlines, perhaps clipping the car in the rain on the way out as Sylvia once did, could have hoped for when they began.

Appendix: Bookshelf.

1. Double whammies

Joint choices of the British Book Society and the American Book-of-the-Month-Club between 1929-49, by date.

Author	Title	Book Society Choice	BOMC Selection
Valentine Kataev	*The Embezzlers**	May-29	Nov-29
Francis Hackett	*Henry the Eighth*	Jul-29	Apr-29
Sigrid Undset	*Kristin Lavransdatter**	Feb-30	Feb-29
Francis Yeats-Brown	*Bengal Lancer*	Jul-30	Nov-30
Vicki Baum	*Grand Hotel**	Sep-30	Feb-31
Charles Morgan	*The Fountain**	Feb-32	Jun-32
R. H. Bruce Lockhart	*Memoirs of a British Agent*	Nov-32	Feb-33
Jean Schlumberger	*The Seventh Age or Saint Saturnin**	Feb-33	Aug-32
Maurice O'Sullivan	*Twenty-Years A-Growing*	May-33	Aug-33
Virginia Woolf	*Flush*	Oct-33	Oct-33
Marguerite Steen	*Matador**	Mar-34	Jul-34
Thornton Wilder	*Heaven's My Destination**	Dec-34	Jan-35
Enid Bagnold	*National Velvet**	Apr-35	May-35
Stuart Cloete	*The Turning Wheels**	Oct-37	Nov-37
Kenneth Roberts	*Northwest Passage**	Jan-38	Jul-37
Pearl S. Buck	*The Patriot**	Apr-39	Mar-39
Ethel Vance	*Escape, a novel of Inside Germany**	Nov-39	Oct-39
Jules Romains	*Verdun**	Apr-40	Jan-40
Ernest Hemingway	*For Whom the Bell Tolls**	Mar-41	Nov-40

Winston S. Churchill, compiled by Randolph S. Churchill	*Into Battle: Winston Churchill's War Speeches*	Feb-41	Jun-41
John P. Marquand	*H. M. Pulham, Esquire**	Feb-42	Mar-41
John Steinbeck	*The Moon is Down**	Jun-42	Apr-42
Franz Werfel	*The Song of Bernadette**	Nov-42	Jun-42
John P. Marquand	*So Little Time**	Jan-Feb 1944	Sep-43
H. E. Bates	*Fair Stood the Wind for France**	Nov-44	Jun-44
Rosamond Lehmann	*The Ballad and the Source**	Sep-44	Apr-45
Evelyn Waugh	*Brideshead Revisited**	May-45	Jan-46
Jim Corbett	*Man-Eaters of Kumaon*	Jul-46	Apr-46
Margery Sharp	*Britannia Mews**	Aug-46	Jul-46
H. R. Trevor-Roper	*The Last Days of Hitler*	Mar-47	Sep-47
Graham Greene	*The Heart of the Matter**	May-48	Aug-48
C. S. Forester	*The Sky and the Forest**	Sep-48	Sep-48
Winston S. Churchill	*The Gathering Storm**	Oct-Nov 1948	Jul-48

*denotes fiction

Joint choices of the British Book Society and the American Book-of-the-Month-Club between 1929-49, by publisher.

Title	UK publisher	US publisher
The Embezzlers	Ernest Behn	Dial Press
Henry the Eighth	Jonathan Cape	Horace Liveright
Kristin Lavransdatter	Alfred A. Knopf (London)	Alfred A. Knopf (New York)
Bengal Lancer	Victor Gollancz	The Viking Press
Grand Hotel	Geoffrey Bles	Grosset & Dunlap
The Fountain	Macmillan	Alfred A. Knopf

Memoirs of a British Agent $	G. P. Putnam's (London)	G. P. Putnam's (New York)
The Seventh Age or Saint Saturnin $	Victor Gollancz	Dodd, Mead
Twenty-Years A-Growing	Chatto & Windus	The Viking Press
Flush	Hogarth Press	Harcourt, Brace & Co.
Matador	Victor Gollancz	Little, Brown & Co.
Heaven's My Destination	Longmans, Green	Harper & Brothers
National Velvet	William Heinemann	William Morrow & Co.
The Turning Wheels	William Collins	Houghton Mifflin
Northwest Passage	William Collins	Doubleday, Doran & Co.
The Patriot	Methen	John Day
Escape, a novel of Inside Germany	William Collins	Little, Brown & Co.
Verdun	Peter Davies Ltd	Alfred A. Knopf
For Whom the Bell Tolls	Jonathan Cape	Charles Scribner's Sons
Into Battle: Winston Churchill's War Speeches $	Cassell & Co.	G. P. Putnam's
H. M. Pulham, Esquire	Robert Hale Ltd	Little, Brown & Co.
The Moon is Down	William Heinemann	The Viking Press
The Song of Bernadette	Hamish Hamilton	The Viking Press
So Little Time	Robert Hale Ltd	Little, Brown & Co.
Fair Stood the Wind for France	Michael Joseph	Little, Brown & Co.
The Ballad and the Source	William Collins	Reynal & Hitchcock
Brideshead Revisited	Chapman & Hall	Little, Brown & Co.
Man-Eaters of Kumaon	Oxford University Press (London)	Oxford University Press (New York)
Britannia Mews	William Collins	Little, Brown & Co.
The Last Days of Hitler	Macmillan (London)	Macmillan (New York)
The Heart of the Matter	William Heinemann	The Viking Press
The Sky and the Forest	Michael Joseph	Little, Brown & Co.
The Gathering Storm	Cassell & Co.	Houghton Mifflin

$ different US title: *Memoirs of a British Agent [US title: British Agent]; The Seventh Age or Saint Saturnin* [US title: Saint Saturnin]; Into Battle: Winston Churchill's War Speeches [US title: Blood, Sweat and Tears]*

2. 'The Book Society Bun'

Margaret Irwin print runs
from the Chatto & Windus archives, University of Reading Special Collections, Profit & Loss ledgers (by title), CW B/3/2 (1927-1933); CW B/3/3 (1933-1945).

- *None So Pretty* (1931): 5000 copies printed by 30 September 1931
- *Royal Flush* (1932) – Book Society Choice*: 24,500 printed by 31 March 1933 [8280 sold to the Book Society]
- *Still She Wished for Company* (1932): 2150 printed by 30 September 1933
- *The Proud Servant* (1934) – Book Society Choice*: 26,050 printed by 31 March 1935
- *Madame Fears the Dark* (1935): 4250 printed by 31 March 1936
- *The Stranger Prince* (1937) – Book Society Choice*: 38,500 printed by 31 March 1937 [8000 sold to the Book Society]
- *The Gay Galliard* (1941) – Book Society Choice*: 40,224 printed by 31 March 1942 [6600 sold to the Book Society]

3. What came next...

Data compiled from the *Bookman* (incorporating *The Book Society News*)

Jan/Feb	1946	*Horned Pigeon: A Record of Adventure*	George Millar
March	1946	*Private Angelo*	Eric Linklater
April	1946	*The White Tower**	James Ramsay Ullman
May/Jun	1946	*That Lady**	Kate O'Brien
July	1946	*Man-Eaters of Kumaon*	Jim Corbett
August	1946	*Britannia Mews**	Margery Sharp

Sep/Oct	1946	*The Westering Sun**	George Blake
November	1946	*The Happy Prisoner**	Monica Dickens
December	1946	*Brensham Village*	John Moore
Jan/Feb	1947	*The Wind Cannot Read**	Richard Mason
March	1947	*The Last Days of Hitler*	H. R. Trevor-Roper
April	1947	*Two Names Upon the Shore**	Susan Ertz
May/June	1947	*The Chequer Board**	Nevil Shute
July	1947	*The Mountain Village**	Chun-Chan Yeh
August	1947	*Chatterton Square**	E. H. Young
September	1947	*Autobiography*	Neville Cardus
October	1947	*The House by the Sea**	Jon Godden
Nov/Dec	1947	*The Purple Plain**	H.E. Bates
January	1948	*Thérèse*	François Mauriac
February	1948	The *Field of the Stranger**	Olivia Robertson
March	1948	*The Walled City**	Elspeth Huxley
April	1948	*Great Morning*	Osbert Sitwell
May	1948	*The Heart of the Matter**	Graham Greene
Jun/Jul	1948	*Before the Deluge**	Mark Aldanov
August	1948	*The Americans*	Geoffrey Gorer
September	1948	*The Sky and the Forest**	C. S. Forester
Oct/Nov	1948	*The Gathering Storm*	Winston Churchill
December	1948	*No Highway**	Nevil Shute
January	1949	*The Jacaranda Tree**	H. E. Bates
Feb/Mar	1949	*The Heat of the Day**	Elizabeth Bowen
April	1949	*I Capture the Castle**	Dodie Smith
May	1949	*The Willow Cabin**	Pamela Frankau
June	1949	*A Sort of Traitors**	Nigel Balchin
Jul/Aug	1949	*Love in a Cold Climate**	Nancy Mitford
September	1949	*Eastern Approaches*	Fitzroy Maclean
October	1949	*A Writer's Note Book*	W. Somerset Maugham
November	1949	*Alice**	Elizabeth Eliot
December	1949	*The White South**	Hammond Innes
January	1950	*A Few Flowers for Shiner**	Richard Llewellyn
Feb/Mar	1950	*The Feast**	Margaret Kennedy

April	1950	*The Kon-Tiki Expedition*	Thor Heyerdahl
May	1950	*The World My Wilderness**	Rose Macaulay
June	1950	*A Town Like Alice**	Nevil Shute
Jul/Aug	1950	*Behold Thy Daughter**	Neil Paterson
September	1950	*Florence Nightingale*	Cecil Woodham-Smith
October	1950	*Strait and Narrow**	Geoffrey Cotterell
November	1950	*The Age of Elegance*	Arthur Bryant
December	1950	*The World is a Bridge**	Christine Weston
Jan/Feb	1951	*The Loved and the Envied**	Enid Bagnold
March	1951	*The Little Madeleine*	Mrs Robert Henrey
April	1951	*World Within World*	Stephen Spender
May	1951	*Festival at Farbridge**	J. B. Priestley
June	1951	*Round the Bend**	Nevil Shute
Jul/Aug	1951	*A Dragon Apparent*	Norman Lewis
September	1951	*The Cruel Sea**	Nicholas Monsarrat
October	1951	*The Long Memory**	Howard Clewes
November	1951	*Children of the Archbishop**	Norman Collins
December	1951	*Lucy Carmichael**	Margaret Kennedy
Jan/Feb	1952	*Venture to the Interior**	Laurens van der Post
March	1952	*Reputation for a Song**	Edward Grierson
April	1952	*Patrice Périot*	Georges Duhamel, trans. by E. F. Bozman
May	1952	*Victory**	Joseph Conrad
June	1952	*A Many-Splendoured Thing*	Han Suyin
Jul/Aug	1952	*Campbell's Kingdom**	Hammon Innes
September	1952	*The Island**	Jean Matheson
October	1952	*Love for Lydia**	H. E. Bates
November	1952	*Annapurna*	Maurice Herzog
December	1952	*The Cardboard Crown**	Martin Boyd
Jan/Feb	1953	*Who Goes Home**	Maurice Edelman
March	1953	*The Singer not the Song**	Audrey Erskine Lindop
April	1953	*The Echoing Grove**	Rosamond Lehmann
May	1953	*Fenny**	Lettice Cooper
June	1953	*Like Men Betrayed**	John Mortimer

Jul/Aug	1953	*The Overloaded Ark*	Gerald M. Durrell
September	1953	*Seven Years in Tibet*	Heinrich Harrer
October	1953	*The Go-Between**	L. P. Hartley
November	1953	*The Reason Why*	Cecil Woodham-Smith
December	1953	*The Gipsy in the Parlour**	Margery Sharp
Jan/Feb	1954	*The Crooked Wall**	Faith Compton Mackenzie
March	1954	*Madame de Pompadour*	Nancy Mitford
April	1954	*The Tortoise and the Hare**	Elizabeth Jenkins
May	1954	*Bhowani Junction**	John Masters
June	1954	*A Wreath for the Enemy**	Pamela Frankau
Jul/Aug	1954	*The Governor's Wife**	David Unwin
September	1954	*The Wilder Shores of Love**	Lesley Blanch
October	1954	*The Faithful Ally**	Eric Linklater
November	1954	*The Corner-Stone**	Zoé Oldenbourg
December	1954	*The Young Have Secrets**	James Courage
Jan/Feb	1955	*The Hidden River**	Storm Jameson
March	1955	*A World of Love**	Elizabeth Bowen
April	1955	*Going to the Wars*	John Verney
May	1955	*We Die Alone*	Daniel Howarth
June	1955	*Memoirs of Hadrian**	Marguerite Yourcenar
Jul/Aug	1955	*The Shiralee**	D'Arcy Niland
September	1955	*The Fall of the Sparrow**	Nigel Balchin
October	1955	*H. M. S. Ulysses**	Alistair MacLean
November	1955	*Portrait of Vincent*	Lawrence & Elizabeth Hanson
December	1955	*The Quiet American**	Graham Greene
Jan/Feb	1956	*Bugles and a Tiger*	John Masters
March	1956	*The Long View**	Elizabeth Jane Howard
April	1956	*The Long Walk*	Slavomir Rawicz
May	1956	*Anglo-Saxon Attitudes*	Angus Wilson
June	1956	*The Proving Flight**	David Beaty
Jul/Aug	1956	*...And the Rain my Drink**	Han Suyin
September	1956	*The Towers of Trebizond**	Rose Macaulay

October	1956	*My Family and Other Animals*	Gerald Durrell
November	1956	*Twilight for the Gods**	Ernest Gann
December	1956	*Madame Solario**	Gerald Bullett
Jan/Feb	1957	*The Fountain Overflows**	Rebecca West
March	1957	*Without Love**	Gerald Hanley
April	1957	*The Last Migration*	Vincent Cronin
May	1957	*This Hallowed Ground*	Bruce Catton
June	1957	*The Awakened**	Zoe Oldenbourg
Jul/Aug	1957	*Bitter Lemons*	Lawrence Durrell
September	1957	*The Grand Catch**	Gil Buhet
October	1957	*The Volcanoes Above Us**	Norman Lewis
November	1957	*March the Ninth**	R. C. Hutchinson
December	1957	*Voss**	Patrick White
Jan/Feb	1958	*A Letter to Elizabeth*	Bettina Linn
March	1958	*The Roots of Heaven**	Romain Gary
April	1958	*Aku-Aku*	Thor Heyerdahl
May	1958	*The Director**	Alan Thomas
June	1958	*They Came to Cordura**	Glendon Swarthout
Jul/Aug	1958	*The Law**	Roger Vaillard, trans. by Peter Wiles
September	1958	*The King Must Die**	Mary Renault
October	1958	*The Time of the Dragons**	Alice Ekert-Rotholz
November	1958	*The Bell**	Iris Murdoch
December	1958	*Mani*	Patrick Leigh Fermor
Jan/Feb	1959	*Women and Thomas Harrow**	John P. Marquand
March	1959	*The Flame Trees of Thika**	Elspeth Huxley
April	1959	*The Dark Dancer**	Balachandra Rajan
May	1959	*Mistress to an Age*	J. Christopher Herold
June	1959	*A Guest and His Going**	P. H. Newby
Jul/Aug	1959	*The Lion**	Joseph Kessel
September	1959	*The Humbler Creation**	Pamela Hansford-Johnson
October	1959	*The Defeat of the Spanish Armada*	Garrett Mattingly
November	1959	*Cider with Rosie*	Laurie Lee

December	1959	*I Can Take It All*	Anthony Glyn
Jan/Feb	1960	*Two Weeks in Another Town**	Irwin Shaw
March	1960	*The Patriots**	James Barlow
April	1960	*The Affair**	C. P. Snow
May	1960	*The Leopard**	Giuseppe di Lampedusa
June	1960	*That Great Lucifer: A Portrait of Sir Walter Ralegh**	Margaret Irwin
Jul/Aug	1960	*A Kind of Loving**	Stan Barstow
September	1960	*The Shorn Lamb**	John Stroud
October	1960	*To Kill a Mocking Bird**	Harper Lee
November	1960	*The L-Shaped Room**	Lynne Reid Banks
December	1960	*The White Nile*	Alan Moorehead
Jan/Feb	1961	*Scenes from Married Life**	William Cooper
March	1961	*The Journey Homeward**	Gerald Hanley
April	1961	*All We Possess**	Edward Hyams
May	1961	*The Business of Loving**	Godfrey Smith
June	1961	*A Tudor Tragedy*	Lacey Baldwin Smith
Jul/Aug	1961	*The Minister**	Maurice Edelman
September	1961	*The Road Past Mandalay*	John Masters
October	1961	*George: An Early Autobiography*	Emlyn Williams
November	1961	*Devil of a State**	Anthony Burgess
December	1961	*A Handful of Time**	Helen Foley
Jan/Feb	1962	*The Road from the Monument**	Storm Jameson
March	1962	*The Bull from the Sea**	Mary Renault
April	1962	*The Birds of Paradise**	Paul Scott
May	1962	*The Wind Off the Sea**	David Beaty
June	1962	*An Unofficial Rose**	Iris Murdoch
Jul/Aug	1962	*Hornblower and The Hotspur**	C. S. Forester
September	1962	*Atlantic Fury**	Hammond Innes
October	1962	*Brendan Behan's Island. An Irish Sketchbook*	Brendan Behan
November	1962	*Get Ready for Battle**	R. Prawer Jhabvala
December	1962	*Lady Jane Grey*	Hester W. Chapman

Jan/Feb	1963	*Bonaparte in Egypt*	J. Christopher Herald
March	1963	*Fail-Safe**	Eugene Burdick and Harvey Wheeler
April	1963	*Before My Time**	Niccolò Tucci
May	1963	*The Knight and the Umbrella**	Ian Anstruther
June	1963	*Diamond River*	Sadio Garavani di Turno
Jul/Aug	1963	*Ice Station Zebra**	Alistair MacLean
September	1963	*Throw Out Two Hands*	Anthony Smith
October	1963	*As The Falcon Her Bells*	Phillip Glasier
November	1963	*The Group**	Mary McCarthy
December	1963	*The Grove of Eagles**	Winston Graham
Jan/Feb	1964	*Coin of Carthage**	Bryher
March	1964	*The Most Dangerous Game**	Gavin Lyall
April	1964	*The Hand of Mary Constable**	Paul Gallico
May	1964	*The Lonely Sea and The Sky*	Francis Chichester
June	1964	*The Ordeal of Major Grigsby**	John Sherlock
Jul/Aug	1964	*Louis XIV*	Vincent Cronin
September	1964	*Victoria R.I.*	Elizabeth Longford
October	1964	*Jvlian**	Gore Vidal
November	1964	*Corridors of Power**	C. P. Snow
December	1964	*The Night in Lisbon**	Erich Maria Remarque
Jan/Feb	1965	*Paris in The Terror. June 1792-July 1794*	Stanley Loomis
March	1965	The General Next to God	Richard Collier
April	1965	*The Berlin Memorandum**	Adam Hall
May	1965	*The Ambassador**	Morris West
June	1965	*Ramage**	Dudley Pope
Jul/Aug	1965	*Lost Empires**	J. B. Priestley
September	1965	*Lucy**	Hester Chapman
October	1965	*The Source**	James Michener
November	1965	*Fruit of the Poppy**	Robert Wilder
December	1965	*Thomas. A Novel of the Life Passion and Miracles of Beckett**	Shelley Mydans

Jan/Feb	1966	*The Fatal Impact. An Account of the Invasion of the South Pacific 1767-1840*	Alan Moorehead
March	1966	*Hall of Mirrors**	John Rowan Wilson
April	1966	*Somerset and all the Maughams*	Robin Maugham
May	1966	*The Magus**	John Fowles
June	1966	*The Double Image**	Helen MacInnes
Jul/Aug	1966	*A Long Way to Shiloh**	Lionel Davidson
September	1966	*Papa Hemingway*	A.E.Hotchner
October	1966	*When Eight Bells Toll**	Alistair Maclean
November	1966	*The Elizabethan Epic*	Lacey Baldwin Smith
December	1966	*The Night is a Time for Listening**	Elliot West
Jan/Feb	1967	*The Secret of Santa Vittoria**	Robert Crichton
March	1967	*Night Falls on the City**	Sarah Gainham
April	1967	*Shark Island**	Maurice Edelman
May	1967	*The Eighth Day**	Thornton Wilder
June	1967	*Hornblower and the Crisis**	C. S. Forester
Jul/Aug	1967	*Sea and Islands**	Hammond Innes
September	1967	*The Gabriel Hounds**	Mary Stewart
October	1967	*The Facemaker**	Richard Gordon
November	1967	*Chips: The Diaries of Sir Henry Channon*	ed. Robert Rhodes James
December	1967	*Michel, Michel**	Robert Lewis
Jan/Feb	1968	*The Nice and The Good**	Iris Murdoch

*denotes fiction

Bibliography

Primary sources

I have consulted diaries, letters, correspondence, and other unpublished papers in various institutions to write this project and am grateful to the librarians and archivists who have enabled me to navigate the following collections:

The Edmund Blunden Papers (Manuscript Collection MS-0426). Harry Ransom Center (HRC), The University of Texas at Austin.

Sylva Blunden/Norman, 'Notes of a lecture tour in Germany', April 1937. Oxford, Merton College archive.

Clemence Dane collection, London, Victoria & Albert.

Papers of C. Day-Lewis and his wife Jill Balcon, Oxford, Bodleian, MSS 6681/1-58.

Family papers of Nannie Dryhurst, MS 49,981, Dublin, National Library of Ireland.

Centre for Ephemera Studies; Lettering, Printing and Graphic Design Collections; Department of Typography & Graphic Communication, University of Reading.

Femina Vie Heureuse Prize, English Committee archive, MS 8900, University of Cambridge.

George Gordon Papers, MC:PR33/1, Oxford, Magdalen College archive.

John Johnson Collection of Printed Ephemera, 'Book Clubs', Oxford, Bodleian Library.

Rosamond Lehmann archive, King's College Cambridge.

Sylvia Lynd Collection, MS 5585, University of Reading Special Collections.

Publishers' archives: Chatto & Windus, Hogarth Press, Macmillan, Jonathan Cape, in the Archive of British Printing and Publishing, University of Reading Special Collections.

National Archives, Ministry of Information (MoI), INF 1/234.

The Hugh Walpole Collection (Manuscript Collection MS-04395). HRC, The University of Texas at Austin.
The Hugh Walpole Collection at the King's School Canterbury.
Hugh Walpole Correspondence, MS 54959, London, British Library.
MSS Walpole, Berg Coll, New York Public Library.

Copies of the *Book Society News* (later *The Bookman*) are held in the British Library from 1936 onwards.

The book could not have been written without the efforts of several earlier biographers. For more on the judges see especially:

Hugh Walpole

Rupert-Hart-Davis, *Hugh Walpole* (1952; Stroud: Sutton Publishing, 1997)
Elizabeth Steele, *Hugh Walpole* (NY: Twayne, 1972)
—— *Sir Hugh Walpole and the United States: A Novelist's View of 1919-36 America* (Lewiston: Edwin Mellen, 2006)
The *Hugh Walpole Review* (The Hugh Walpole Society), 2020-

Clemence Dane

Louise McDonald, *Clemence Dane. Forgotten Feminist Writer of the Inter-War Years* (London: Routledge, 2021)

J. B. Priestley

John Baxendale, *Priestley's England. J. B. Priestley and English Culture* (Manchester: MUP, 2007)
Vincent Brome, *J. B. Priestley* (London: Hamish Hamilton, 1988)
Judith Cook, *Priestley* (London: Bloomsbury, 1997)

George Gordon

M. C. Gordon, *The Life of George S. Gordon 1881-1942* (Oxford: OUP, 1945)
M. C. Gordon, ed., *The Letters of George S. Gordon 1902-1942* (Oxford: OUP, 1943)

Sylvia Lynd

Victor Gollancz, *Reminiscences of Affection* (London: Gollancz, 1968)

Sarah LeFanu, *Rose Macaulay* (London: Virago, 2003)

Sean McMahon, ed., *Robert Lynd: Galway of the Races, Selected Essays* (Dublin: Lilliput Press, 1990)

Nicola Wilson, '"So now tell me what you think!": Sylvia Lynd's Collaborative Reading and Reviewing', *Literature & History*, 28.1 (2019), 49-65

Edmund Blunden

Barry Webb, *Edmund Blunden: A Biography* (New Haven: Yale UP, 1990)

Sumie Okada, *Edmund Blunden and Japan. The History of a Relationship* (Houndmills: Macmillan, 1988)

ed. Carol Z. Rothkopf, *Selected Letters of Siegfried Sassoon and Edmund Blunden, 1919-1967*, 3 vols (London: Pickering & Chatto, 2012)

Cecil Day-Lewis

Sean Day-Lewis, *C. Day-Lewis: An English Literary Life* (London: Weidenfeld and Nicolson, 1980).

Peter Stanford, *C Day-Lewis. A Life* (London: Continuum, 2007)

Secondary sources that have informed this book

Angus Calder, *The People's War. Britain 1939-45* (Jonathan Cape, 1969)

Margaret Cole, *Books and the People* (London: Hogarth Press, 1938)

Patrick Collier, *Modernism on Fleet Street* (Aldershot: Ashgate, 2006)

Melba Cuddy-Keane, *Virginia Woolf, the Intellectual, & the Public Sphere* (Cambridge: Cambridge UP, 2003)

Steve Ellis, *British Writers and the Approach of World War II* (Cambridge: CUP, 2015)

John Hampden (ed.), *The Book World* (London: Nelson, 1935)

Robert Hewison, *Under Siege: Literary Life in London 1939-45* (London: Weidenfeld and Nicolson, 1977)

Valerie Holman, *Print for Victory: Book Publishing in England 1939-1945* (London: The British Library, 2008)

Q. D. Leavis, *Fiction and the Reading Public* (1932; Harmondsworth: Peregrine, 1979)
Corinna Norrick-Rühl, *Book Clubs and Book Commerce* (Cambridge: CUP, 2019)
Jenni Ramone and Helen Cousin (eds), *The Richard & Judy Book Club Reader: Popular Texts and the Practices of Reading* (Farnham: Ashgate, 2011)
Joan Shelley Rubin, *The Making of Middle/brow Culture* (Chapel Hill: University of North Carolina Press, 1992)
Janice Radway, *A Feeling for Books: The Book-of-the-Month Club, Literary Taste and Middle-Class Desire* (University of North Carolina Press, 1997)
Alexis Weedon, *The Origins of Transmedia Storytelling in Early Twentieth Century Adaptation* (Houndmills: Palgrave Macmillan, 2021)

For more on the Book Society see my website:
<https://research.reading.ac.uk/thebooksociety/>

Permissions

Extracts from diaries, correspondence and the unpublished papers of Edmund Blunden, along with extracts from the following poems: (i) 'Chapters of Literary History, Very Little Known (from *Choice or Chance*, 1934) (ii) 'Exorcised' (first published in the *TLS*) (iii) 'The Gift: for C.M.P' (from *Shells in a Stream*, 1944) (iv) 'On Rupert Hart-Davis: A Good Friend' (v) 'Time Together' (from *Shells in a Stream*, 1944) are reproduced with thanks to the estate of Edmund Blunden, managed by Georgia Glover for David Higham Associates Ltd.

Poems and Letters by C. Day-Lewis all reproduced by permission of Peters Fraser & Dunlop (www.petersfraserdunlop.com) on behalf of the Estate of C. Day-Lewis.

Thanks to Penguin Random House Archive and Library for permission to quote from the Archive of British Printing and Publishing held at University of Reading Special Collections.

Acknowledgements

This book has been a long time coming and I have many people to thank for reading drafts and sharing insights, for checking in and sustaining me through the research and writing process, and for offering practical and/or archival support.

For funding the early stages, I'm grateful to the British Academy for a Postdoctoral Fellowship (2013-16) which enabled me to begin work on this book and, crucially, to stay in academia while juggling young children. For funding later stages, I thank the University of Reading for a University Research Fellowship (2022-3) and the Harry Ransom Center for a Research Fellowship in the Humanities (2020-21) which I took up after Covid, in 2022.

I'm grateful to the many librarians and archivists who've shown interest in this project and helped in so many ways, some of which they won't realise, but which I have hugely appreciated: Peter Henderson, Walpole Librarian at The King's School Canterbury; Danni Corfield and Caroline Gould at University of Reading Special Collections; Emma Minns, Lettering, Printing and Graphic Design Collections, Department of Typography & Graphic Communication at the University of Reading; Wunmi Odeyingbo and Antonio Hernandez at the British Library; Bruce Kirby at the Manuscripts division, Library of Congress; Julie-Anne Lambert of the John Johnson Collection; Rachel Marsay, cataloguer of the C. Day-Lewis papers at the Bodleian; Verity Parkinson, Merton College archive, Oxford; Ben Taylor, Magdalen College archive, Oxford; Rick Watson, Jim Kuhn, Elizabeth L. Graver and Joan M. Sibley at the Harry Ransom Center, The University of Texas at Austin; Tom Davies, King's College Cambridge; and Carolyn Vega and Emma Davidson at the Berg, New York Public Library. Richard M. Ford, dealer in literary manuscripts, gave me advice on where some of Sylvia Lynd's letters had been sold, and I'd like to thank Guy Baxter, Andrew Nash, and the Friends of National Libraries for supporting the University of

Reading's bid to purchase the diaries and autobiographical writings of Sylvia Lynd and put them in the public domain. Back in 2015, Luke Turner of Hemsley Turner Group offered me a warm welcome and tour of 13 Grosvenor Place SW1, once 'Book Society House', where the old clubroom remained largely as it was.

Thank you to the estates and author's societies who have supported this project: Lydia Syson, representative of Sylvia Lynd's family; Duff Hart-Davis and the Hugh Walpole Society – especially Nicholas Redman and Mark Egerton; Margi Blunden; and the estate of Cecil Day Lewis. Lydia Syson and Nicholas Redman have read and offered advice on parts of this book in draft, for which I am truly grateful. Nicole Reynolds at the University of Ohio, where Edmund Blunden's library now resides, has read several chapters: thanks to her expert eyes and guidance. And thanks to Kate McKinnon who reached out in the final stages of this book and helped make it real.

For inviting me to give talks on the Book Society, I'd like to thank Flora de Giovanni at the University of Salerno; Paul Nash of the Oxford Bibliographical Society; Anthony Mandal at Cardiff University; Corinna Norrick-Rühl at the Johannes Gutenberg University of Mainz; Emily J. Hogg and Charlotte Johanne Fabricius at the University of Southern Denmark, Odense; and Caroline Knowles of the University of Reading's Community Festival. And to the editors and reviewers who have shaped my previously published work on the Book Society, huge thanks: 'Virginia Woolf, Hugh Walpole, the Hogarth Press, and the Book Society', *ELH*, 79:1 (2012), 237-60; 'Virginia Woolf and the Book Society Limited', in *Virginia Woolf and her Female Contemporaries*, eds. Julie Vandivere and Megan Hicks (Liverpool: Liverpool UP, 2016) pp. 48-55; 'Bloomsbury, the Hogarth Press and the Book Society Limited', in *Democratic Highbrow: Bloomsbury between elite and mass culture*, eds. Flora di Giovanni, Antonella Troota and Marina Lops (Mimesis, 2017), pp. 153-70; 'Middlemen, middlebrow, broadbrow', in *British Literature in Transition, 1920-40*, eds. Dougal McNeill and Charles Ferrall (Cambridge: CUP, 2018), pp. 315-330; '"So now tell me what you think!": Sylvia Lynd's Collaborative Reading and Reviewing', *Literature & History*, 28.1 (2019), 49-65; 'Five's better than one': Hugh Walpole and the Book Society', The *Hugh Walpole Review*, 3.2 (2022), 5-14; 'The British Book Society and the American Book-of-the-Month Club, 1929-1949: Joint Choices and transatlantic Connections',

Book History, 27.1 (2024), 144-70; 'Feminist Bibliography: Aki Hayashi, Literary Assistant', in *Feminized Work and the Labour of Literature: New Literary Perspectives on the Times, Spaces and Forms of Women's Work*, eds. Emily J. Hogg and Charlotte J. Fabricius (EUP, 2025 forthcoming). In 2011 I was invited to contribute to BBC Radio 4's 'The Walpole Chronicle' on the relationship between Virginia Woolf and Hugh Walpole: I am grateful for this interest in my early research which convinced me that there was a wider audience for this story.

For building collegiality and a dynamic, inspiring research community I thank Sophie Heywood; Daniela La Penna; Sue Walker; Nicola Abram; Sue Walsh; Michelle O'Callaghan; Andrew Mangham; Claire Battershill; Alice Staveley; Helen Southwood; and Elizabeth Willson Gordon. Several individuals have provided crucial advice at points in this rambling project for which I'd like to thank Sarah LeFanu; Alison Light; Shelley Harris; Alanna Skuse; John Scholar; Yasmine Shamma; Dennis Duncan; Cathy Clay; Katsura Sako; Xander Ryan; D-M Withers; Mark Hussey; Alison Donnell; Simon Eliot; Patrick Parrinder; Clara Farmer; and Roberta Gilchrist.

Starting out as an academic project, the writing has gone through various iterations. Thanks to the Arvon tutors and staff at Totleigh Barton, online (covid!) and Lumb Bank who helped me steer a course into non-fiction, especially Laura Barton; John-Paul Flintoff; and Elise Valmorbida; thanks to the writing friends I made there, and most of all 'The Red Herrings': Helen Meller, Sue Tangney and Louise Kenward. I spent more time than I'd care to admit chasing literary agents for this book and I'd like to thank those who gave me their time and consideration, especially Anna Power. Robert Peett took it on as an editor of a small independent and I am very grateful for his input and enthusiasm.

Some of my first readers have been those nearest and dearest to me. Thanks to Kate Whiting, Peter and Emily Mathias who have offered advice, support, and the occasional red-pen in places. To my parents, Julie and Graham Wilson, my in-laws Roy and Wendy Mathias, and the friends who've kept asking me how it's going, thanks Julia and Rich Paterson, Lou and Paul Ramage, Liz Ellis, Claire Jenkins, and Lucy Latchmore.

Peter, Emily, and Michael Mathias have lived with this book a long time and were forced, on some occasions, to read bits 'hot off the press'. They've hiked above Hugh Walpole's home in the Lakes and stalked Cecil Day-Lewis's home Box Cottage. Thanks to them for being everything.

Endnotes

Introduction

[1] Q. D. Leavis, *Fiction and the Reading Public* (1932; Harmondsworth: Peregrine, 1979), p. 34.
[2] Margaret Cole, *Books and the People* (London: Hogarth Press, 1938), p. 5.
[3] 'Twopenny' libraries – where you could borrow a book for two pence, with no annual subscription - were common in the 1930s, catering largely for working-class readers.
[4] F. R. Richardson, 'The Circulating Library', in *The Book World*, ed. John Hampden (London: Nelson, 1935), 195-202, p. 197.
[5] H. G. Wells, 'Interviews with Famous Authors,' *The Book Window: A Guide to Book Buying and Book Reading* 1.1 (July 1927): 3-4 (3).
[6] Clemence Dane in *The Book Window*, Spring 1929, p. 52.
[7] Cole, *Books and the People*, p. 6.
[8] Hugh Walpole, *Vanessa*, in *The Herries Chronicle* (Macmillan, 1939), p. 1467.
[9] HW to Frere, May 1928, qtd in Rupert Hart-Davis, *Hugh Walpole* (1952; Stroud: Sutton, 1997), p. 299.
[10] 'Bloomsberries' is associated with Molly MacCarthy. See 'Clive Bell: Bloomsbury' in *The Bloomsbury Group. A Collection of Memoirs and Commentary*, ed. S. P. Rosenbaum (Toronto: University of Toronto Press, 1995), pp. 114-23 (p. 117). Ellen Wilkinson, *Clash* (1929; Virago, 1989), p. 17.
[11] Woolf makes this remark about Máire (B. J.) Lynd, Sylvia's youngest daughter. Woolf, *The Diary of Virginia Woolf. Vol. 4 1931-35*, ed. A. O. Bell (Harmondsworth: Penguin, 1983), 30 October 1935, p. 349.
[12] J. B. Priestley, *Margin Released: A Writer's Reminiscences and Reflections* (London: Reprint Society, 1963), p. 153-4.
[13] JBP, 'High, Low, Broad' in *Open House: A Book of Essays* (London: Heinemann, 1930), pp. 162, 166. This book of essays is dedicated to Robert and Sylvia Lynd.
[14] George Gordon, *Companionable Books*, series I (London: Chatto & Windus, 1927), p. vi.
[15] GG to HW, 31 Oct. 1928. *The Letters of George S. Gordon, 1902-42*, ed. Mary C. Gordon (Oxford: OUP, 1943), p. 188.
[16] Mary C. Gordon, 'Preface', *Letters of George S. Gordon*, p. vii.
[17] S.P.B. Mais, *Books and their Writers* (London: Grant Richards, 1920), p. 67.
[18] Book Society flyer, c. 1932, p. 4. John Johnson Collection of Printed Ephemera, Oxford, Bodleian Library, Book Clubs box 1.
[19] Clemence Dane, *Tradition and Hugh Walpole* (Port Washington, NY: Kennikat Press, 1973), p. 245.

[20] HW Diary, 1 Feb. 1928. The Hugh Walpole Collection at the Harry Ransom Center, The University of Texas at Austin.
[21] Rose Macaulay to Sylvia Lynd, n.d. 1930, in *The Correspondents of Sylvia Lynd, Poet*, catalogue compiled by Richard M. Ford.
[22] JBP to Rupert Hart-Davis, qtd in Rupert Hart-Davis, *The Power of Chance: A Memoir* (London: Sinclaire-Stevenson, 1991), p. 61.
[23] For the full story see my article 'Virginia Woolf, Hugh Walpole, The Hogarth Press, and the Book Society', *Literature and History* 79.1 (2012), 237-60.
[24] HW, *Reading: Being one of a series of essays edited by J. B Priestley and entitled: These Diversions* (London: Jarrolds, 1926), p. 88.
[25] HW, 'Notes from a Northern Cottage' [undated]. Hugh Walpole Collection, HRC, Box 27.

Chapter 1

[26] Sylvia Lynd, 'Hugh Walpole', *The Cantuarian*, July 1941, p. 114. HW to St John Ervine, 19 January 1921, qtd in Hart-Davis, *Hugh Walpole*, p. 204.
[27] SL, 'HW', *Cantuarian*, p. 114.
[28] JBP, *Margin Released*, p. 171-72.
[29] HW, *The Apple* Trees*: Four Reminiscences* (Waltham St. Lawrence: Golden Cockerel Press, 1932), p. 7. HW, *Open Letter of an Optimist* (London: Macmillan, 1941), p. 5.
[30] HW, *Open Letter of an Optimist*, p. 6.
[31] HW, *Apple Trees*, p. 5, p. 8.
[32] HW, *Apple Trees*, p. 10.
[33] HW, 'Reading for Education. The Literary Snob,' *John O' London's Weekly*, 6 March 1926, 853-54. HW, *Reading*, p. 88, p. 11.
[34] Hart-Davis, *Hugh Walpole*, p. 39.
[35] HW, *Apple Trees*, p. 22, p. 25.
[36] Qtd in JBP, *Margin Released*, p. 172.
[37] Clemence Dane, 'HW', *Cantuarian*, July 1941, p. 116.
[38] Richardson, 'Circulating Library', p. 200.
[39] HW, '*Rogue Herries*', in *Titles to Fame*, ed. Deny Kilham Roberts (London: Nelson, 1937), pp. 1-20, p. 5.
[40] *The Times*, 29 December 1928, p. 6.
[41] 'New Book Society', *Guardian*, 10 March 1929, p. 12.
[42] 'The Book Society: Some Privileges of Membership', undated flyer, John Johnson Collection.
[43] HW to SL, 1 November 1928. The Hugh Walpole Collection at the King's School Canterbury.
[44] Bott was a great disrupter, later involved with The Reprint Society, founder of Pan paperback books in 1944, and co-founder of The Folio Society in 1947.
[45] HW to SL, 12 March 1929. King's School Canterbury.
[46] HW Journal, qtd in Hart-Davis, *Hugh Walpole*, p. 304.
[47] HW Diary, 7 March 1929, qtd in Hart-Davis, *Hugh Walpole*, p. 304.

[48] HW to SL, 12 March 1929. King's School Canterbury.
[49] SL to HW, 16 March 1929. HRC.
[50] Charles Lee, *The Hidden Public: The Story of the Book-of-the-Month Club* (NY: Doubleday, 1958), p. 47-8.
[51] HW to SL, 12 March 1929. King's School Canterbury.
[52] HW Diary, 29 May 1929.
[53] HW, 'The First Soviet Humorist', 25 May 1929, *The Graphic*, p. 385.
[54] SL, *Slices of Autobiography*, n.p. Sylvia Lynd Collection, MS 5585, University of Reading Special Collections, Box 3.
[55] Francis Hackett, *Henry the Eighth* (London: Cape, 1929), p. 7.
[56] HW, 'The Most-Married Monarch', 3 August 1929, *The Graphic*, p. 220.
[57] Clemence Dane, 'Henry VIII Francis Hackett.' Draft article in Clemence Dane Collection, Victoria & Albert, HM/120/4/22.
[58] HW, 'The Most-Married Monarch'.
[59] Richardson, 'Circulating Library', p. 196.
[60] SL to HW, 19 July 1929. HRC.
[61] Mazo de la Roche to HW, 26 August 1936. HRC.
[62] HW, 'Life Comes Back to the Novel', 26 Oct. 1929, *The Graphic*, p. 172.
[63] Virginia Woolf, 'Modern Fiction', in *The Common Reader* (London: Hogarth Press, 1925), pp. 184-95 (p. 189).
[64] HW, *Letter to a Modern Novelist* (London: Hogarth Press, 1932), p. 1, p. 18.
[65] HW Diary, 2 May 1928.
[66] HW Diary, 8 November 1929.
[67] VW describing HW to Vanessa Bell, 18 May 1929, *The Letters of Virginia Woolf*, vol. 4, eds. Nigel Nicolson and Joanne Trautman (London: Hogarth Press, 1978) p. 60. VW Diary, 13 April 1929; *The Diary of Virginia Woolf*, vol. 3, ed. Anne Olivier Bell and Andrew McNeillie (NY: Harcourt Brace Jovanovich, 1980), p. 221.
[68] HW, *Hans Frost* (London: Macmillan, 1929), p. 68.
[69] VW to HW, 18 September 1929, *Letters*, v.4, p. 89.
[70] HW, 'London Letter', October 1929, HRC. VW to HW, 8 November 1931, *Letters*, v.4, p. 401.
[71] Elizabeth Steele, *Sir Hugh Walpole and the United States: A Novelist's View of 1919-36 America* (Lewiston: Edwin Mellen, 2006), p. 57.
[72] HW, *Wintersmoon* (London: Macmillan, 1928), p. 95-6.
[73] JBP, *Literature and Western Man* (Harmondsworth: Penguin, 1969), p. 338.
[74] HW, 'Life Comes Back to the Novel'.
[75] SL to HW, 20 September 1929. HRC.
[76] HW, 'A War Novel with Wit and Humanity', *The Graphic*, 16 November 1929.
[77] *New York Times*, 1 January 1930; in Steele, p. 73.
[78] HW letter 1933, qtd in Hart-Davis, *Hugh Walpole*, p. 269.
[79] HW to Ethel Cheevers, May 11? 1925. HRC
[80] HW to HC, Whit Monday 1926, HRC.
[81] HW to Ethel Cheevers, 13 May 1931. HRC.
[82] HW Diary, 15 January 1928.
[83] HW Diary, 23 February; 16 March 1930.
[84] HW Diary, 10, 11 March 1930.

[85] Harold Macmillan to HW; qtd in Hart-Davis, *Hugh Walpole*, p. 321.
[86] HW to Harold Macmillan, 17 and 2 April, 1930. Hugh Walpole Correspondence, MS 54959, British Library.
[87] Thomas Mark to Rupert Hart-Davis; in Elizabeth Steele, *Hugh Walpole* (NY: Twayne, 1972), p. 117.
[88] HW, *Rogue Herries* (London: Pan, 1971), p. 113, 110.
[89] L. C. Hartley, in Steele, *Hugh Walpole*, p. 119-20.
[90] HW Diary, in Hart-Davis, *Hugh Walpole*, p. 236.
[91] HW, *Apple Trees*, p. 67.
[92] HW Diary, 29 April 1930.
[93] Harold Raymond to Margaret Irwin, 16 October 1936. Chatto and Windus archive, University of Reading Special Collections, 63/2.
[94] Harold Raymond to Margaret Irwin, 30 April 1930, C&W archive, LB 128.
[95] 'Our Candid Camera Sees Double', *The Graphic*, 10 May 1930.
[96] SL to HW, 24 March 1930. HRC.
[97] Linklater to Howard, 9 January 1931. Jonathan Cape archive, University of Reading, A27.
[98] HW to SL, 7 April 1930. King's School Canterbury.
[99] Richard Aldington to Charles Prentice, 4 July 1929, C&W archive, CW 48/3.
[100] VW to Vita Sackville-West, 8? May 1930. *Letters*, v. 4, p. 165.
[101] HW to Harold Macmillan, 23 May 1930. BL.
[102] HW to Harold Macmillan, 24 May 1930. BL.
[103] HW Diary, 27 June 1930.
[104] HW, 'Notes from a Northern Cottage', Dec 1930, in *The Golden Book Magazine*; rpr. in *The Hugh Walpole Review*, 2:1 (2021), 89-90 (89).
[105] HW to Harold Macmillan, 7 June 1930. BL.
[106] HW Diary, 25 September 1930.
[107] HW to SL, 1 Aug 1930. King's School Canterbury.
[108] HW Diary, 26 and 25 September 1930.
[109] VW *Diary*, v.3, 5 Nov 1930, p. 328.
[110] W. Somerset Maugham, *Cakes and Ale* (1930; repr. London: Vintage, 2000), pp. 8-13.
[111] VW *Diary*, v.3, 5 Nov 1930, p. 328.
[112] Maugham to HW, in Hart-Davis, *Hugh Walpole*, p. 317.
[113] HW Diary, 26 September 1930.
[114] Hart-Davis, *Hugh Walpole*, p. 318.
[115] HW Diary, Notes for 1931.

Chapter 2

[116] SL, *Slices of Autobiography*.
[117] Sheila Lynd (Wheeler), 'Fragment of Autobiography', Family papers of Nannie Dryhurst. MS 49,981, National Library of Ireland, MS 49,981/11.
[118] David Garnett, *The Golden Echo*, in Family papers, MS 49,981/18-/1-20.
[119] Arthur Ransome, *Autobiography* (1976) in McMahon, p. 26.

[120] Máire Gaster, 'N. F. Dryhurst, Anarchist, internationalist and Irish Nationalist, 1856-1930', Family papers, MS 49,981/10, p. 13.
[121] Gaster , 'N. F. Dryhurst, Anarchist, internationalist', p. 12
[122] Robert Lynd, 'Should Kissing on the Stage by Stopped?', 1941, in Robert Lynd, *Galway of the Races: Selected Essays*, ed. Sean McMahon (Dublin: Lilliput Press, 1990), p. 26.
[123] SL letter 30 December 1907. Family papers, MS 49,981/18/21-24.
[124] R. A. Scott-James, 'Robert Lynd', *Dictionary of National Biography*, in McMahon, p. 14.
[125] Lynd (Wheeler), 'Fragment of Autobiography', p. 2.
[126] Ransome, *Autobiography* (1976) in McMahon, p. 26.
[127] Thanks to Lydia Syson for sharing Sylvia's membership card.
[128] RL, 'James Connolly: An Appreciation' (1916), in McMahon, p. 90.
[129] Victor Gollancz, *Reminiscences of Affections* (London: Gollancz, 1968), p. 90.
[130] Gollancz, *Reminiscences*, p. 85-6.
[131] VW, *Diary*, v.3, 27 March 1926, p. 70-1.
[132] SL Diary, 21 October 1935, Sylvia Lynd Collection, MS 5585, University of Reading Special Collection, Box 1.
[133] J. B. Morton, 'Mrs. Sylvia Lynd', *The Times*, 8 March 1952.
[134] SL Diary, 30 January 1936.
[135] SL, 'Book Reviews', *Time and Tide*, 24 November 1922, 19 March 1926.
[136] SL, 'The Critic in Relation to both Writer and Reader', *Time and Tide*, 7 February 1930.
[137] Clemence Dane, draft article, V&A, THM/120/4/22. HW Diary, 5 November 1928.
[138] E. M. Delafield, 'The Diary of a Provincial Lady', in *Titles to Fame*, ed. Denys Kilham Roberts (Nelson, 1937), p. 129.
[139] E. M. Delafield, *The Diary of a Provincial Lady* (London: Virago, 1984), p. 8 and 11.
[140] *Diary of a Provincial Lady*, p. 6.
[141] Margaret Cole, *Books for the People* (London: Hogarth Press, 1938), pp. 22, 25, 26.
[142] *Diary of a Provincial Lady*, p. 17.
[143] *Diary of a Provincial Lady*, p. 6.
[144] J. M. Denwood, *Rosley Hill Fair* (London: Jarrolds, 1933), Author's biography.
[145] J. M. Denwood, *Cumbrian Nights: 'Red Ike's' Poaching Life* (London: Jarrolds, 1932), p. 17.
[146] HW, 'A Word as Preface', to *Red Ike* (London: Hutchinson, 1931), p. 6.
[147] Fowler Wright, 'Foreword', *Red Ike*, p. 5.
[148] HW to SL, May 11 1931. King's School Canterbury; SL to HW, 12 May 1931. HRC.
[149] Helen Fletcher, 'New Fiction', *Time and Tide*, 4 July 1931.
[150] SL to HW, 5 April 1931. HRC.
[151] HW to SL, 7 April 1931. King's School Canterbury.
[152] Anon, 'The Thrush and The Jay', *TLS*, 4 January 1917, p. 7. Quotes on Gollancz ad, *TLS*, 7 May 1931. Ed. 'Baskerville', 'Books of the Week', *Birmingham Gazette*, 16 April 1931, p. 4.

[153] Máire Gaster, 'Introduction to Sylvia Lynd's Autobiography', in *Writers and Hampstead: Observations on the Place and the People*, ed. Ian Norrie (Hampstead: High Hill Press, 1987), p.106.
[154] Gollancz, *Reminiscences*, p. 90.
[155] *Publishers Circular*, 26 December 1931, p. 793.
[156] Christopher Morley to HW, 1 April 1926. Berg Coll MSS Walpole, New York Public Library.
[157] T. S. Stribling to Mary Hall, 25 July 1931. Qtd in Edward J. Piacentino, 'Selected Letters of T. S. Stribling, 1910-34', *Mississippi Quarterly* 38.4 (1985), 465.
[158] T. S. Stribling, *The Forge* (London: Heinemann, 1931), p. 192.
[159] Clemence Dane, 'T. S. Stribling, Bk. Soc. Aug 1931'. Draft article, V&A, THM/120/4/22.
[160] 'Postscript', *The Crisis*, August 1931, p. 279.
[161] SL to HW, 29 June 1931. HRC.
[162] Kate O'Brien, *Without my Cloak* (London: Virago, 1986), p. 434.
[163] Notes from the meeting of the Femina Vie Heureuse Prize committee, 6 Dec 1932. Femina Vie Heureuse Prize, English Committee archive, University of Cambridge, MS 8900.
[164] SL to HW, 4 September 1931. HRC.
[165] SL Diary, 2 February 1937; 23 October 1935.
[166] Qtd in Bridget Hourican and Patrick R. Dempsey, 'Beatrice Campbell', *Dictionary of Irish Biography* (2009) <Campbell, Beatrice Moss | Dictionary of Irish Biography (dib.ie)≥
[167] SL Diary, 1 December 1935.
[168] SL Diary, 14 December 1935; 11 December 1935; 23 October 1935.
[169] Gollancz, *Reminiscences*, p. 91.
[170] SL, *Slices of Autobiography*; Diary, 30 November 1935; 2 February 1937.
[171] HW Diary, 3 August 1931.
[172] HW Diary, 21 February 1932.
[173] HW to JBP, 18 July 1931. HRC.
[174] HW Diary, 23 September 1927; qtd in Hart-Davis, *Hugh Walpole*, p. 282.
[175] HW in Judith Cook, *Priestley* (London: Bloomsbury, 1987), p. 92.
[176] Edmund Blunden, *Undertones of War* (1928; London: Penguin, 2000), p. 53; EB to his mother, 31 March 1916 in Barry Webb, *Edmund Blunden: A Biography* (New Haven: Yale UP, 1990), p. 60.
[177] Robert Lynd, 'Mr. Edmund Blunden', *Daily News* (London, 2 May 1922), p. 7. Thanks to Ben Bruce for this reference.
[178] SL, 'If You have Tears', *Time and Tide*, 21 December 1928, p. 1254.
[179] Graves qtd in Webb, *Edmund Blunden*, p. 3.
[180] Delafield, *The Provincial Lady Goes Further* in *The Diary of a Provincial Lady* (London, Virago, 1984), p. 172.
[181] HW to SL, 1 June 1931, King's School Canterbury.
[182] 'The Book Society', *Time and Tide*, 13 February 1932.
[183] HW, GG, EB, CD, SL, 'The Book Society', *Time and Tide*, 12 March 1932, p. 287. Rose Macaulay, 'The Book Society', *Time and Tide*, 5 March 1932, p. 261.
[184] Lady Margaret Rhonda to SL, 28 February 1932, private archive. SL, 'The Book Society', *Time and Tide*, 27 February 1932, p. 227.
[185] Leavis, *Fiction and the Reading Public*, p. 34.

Chapter 3

[186] EB to his mother, 8 March 1932; EB to E. L. Griggs, 16 January 1933 in Webb p. 183.
[187] EB to Sylva Norman, 10 February 1932 in Webb, p. 195.
[188] EB to Aki Hayashi, 7 February 1932 in Webb, p. 195.
[189] EB to Siegfried Sassoon, 14 February 1932. *Selected Letters of Siegfried Sassoon and Edmund Blunden, 1919-1967*, 3 vols, ed. Carol Z. Rothkopf (London: Pickering & Chatto, 2012), vol. 2, p. 4.
[190] HW Diary, 25 February 1932; EB to Claire Blunden, nd, in Webb p. 192.
[191] HW Diary, 4 March 1932.
[192] RH-D to EB, 11 April 1932. HRC.
[193] RH-D to EB, 8 March 1952 in Philip Ziegler, *Rupert Hart-Davis: Man of Letters* (London: Chatto & Windus, 2004), p. 79
[194] RH-D to EB, 23 May 1932. HRC.
[195] EB to Siegfried Sassoon, 1 June 1932 in Webb, p. 194.
[196] RH-D to EB, 23 May 1932. HRC.
[197] EB to SS, 14 February 1932. *Selected Letters,* v.2, p. 4
[198] Sylva Norma to EB, 30 September 1931. HRC.
[199] EB to SS, 14 February 1932. *Selected Letters*, v.2, p. 4.
[200] EB to Sylva Norman, 6 February 1932 in Webb, p. 199.
[201] EB to AH, 31 August 1925 in Sumie Okada, *Edmund Blunden and Japan. The History of a Relationship* (Houndmills: Macmillan, 1988), p. 97.
[202] EB to Sylva Norman, 6 February 1932 in Webb, p. 199.
[203] EB to AH, 17 January 1927 in Okada, p. 128.
[204] EB to AH, 7 March 1932 in Okada, p. 148.
[205] EB to AH, 9 March 1932 in Webb, p. 202.
[206] EB to AH, 8 September 1932 in Okada, p. 151.
[207] EB to AH, 24 October 1932 in Okada, p. 152.
[208] EB to SS, 6 May 1933, v.2, p. 48.
[209] EB, 'British Writing in Wartime', article draft, HRC. Thanks to Nicole Reynolds for alerting me to this and other papers referencing the Book Society in the enormous Blunden archive at the HRC. EB to SS, 6 May 1933, v. 2, p. 48.
[210] Mary C. Gordon, *The Life of George S. Gordon 1881*-1942 (Oxford: OUP, 1945), p. 91.
[211] EB, 'Laconies on New Books'. HRC.
[212] EB to RH-D, 21 March 1932. HRC.
[213] Ziegler, p. 81.
[214] GG to RH-D, 26 September 1932 in Ziegler, p. 80.
[215] Graham Greene, *Ways of Escape*, in Cook, *Priestley,* p. 113.
[216] Graham Greene to Hugh Greene, 30 November 1932 in *Graham Greene. A Life in Letters*, ed. Richard Greene (London: Little, Brown, 2007), p. 47.
[217] EB to SS, 26 Feb 1933, *Selected Letters*, v.2, pp. 34-5.
[218] SS to EB, 28 Feb 1933, *Selected Letters*, v.2, p. 36.
[219] EB, *Undertones of War*, p. xi.
[220] EB to SS, 2 January 1931, *Selected Letters*, v.1, p. 311.

[221] *An Encyclopaedia of Fascism*, ed. Aldous Huxley (London: Chatto & Windus 1937, published under the auspices of The Peace Pledge Union), p. 89.
[222] We know from meeting transcripts that Sylvia talked these books down on the *Prix Femina* committee and there is no reason to suggest she would have acted differently on the Book Society. Cambridge, Femina. MS8900, box 1, 1/2/23 and 1/2/28. Minutes, 14 November 1933 and 14 November 1934.
[223] Cambridge, Femina, 1/2/22, 24 October 1933, p. 5.
[224] *The Scotsman*, 7 December 1933, p. 2.
[225] EB to Takeshi Saito, 4 January 1930 in Webb, p. 170. For more see Nicole Reynolds, 'Margins of Error: Edmund Blunden Annotates *Goodbye to All That*', *Book History*, 27.1 (2024), 102-37.
[226] EB to SS, 9 October 1934 and 6 March 1934, *Selected Letters* v.2, p. 93, p. 84.
[227] HW Diary, 21 May 1934.
[228] HW to Dorothy in Hart-Davis, *Hugh Walpole*, p. 350.
[229] Lenore Coffee, *Storyline: Recollections of a Hollywood Screenwriter* (London; Cassell, 1973), p. 197. Thanks to Alexis Weedon, *The Origins of Transmedia Storytelling in Early Twentieth Century Adaptation* (Houndmills: Palgrave Macmillan, 2021) for details in this section, and Rod Boroughs, 'Becoming a Hollywood Screenwriter: Walpole's "grand opening in films"', *The Hugh Walpole Review*, 2.1 (2021), pp. 57-67.
[230] 'The Cinema: Hugh Walpole in Hollywood', *The Scotsman*, 19 March 1935, 13; in Weedon, p. 154.
[231] CD to HW, 18 March 1933, private collection, in Rose Collis, 'The Friendship of Clemence Dane and Hugh Walpole', in *The Hugh Walpole Review*, 4.2 (2023), pp. 14-34 (p. 29).
[232] HW to Dorothy; in Hart-Davis, *Hugh Walpole*, p. 352.
[233] GG to HW, 16 June 1935, HRC.

Chapter 4

[234] SL Diary, 21 Oct 1935. Unattributed quotes in this chapter are from the diary, unless clearly a reference to a review published in the *Book Society News*.
[235] Thomas Sturge Moore (1870-1944) was a prominent poet, designer, and wood engraver who lived in Hampstead. He collaborated with W. B. Yeats and helped translate the poetry of Rabindranath Tagore into English, nominating Tagore for the Nobel Prize (which he was awarded) in 1913.
[236] George Blake to SL, 12 January 1935 in *The Correspondents of Sylvia Lynd, Poet*, catalogue compiled by Richard M. Ford.
[237] SL, 'August 1938 Choice – *Rebecca*', *Book Society News*, 5-6.
[238] Ann Bridge, *Illyrian Spring* (London: Daunt Books, 2012), p. 16.
[239] *Illyrian Spring*, p. 14.
[240] HW to SL, 15 October 1934, King's School Canterbury.
[241] SL, *BSN*, May 1938, p. 5.
[242] Julian Huxley, *Africa View* (London: Chatto & Windus, 1932), p. 32.
[243] Sally Chilver 1957, qtd in David Mills, 'British Anthropology at the End of Empire: the Rise and Fall of the Colonial Social Science Research Council, 1944-

1962', *Revue d'Historie des Sciences Humaines*, 6.1 (2002), 161-88.
[244] This is from Margaret Cole, *Books and the People*, p. 26.
[245] For more on this 'gentleman's agreement' (which lasted until 1976) see my 'British Publishers and Colonial Editions' in *The Book World: Selling and Distributing British Literature*, ed. Nicola Wilson (Brill, 2016); and the work of Hyei Jin Kim, <CBCP Fellow update: What's in a name?: Tracing the Evolution of the Traditional Market Agreement - Centre for Book Cultures and Publishing>
[246] *Bengal Lancer* also won the backing of the James Tait Black Memorial Prize.
[247] H. J. Lethbridge, 'Introduction' to *The Ginger Griffin* (Hong Kong: OUP, 1985), p. viii.
[248] Thanks to Lydia Syson for this detail. See <The Battle of Bermondsey | Lydia Syson The Battle of Bermondsey | Official Website of the Author Lydia Syson>
[249] Valentine Cunningham, *British Writers of the Thirties* (Oxford: OUP, 1988), pp. 211-12.
[250] Sheila Lynd to SL, 1 April 1935, private collection, with thanks to Lydia Syson.
[251] SL, 'Books for Everyman', *Sunday Times*, 6 December 1936, p. 1.
[252] SL Diary, 19 February 1936.

Chapter 5

[253] HW to CDL, 6 February 1937. Berg, Walpole.
[254] *Sheffield Independent*, 27 July 1937.
[255] Geoffrey Grigson, *New Verse*, 25 May 1937, 23-4.
[256] Grigson, *New Verse*, 15 June 1935, 20.
[257] CDL to Stephen Spender, undated in Peter Stanford, *C Day-Lewis. A Life* (London: Continuum, 2007), p. 153.
[258] The Popular Front, or the 'people's front', came from 'le Front Populaire', an agreement signed by the French Communist Party with other left-wing groups in the summer of 1934 to form an alliance against fascism. In Spain a similar movement was called the 'Frent Popular'.
[259] There were meaner tags: the 'Homintern' combined the homosexuality and communist leanings of the group; then later, poet Roy Campbell coined 'MacSpaunday' from MacNeice, Spender, Auden and Day-Lewis. See Stanford, p. 110-11.
[260] C Day Lewis, *The Buried Day* (London: Chatto & Windus, 1960), p. 217. They may have been together earlier at the BBC for a recording on 'The Modern Muse' in October 1938. See Stanford, p. 112.
[261] Virginia Woolf, 'The Leaning Tower' (May 1940), in *The Essays of Virginia Woolf, vol 6: 1933 to 1941*, ed. Stuart N. Clarke (London: The Hogarth Press, 2011), pp. 259-83 (p. 2670.
[262] CDL, from *The Magnetic Mountain* in *Collected Poems 1929-1933* (London: The Hogarth Press, 1938), p. 151.
[263] CDL, 'The Thirties in Retrospect' in Stanford, p. 71.
[264] CDL, *The Buried Day*, p. 218
[265] CDL, *A Hope for Poetry* (Oxford: Blackwell, 1936), p. 65, 98.
[266] CDL to Spender 1935 in Stanford, p. 140.

[267] Stanford, p. 129.
[268] CDL, *A Question of Proof* (1935; London: Vintage, 2012), p. 3, 21.
[269] CDL, *Noah and the Waters* (London: The Hogarth Press, 1936), p.22, 9.
[270] CDL, *We're not going to do nothing. A reply to Aldous Huxley's 'what are you going to do about it?*, *Left Review*, 1936, p. 30, 16.
[271] 'Spain: The World's "Civil" War', *Peace News*, 1 August 1936.
[272] CDL, *The Buried Day*, p. 219.
[273] CDL ed., *The Mind in Chains: Socialism and the Cultural Revolution* (London: Frederick Muller, 1937), p. 13.
[274] CDL to J. Crump, September 1937 in Stanford, p. 152.
[275] CDL, *The Mind in Chains*, p. 16-17.
[276] Victor Gollancz to G. D. H. Cole, December 1936 in Ruth Dudley Edwards, *Victor Gollancz: A Biography* (London: Gollancz, 1987), p. 238.
[277] 25 April 1937, *Observer*, p. 12 in Terence Rodgers, 'The Right Book Club: Text Wars, Modernity and Cultural Politics in the Late Thirties', *Literature & History*, 12.2 (2003), 1-15.
[278] 28 September 1937, *The Times*, p. 15.
[279] Winston Churchill, 10 November 1937, *The Bookseller*, p. 412. Thanks to Terence Rodgers for this detail.
[280] W. H. Auden and Louis MacNeice, *Letters from Iceland* (London: Faber & Faber, 1937), p. 35.
[281] *Letters from Iceland*, p. 30.
[282] EB, 'The Klosterhaus Readings, 1937', *German Life and Letters*, 2:1 (October 1937), 33-38.
[283] Sylva Blunden/Norman, Notes of a lecture tour in Germany, April 1937. Oxford, Merton College archives.
[284] Sylva Blunden, Notes of a lecture tour in Germany.
[285] EB to Rupert Hart-Davis, 14 August 1939 in Webb, p. 210.
[286] Sylva Blunden to EB, 20 July and 4 August 1939, HRC.
[287] Sylva Blunden, Notes of a lecture tour in Germany. Göttingen was founded by George II in 1734.
[288] EB, 'The Göttingen Celebrations', *The Times,* 1 May 1937.
[289] EB to Enid Bagnold in Webb, p. 217.
[290] EB, *BSN*, November 1938, p. 19.
[291] EB, *BSN*, January 1938.
[292] SL to HW, 23 February 1938, HRC.
[293] Virginia Woolf, *A Room of One's Own and Three* Guineas (Harmondsworth: Penguin, 1993), p. 270.
[294] Woolf, *A Room of One's Own and Three* Guineas, p. 272.
[295] Eric Linklater, *The Impregnable Women* (London: Cape, 1938), p. 12, 33.
[296] 'Members' Room', *BSN*, October 1938, p. 39.
[297] SL to Alfred Robert Dryhurst, 8 October 1938. From the catalogue of Richard M. Ford, shared by Lydia Syson.
[298] HW to EB, 10 October 1938, HRC.
[299] Sylva Norman to EB, 28 and 30 September 1938, HRC.
[300] Grigson in Webb, p. 189.
[301] Elizabeth Bowen, *The Death of the Heart* (London: Vintage, 1998), p. 42, 80, 32.

[302] Elizabeth Bowen to CDL, 25 November 1938. Oxford, Bodleian, CDL papers, Correspondence MS 6681/1.
[303] CDL, 'Overtures to Death', *Selected Poems* (London: Hogarth Press, 1940), p. 72.
[304] E. M. Forster to CDL, 30 October 1938. Bodleian, CDL papers.
[305] CDL, 'Self-Criticism and Answer', in *Complete Poems of C. Day Lewis*, ed. Jill Balcon (London: Sinclair-Stevenson, 1992), pp. 309-10.
[306] CDL, *The Buried Day*, p. 222.
[307] CDL, *The Buried Day*, p. 224.
[308] 'A Black Day for Germany', *The Times*, 11 November 1938.
[309] CDL, *Complete Poems*, p. 289-90.
[310] CDL, *A Hope for Poetry*, p. 83.

Chapter 6

[311] SL Diary, 2 February 1937.
[312] SL Diary, 20 April 1939.
[313] SL Diary, 13 May 1939.
[314] SL Diary, 18 April 1939.
[315] Sheila Lynd to Victor Gollancz. Modern Records Centre, Warwick, 157/3/DOC/1, in Dudley Edwards, *Victor Gollancz*, p. 303.
[316] SL Diary, 26 June 1939.
[317] HW, 'Our First Ten Year's, *BSN*, April 1929, p. 46.
[318] Alan Bott, 'Do You Remember?', *BSN*, April 1939, pp. 50-2.
[319] *BSN*, August 1937, p. 13.
[320] *BSN*, May 1939, p. 38.
[321] Both the Print Society and Sequana were described as the Book Society's 'friend and offshoot' (*BSN*, February 1939, p. 31). In the absence of surviving financial or company records, it is not possible to determine the precise connections, but both were likely subsidiaries. Judges on *Sequana* included Andre Maurois, Paul Valery, Pierre Benoit, Francois Mauriac, and Georges Duhamel.
[322] SL Diary, 2 April 1939.
[323] E. M. Forster, 'The 1939 State', *New Statesman and Nation*, 10 June 1939, pp. 888-9.
[324] Geoffrey Faber, *Spectator*, 15 September 1939 in Robert Hewison, *Under Siege: Literary Life in London 1939-45* (London: Weidenfeld and Nicolson, 1977), p. 9.
[325] *BSN*, June 1939, p. 40.
[326] Twenty years later, Pamela Frankau would join the Selection Committee for a spell in the late 1950s.
[327] H. G. Wells, *The Holy Terror* (London: Michael Joseph, 1939), p. 101.
[328] HW qtd in 'Taxing of Books. Effect on Public Morale', *The Times*, 6 July 1940, p. 2.
[329] HW Diary, 22 August 1939.
[330] SL Diary, 19 September 1939.
[331] SL Diary, 4 October 1939.

[332] Mary C. Gordon, *The Life of Geroge S. Gordon*, p. 154.
[333] On the outbreak of war, conscription was ramped up to include all men aged between eighteen and forty-one; in December 1941 unmarried women and childless widows between twenty and thirty were liable to be called up, older men up to the age of sixty were required to do some form of National Service.
[334] EB Diary, 9 September 1939.
[335] HW Diary, 4 September 1939.
[336] HW Diary, 10 September 1939.
[337] HW Journal, 16 June 1940. Vol XIII. HRC.
[338] SL Diary, 3 September 1939.
[339] SL Diary, 1 September 1939.
[340] SL Diary, 14 September 1939.
[341] SL Diary, 6 October 1939.
[342] EB Diary, 5 September 1939.
[343] EB Diary, 3 and 4 September 1939.
[344] EB Diary, 16 September 1939.
[345] EB Diary, 7 September 1939; 21 September 1939.
[346] EB Diary, 26 September 1939.
[347] RHD to EB, 28 November 1939. HRC.
[348] Valerie Holman, *Print for Victory: Book Publishing in England 1939-1945* (London: The British Library, 2008), p. 28.
[349] Alan Bott, *BSN*, October 1939, p. 24.
[350] EB Diary, 27 September 1939.
[351] CDL to HW, undated. HRC.
[352] CDL, *The Buried Day,* p. 233.
[353] CDL to Frank Halliday, 15 March 1941 in Sean Day-Lewis, *C. Day-Lewis: An English Literary Life* (London: Weidenfeld and Nicolson, 1980), p. 137.
[354] EB Diary, 29 November 1939.
[355] Hungary officially joined the Axis powers in November 1940.
[356] SL Diary, 18 September, 20 November, 12 October, 13 November 1939.
[357] EB Diary, 29 November 1939.
[358] CDL, *The Buried Day,* p. 85.
[359] HW, 'Re-reading in Wartime', BSN, Dec 1939, p. 35.

Chapter 7

[360] EB Diary, 2 January 1940.
[361] EB Diary, 19 February, 14 March 1940.
[362] EB Diary, 22 February 1940.
[363] EB Diary, 16 April 1940.
[364] EB, 'Bombing of Cities. To the editor of *The Times*', *The Times*, 16 April 1940, p. 4.
[365] EB Diary, 16 April 1940.
[366] EB Diary, 5 March 1940. HW Diary, 2 July 1940.
[367] EB Diary 29 November 1939; 5 March 1940.

[368] EB Diary, 15 and 16 March 1940.
[369] GG to Tony Gordon, 24 May 1940, *Letters of George S. Gordon*, p. 221.
[370] EB Diary, 20, 21 May 1940.
[371] EB Diary, 3 June 1940.
[372] HW, *Open Letter of an Optimist* (London: Macmillan, 1941), p. 5.
[373] HW Diary, 30 June 1940.
[374] *BSN*, April 1940, p. 32.
[375] Holman, *Print for Victory*, p. 250.
[376] 'Members' Room', *BSN*, June 1940, p. 25.
[377] National Archives, Ministry of Information (MoI), 9 May 1940, INF 1/234. Valerie Holman has led the charge with this fascinating story, see *Print for Victory* and 'Carefully Concealed Connections: The Ministry of Information and British publishing, 1939-46', *Book History*, 8 (2005), 197-226.
[378] MoI, Memorandum for Policy Committee, Paper Rationing, INF 1/234.
[379] MoI, Bamford to Cooper, Ministry of Supply, 30 May 1940, INF 1/234.
[380] EB Diary, 16 March 1940.
[381] *Book-of-the Month Club News*, April 1940, pasted into book <FAILURE OF A MISSION by Henderson, Sir Nevile (amazon.co.uk)≥
[382] EB Diary, 5, 16 March 1940.
[383] 'HW Talking', 5 April 1941. BBC radio broadcast, transcript at HRC.
[384] GG to Tony Gordon, 24 May 1940. *Letters of George S. Gordon*, p. 221.
[385] GG to W.G.N. (unspecified), 24 May and 14 July 1940, *Letters of George S. Gordon*, p. 221-2.
[386] 'The Stand-To' and 'Watching Post' rpr in *Word Over All* (London: Cape, 1943), pp. 27, 28-9.
[387] CDL, *The Buried Day*, pp. 225-6, 231, 234.
[388] JBP to CDL, 21 October 1939, Bodleian, CDL papers, MS 6681/3.
[389] 193/HRC IMG 1218 – thanks to Nicole for sending* HRC
[390] EB Diary, 11 June, 9 July 1940.
[391] EB Diary, 21 October 1940.

Chapter 8

[392] *BSN*, November 1940, p. 25.
[393] *BSN*, December 1940, p. 25 and p. 8.
[394] 'Taxing of Books', 6 July 1940, *The Times*.
[395] *BSN*, December 1940, p. 25.
[396] SL, *Slices of Autobiography*, Box 3, B1-B3.
[397] Sheila and B. J. moved with their husbands out of London to Charlbury in Oxfordshire during the Blitz, sharing the housework and childcare between them. Co-habiting enabled Sheila to manage work for the *Daily Worker* and B. J. for Heinemann alongside their commitments to the Communist Party. They maintained the shared household arrangement in London after the war, living next to their mother at 6 Keats Grove.
[398] EB Diary, 24 October, 29 October, 28 December 1940.

[399] Aki Hayashi to EB, 17 September 1940, HRC.
[400] HW Diary, 9-11 September 1940.
[401] Hart-Davis, *Hugh Walpole*, p. 433.
[402] Harold Cheevers to Grace Hubble, 8 October 1941. <Harold Cheevers, chauffeur/companion to writer Hugh Walpole, writes to Grace Hubble. - Manuscripts - Huntington Digital Library>
[403] 'HW Talking', 1 March 1941, BBC overseas broadcast transmission, transcript, HRC.
[404] 'Petrel', *The Bookseller*, 2 January 1941 in Holman, *Print for Victory*, p. 30. For a list of the firms whose premises were destroyed see Holman, p. 256.
[405] GG, *BSN*, February 1941, p. 3-4. Other quotes from critics are from the inside wrapper, *Into Battle* (London: Cassell, 1941).
[406] HW Diary, 20 August 1940.
[407] HW Diary, 27, 24 January 1941.
[408] HW Diary, 8 March 1941. In his diary, Hugh notes making broadcasts for America, Australia and the Dominions – programmes that would have aired on the English-language Empire Service, reaching Australia, Canada, New Zealand, South Africa; the transcripts of 'Hugh Walpole Talking' preserved at the HRC record times for 'Eastern transmission', suggesting they were also shared with the new Eastern Service (begun May 1940) for India.
[409] 'HW Talking', 1 March 1941, BBC transcript, HRC.
[410] 'HW Talking', 8 March, 5 April 1941, BBC transcripts, HRC.
[411] 'HW Talking', BBC transcripts, 1 March, 19 April, 26 April 1941.
[412] Mass Observation, File Report 1332, July 1942, 'Books and the Public', p. 70, 180. See Katie Halsey, '"Something light to take my mind off the war: Reading on the Home Front during the Second World War' in *The History of Reading. Evidence from the British Isles, c. 1750-1950*, vol 2, eds. Halsey and Owens (Palgrave Macmillan, 2011), p. 96-7.
[413] 'HW Talking', 12 April 1941.
[414] 'HW Talking', 19 April 1941.
[415] SL to HW, 21 April 1941. HRC
[416] 'Sir Hugh Walpole', *The Times*, 2 June 1941.
[417] 'Sir Hugh Walpole', *The Times*, 6 June 1941.
[418] RHD to EB, 21 September 1941. HRC.
[419] EB Diary, 9 June 1940.
[420] SL, *BSN*, July 1941, p. 13.
[421] SL, 'Hugh Walpole', *The Cantuarian*. July 1941, p. 115.
[422] EB Diary, 30 June 1941.
[423] EB Diary, 26, 29 May 1941.
[424] Cook, *Priestley*, p. 181.
[425] John Baxendale, *Priestley's England. J. B. Priestley and English Culture* (Manchester: MUP, 2007), p. 154.
[426] EB Diary, 20 October 1940.
[427] EB Diary, 11 July 1941.
[428] HW, *The Blind Man's House* (London: Macmillan, 1941), p. 422.
[429] Marguerite Steen, *The Sun is My Undoing* (London: The Companion Book Club, 1957), p. 9.
[430] EB Diary, 8 October 1941.

431 EB Diary, 8 December 1941.
432 EB to AH, 8 December 1941 in Okada, p. 165.
433 EB Diary, 9 December 1941.
434 AH to EB, Monday [8 December 1941]. HRC.
435 RHD to EB, 11 December 1941. HRC.
436 AH to EB, 11 December 1941. HRC.
437 EB to Aki Hayashi, 24 September 1949 in Okada, p. 28.
438 'The Members' Room', *BSN*, December 1941.
439 Margaret Irwin to Harold Raymond, 1 January 1942, UoR, Chatto & Windus archives, CW 95/12.
440 Harold Raymond to Jack Monsell, 29 October 1942. CW 95/12.

Chapter 9

441 Vaughan to D. D. G, 15 April 1942, National Archives, MoI, INF 238 part 3/c.
442 Holman, *Print for Victory*, p. 65.
443 National Archives, MoI, Book publishers Advisory Committee on Special Allocations of Paper, I.A.2632/1942, BT 96/132.
444 CDL, 'Do We Read Better Books in Wartime?', *Picture Post*, 25 March 1944, 23-6.
445 J. M. Dent, 'Everyman Library. New Year Letter of Explanation', *The Bookseller*, 1 January 1942, p. 9.
446 'The Members Room', *BSN*, April 1942, p. 20; December 1942, p. 64.
447 MoI, INF 1/123, Fraser, 'Books and Pamphlets Programme', 2 December 1941, p. 1 in Herny Irving, 'Towards "A New Kind of Book": Publishing and the Ministry of Information, 1939-47', *Publishing History*, 75 (2016), 53-75 (pp. 65).
448 CDL to Rosamond Lehmann, Christmas Day [?] and undated. Rosamond Lehmann archive, King's College Cambridge.
449 Selina Hastings, *Rosamond Lehmann* (London: Vintage, 2003), p. 223.
450 Hastings, *Rosamond Lehmann*, p. 218.
451 *Dusty Answer* (1927) and *Invitation to the Waltz* (1932) were BOMC nominations. *A Note in Music* (1930), *The Weather in the Streets* (1936) and *The Echoing Grove* (1953) were Book Society choices. *The Ballad and the Source* was chosen by both clubs (BS September 1944; BOMC April 1945). Lehmann's connections to the BOMC and the Book Society are discussed in Wendy Pollard, *Rosamond Lehmann and Her Critics. The Vagaries of Literary Reception* (Aldershot: Ashgate, 2004).
452 RL to John Hayward, 17 October 1942 in Hastings, p. 226.
453 *The Letters of Evelyn Waugh*, ed. M. Amory (1980), p. 153 in Martin Stannard, 'Evelyn Arthur St John Waugh', *Oxford Dictionary of National Biography* (2011).
454 Evelyn Waugh, *Put Out More Flags* (London: The Book Club, 1943), p. 11, 56, 28.
455 *Put Out More Flags*, pp. 73-4, 38, 48.
456 CDL, *BSN*, March 1942, p. 1-2.
457 GG to R. B. S., 22 December 1941, *Letters of George S. Gordon*, p. 242.

[458] EB Diary, 12 March 1942.
[459] EB Diary, 19 March 1942.
[460] 'Obituary notice', *The Times*, 13 March 1942, p. 7.
[461] R. W. Chapman, 'Prefatory Note', in George Stuart Gordon, *Anglo-American Literary Relations* (Oxford: OUP, 1942), p. 6.
[462] M. C. G., 'Introduction', *Life of George S. Gordon*, p. viii.
[463] EB Diary, 17 April, 4 June 1942.
[464] SL, *Slices of Autobiography*, Box 3, B1-B3.
[465] CDL to Frank Halliday, June 1942 in Sean Day-Lewis, *C. Day-Lewis*, p. 146.
[466] CDL to RL, undated. RL archive, King's College Cambridge.
[467] EB Diary, 11 March 1942.
[468] CDL, *BSN*, March 1942, p. 6.
[469] Martin Gilbert, *Churchill: The Power of Words* (Boston: Da Capo Press, 2012), p. 312.
[470] Hillary, *The Last Enemy* (London: Macmillan, 1942), p. 14.
[471] J. B. Priestley, *BSN*, May 1942, p. 5.
[472] CDL, 'Do We Read Better Books in Wartime?'
[473] EB, *BSN*, May 1942.
[474] CDL, 'Do We Read Better Books in Wartime?'
[475] CDL to RL, undated [Wednesday night], RL archive, King's College Cambridge.
[476] Hugh MacLennan, 'Foreword', *Barometer Rising* (Penguin Canada, 2017).
[477] EB Diary, 2 November, 1 September 1942.
[478] EB to AH, 29 May 1942 in Okada, p. 167.
[479] EB Diary, 21 Oct 1942.
[480] EB Diary, 1 September 1942; EB to AH, 15 April 1943 in Okada, p. 168.
[481] EB Diary, 2 November, 1 September 1942.
[482] EB Diary, 13 September, 21 and 31 October 1942.
[483] Qtd in Pollard, p. 109.
[484] RL to Laurie Lee, 23 April 1943 in Hastings, p. 237.
[485] CDL to RL, n.d. [Sunday]. RL archive, King's College Cambridge.
[486] RL to Laurie Lee, 23 April 1943 in Hastings, p. 237.
[487] RL, *The Ballad and the Source* (London: Collins, 1944), p. 101.
[488] RL to Jean MacGibbon, 1 November 1944 in Hastings, p. 245.
[489] *The Ballad and the Source*, p. 110.
[490] CDL to RL, n.d. [Wednesday], King's College Cambridge.
[491] CDL, 'Introduction' to *Anna Karenina* (London: The Book Society, 1943), p. viii, xi, xii.
[492] CDL, *BSN*, May/June 1943.
[493] CDL to RL, n.d., King's College Cambridge.
[494] *BSN*, May/June 1943, p. 3.
[495] With thanks to Stanford, p. 200.
[496] CDL, 'Do We Read Better Books in Wartime', p. 24.
[497] CDL to RL, n.d. [Wednesday], King's College Cambridge.
[498] CDL to RL, n.d. [Thursday], King's College Cambridge.
[499] Sean Day-Lewis, *C. Day-Lewis*, p. 151.
[500] Stanford, p. 205.
[501] Dorothy Whipple, *They Were Sisters* (London: Persephone, 2007), p. 406, 433.

Chapter 10

[502] EB to Sylva Blunden, undated draft in Webb, p. 240.
[503] Sylva Blunden to CMB, 8 February 1944 in Webb, p. 241.
[504] EB to Siegfried Sassoon, 7 February 1944, *Selected Letters*, v.2, p. 373; SS to EB, 28 February 1944, *Selected Letters*, v.2, p. 374.
[505] RHD to EB, 1 March 1944. HRC.
[506] EB to SS, 9 May 1944, *Selected Letters*, v.2, p. 381.
[507] John P. Marquand, *So Little Time and Point of No Return: Two Complete Novels* (Boston: Little, Brown and Company, 1949), p. 99
[508] SS to EB, 15 May, 14 April 1944, *Selected Letters*, v.2, p. 382, 377.
[509] EB to SS, 6 June 1944, *Selected Letters*, v.2, p. 383.
[510] Priestley, *BSN* May/June 1944.
[511] *The Ballad and the Source*, p. 219.
[512] EB, 'Introduction', *Persuasion* (London: The Book Society, 1944), p.
[513] SS to EB, 28 June 1944, *Selected Letters*, v.2, p. 384.
[514] EB to SS, 4 April 1945, *Selected Letters*, v.2, p. 410.
[515] CDL to RL, n.d. [Thursday]. King's College Cambridge.
[516] CDL, *Minute for Murder* (London: Vintage, 2012), p. 94.
[517] RL to John Lehmann, n.d. in Hastings, p. 241.
[518] SS to EB, 20 April 1945, *Selected Letters*, v.2, p. 413.
[519] Evelyn Waugh, 'Preface' (1959), *Brideshead Revisited*, revised edition (London: Chapman & Hall, 1960).
[520] Waugh, *Brideshead Revisited* (London: Chapman & Hall, 1945), p. 11.
[521] 'Hugh Walpole Talking', 5 April 1941, BBC transcript, HRC.
[522] Peter Henderson, 'Hugh Walpole, the King's School, and the Walpole Collection', King's School Canterbury, p. 5.
[523] Peter Henderson, archivist at the King's School Canterbury, and members of the Hugh Walpole Society are still trying to ascertain where parts of the library ended up.
[524] Thanks to Nicholas Redman, 'J. B. Priestley on Walpole's Art Collection', *The Hugh Walpole Review*, 5.1 (2024), p. 54.
[525] EB to SS, 10 May 1945 and 16 May 1945, *Selected Letters*, v.2, p. 416 and 418.
[526] EB to SS, 28 August 1945, *Selected Letters*, v.2, p. 424.
[527] RHD to EB, 13 August 1945. HRC.
[528] EB to Lance Blunden, 31 August 1945 in Webb, p. 272.
[529] EB to SS, 28 August 1945, *Selected Letters*, v.2, p.424.
[530] SS to EB, *Selected Letters*, v.2, p. 388.
[531] EB to SS, 28 August 1945, *Selected Letters*, v.2, p. 424.

Postscript

[532] 'A Bookman's Jottings', *The Bookman* (incorporating *The Book Society News*), 1.2, April 1946, p. 12.
[533] Pan was founded in 1944 by Alan Bott as an independent subsidiary of the Book

Society, becoming a consortium of publishers including Macmillan, Collins, Hodder & Stoughton, Heinemann and Cape. Thanks to David Finkelstein and Alistair McCleery, 'Publishing', *The Cambridge History of the Book in Britain*, p. 168.

[534] Finkelstein and McCleery, p. 169.

[535] *Arts Council 25th Annual Report* (London: Arts Council of Great Britain, 1970), p. 10 in Asha Rogers, *State Sponsored Literature: Britain and Cultural Diversity after 1945* (Oxford: OUP, 2020), p. 61.

[536] *Bookman*, June 1960, p. 19.

[537] *Bookman*, May 1959, p. 25.

[538] *Bookman*, July/August 1959, 1.1, p. 1.

[539] HW, *Reading* (London: Jarrolds, 1926), p. 88.

[540] MS in EB Papers, Works, 21.9, On-Oz, HRC.

[541] See Elizabeth McHenry, *Forgotten Readers: Recovering the Lost History of African American Literary Societies* (Durham: Duke UP, 2022), p. 308.

[542] Corinna Norrick-Rühl, *Book Clubs and Book Commerce*, p. 74.

[543] Michael Bhaskar, *Curation: The Power of Selection in a World of Excess* (Piatkus, 2016), p. 3.

[544] <Book of the Month Reviews: Everything You Need To Know (mysubscriptionaddiction.com)≥

[545] Indian jute manufacture overtook the Scottish industry in the early twentieth century. For more see Jim Tomlinson, *Dundee and the Empire: 'Juteopolis' 1850-1939* (EUP, 2014).

Index